A Polemical Preacher of Joy

A Polemical Preacher of Joy

An Anti-apocalyptic Genre for Qoheleth's Message of Joy

JEROME N. DOUGLAS

◆PICKWICK *Publications* • Eugene, Oregon

A POLEMICAL PREACHER OF JOY
An Anti-apocalyptic Genre for Qoheleth's Message of Joy

Copyright © 2014 Jerome N. Douglas. All rights reserved. Except for brief quotations in critical publications or reviews, no part of this book may be reproduced in any manner without prior written permission from the publisher. Write: Permissions. Wipf and Stock Publishers, 199 W. 8th Ave., Suite 3, Eugene, OR 97401.

Pickwick Publications
An Imprint of Wipf and Stock Publishers
199 W. 8th Ave., Suite 3
Eugene, OR 97401

www.wipfandstock.com

ISBN 13: 978-1-62564-064-2

Cataloguing-in-Publication Data

Douglas, Jerome N.

    A polemical preacher of joy : an anti-apocalyptic genre for Qoheleth's message of joy / Jerome N. Douglas.

    viii + 177 p. ; 23 cm. Includes bibliographical references.

    ISBN 13: 978-1-62564-064-2

    1. Bible. Ecclesiastes—Criticism, interpretation, etc. I. Title.

BS1475.52 D693 2014

Manufactured in the U.S.A.   10/10/2014

Contents

Acknowledgments | vii

Chapter 1
The Question | 1

Chapter 2
Genre: A Definition | 25

Chapter 3
Wisdom and Apocalyptic Genre and Thought Meld/Clash in Second Temple Judaism | 46

Chapter 4
Setting and Function of Ecclesiastes | 101

Chapter 5
The Rhetorical Strategy of Ecclesiastes | 146

Bibliography | 169

Acknowledgments

I am indebted to a host of people and friends for their encouragement, advice, and support during my doctoral program and the culminating task of this book. Time and space would not allow me to thank all of those who, through their words and kind deeds, brought refreshing winds in what can often be like a long, albeit rewarding and fulfilling, trek on a hot, humid day. There are a few that I would like to highlight for their contribution to me on this transformative journey.

The seeds for this book germinated during my doctoral studies at Marquette University. I am grateful to the faculty under whom I have studied and have been greatly enriched in my scholarly endeavors. I would like to mention a few whose impact directly influenced this work. While in the seminar on Hermeneutic Theory with Dr. Bradford Hinze my understanding and explorations on the topic of genre, which is central to this project, expanded significantly. In fact, my seminar paper on the genre of Ecclesiastes served as a launching pad for my later work. The idea of recognizing an anti-apocalyptic genre in Ecclesiastes began to form during the academic year when I engaged in an independent study of Wisdom literature under the direction of Dr. Deirdre Dempsey as well as the seminar on Jewish Apocalyptic literature with Dr. Andrei Orlov. An independent study on inter-testamental literature, as well under the direction of Dr. Orlov, also enabled me to further my knowledge in this area of study as well as fine tune the direction I would later pursue for this book. I am grateful to these faculty members for their diligent investment of time and consultation.

I am immensely grateful to my mother, Ives Douglas, whose endless and loving encouragement has consistently invigorated me on this educational journey. Her selfless love and support have been immeasurable during these years, as well as my whole life.

Chapter 1

The Question

How is the reader to interpret Ecclesiastes? What is the message of the author? What is the genre of this book? Many scholars have observed the number of statements in the book that appear to be conflicting or, at the very least, in tension with one another. Is Qoheleth[1] communicating a message of complete pessimism, qualified pessimism, realism, repentance and regret, or even possibly a message of joy? What is one to make of the number of statements in Ecclesiastes that would seem to support more than one of the afore-mentioned views?

In his work *Validity in Interpretation,* Eric D. Hirsch writes "Valid interpretation is always governed by a valid inference about genre. . . . Every disagreement about an interpretation is usually a disagreement about genre . . ."[2] Discussions about the message and genre label(s) of or in Ecclesiastes have not fully considered Qoheleth's polemics against the apocalyptic thought of his day, 200 B.C.E.

This work will propose that Qoheleth, in part, utilizes a hybrid genre[3] in his work. He, in part, employs what this book will call an "anti-apocalyptic genre" in Ecclesiastes, and the presence of this genre serves to further

---

1. In this book, I refer to the author of Ecclesiastes by the name Qoheleth, and I refer to the book by the name Ecclesiastes. The preferred, but not exclusive, translation is the New Revised Standard Version.

2. Hirsch, *Validity in Interpretation,* 98.

3. A definition of genre will appear in chapter 2. Chapter 3 will address a definition of apocalyptic genre and thought, the genre of wisdom literature, and the melding/clashing of these two.

A Polemical Preacher of Joy

Qoheleth's overall message of joy. Recognizing the presence of an anti-apocalyptic genre within the tapestry of Ecclesiastes will assist the interpreter in understanding Qoheleth's message. Surely the identification of this anti-apocalyptic genre label will not solve and answer all of the problems and questions with this text but will greatly bolster understanding. The first chapter will discuss the state of the question regarding both the genre and message of Ecclesiastes. It will survey the fruits of scholarship over the past century with regard to the overarching message and sub-genres of Ecclesiastes. This overview and discussion will serve as an historical backdrop for the work that continues in the following chapters.

The second chapter will present a definition of genre that will be crucial for the rest of the treatment of the genre and message of Qoheleth in Ecclesiastes. For this discussion the works of Harry Nasuti and Eric Hirsch will serve as foils resulting in the particular definition adopted for this book. This book will argue for a definition of genre that encircles the central *foci* of setting and function.

The third chapter will address the interaction of apocalyptic and sapiential or wisdom thought. This discussion will present examples of the interaction where apocalyptic and sapiential thought meld/clash. The purpose of this chapter is also to demonstrate that such an interaction was not uncommon for this Second Temple Judaism period.

The fourth chapter will concentrate on demonstrating the clash between Qoheleth and the apocalyptic thought of the day, approximately around 200 B.C.E., and demonstrating the anti-apocalyptic genre that Qoheleth utilizes. Key to the foundation of this chapter will be the setting (date and social location) and function of Qoheleth; passages that will receive particular attention will include 7:1–10, 3:10–22, and 9:1–10. Understanding genre in terms of setting and function, this chapter will demonstrate how Qoheleth argues against crucial apocalyptic thoughts such as the final judgment, the afterlife, and humanity's ability to know the actions of God.

The fifth chapter will show how Qoheleth's use of the anti-apocalyptic genre impacts the message of joy that he presents. Melding this genre label of anti-apocalyptic with present scholarship on the message of joy in Ecclesiastes, this chapter will show Qoheleth's rhetorical strategy and how it receives reinforcement by the presence of this hybrid genre of wisdom and apocalyptic, this anti-apocalyptic genre.

THE STATE OF THE QUESTION: MESSAGE

Twentieth-Century Interpretation

Historical Critical Interpretation

The three key words for this book are setting, function, and genre. In chapter two I will define genre around the two *foci* of setting and function. I will discuss the setting of the author and audience of Ecclesiastes in chapter four. Function and genre will receive preliminary attention in this present chapter. By function, I also refer to the message of the book. What does the author intend to accomplish with this writing, or what response does the author intend to elicit from the reader? This chapter begins to place my forthcoming suggestion in a historical context by reviewing what scholars have said about the message (or function) of Ecclesiastes.[4] My definition for genre will appear in chapter two, but in this chapter I will review what

---

4. I acknowledge my indebtedness to Ginsburg, *Coheleth*, 27–240. I am also indebted to Izak Spangenberg, "A Century of Wrestling with Qohelet," 61–91. I. J. J. Spangenberg's overview of the history of the interpretation of Qoheleth takes into consideration the different interpretive paradigms used for the book at different times in history. He recognizes that at least three paradigms have impacted the interpretation of Ecclesiastes: the pre-critical paradigm, the historical critical, and the modern literary criticism paradigms. He discusses these paradigms, considers when and how they arose in response to different crises or shifts in interpretation of the respective time periods, and assesses how these different paradigms impacted the interpretation of Ecclesiastes. The majority of my attention in this chapter will be devoted to the second and third paradigms of interpretation as seen in scholarly treatment of the book. Ibid., 61–91.

During the pre-critical period and before the Reformation there was a strong emphasis on tradition and the role of the church on the interpretation of Ecclesiastes. (Spangenberg uses what he calls "the Word of God" paradigm to describe the shift that takes place during the Reformation. I am broadening this term with the use of "pre-critical" to refer to the shift not only at the Reformation but also before the Reformation.) The Reformation brought about a shift in thinking that now allowed the individual interpreter to approach Scripture. The reformers emphasized that Scripture was clear, and the individual did not have to turn to a fourfold interpretation to understand it properly.

In response to three crises, according to Spangenberg (Galileo proposing a heliocentric universe, Descartes espousing the position that only the truth that could be grasped mentally through reason was valid, and the shift in the view of history to where the Bible was now examined through history), the historical- critical paradigm arose. Ibid., 64, 65.

During the latter part of the twentieth century, Spangenberg continues, attention began to shift from the author and then to the text and later to the reader. This shift along with the conclusion that the historical-critical approach was not the sole set of tools which the interpreter had to use brought about the shift to modern literary criticism paradigm. Ibid., 66.

commentators have written about the sub-genres of Ecclesiastes. In chapter four I will present my suggestion for another sub-genre that will reflect the setting and message (or function) of Ecclesiastes.

In the twentieth century and beyond, there have been some points of consensus that emerged from a historical critical treatment[5] of Ecclesiastes. Most agree that Solomon was not the author of the book and that the date for the book, many would argue, is approximately the third century B.C.E. Scholars agree on the unity of the book, with the understanding that the epilogue is the result of another hand. Interpreters commonly hold that the author of Ecclesiastes places distance between other biblical traditions such as the conventional wisdom tradition and himself. There is, however, not a consensus on what the message of the book is—whether positive or pessimistic.[6]

Interpreters in the twentieth century can be divided into those that are in the perspective of historical criticism and those that engage in more modern literary approaches. First, I discuss the contributions of historical-critical commentators—particularly regarding their understanding of the message (or function) of Ecclesiastes—and then attention turns to modern literary interpreters. Although not an exhaustive list, the interpreters that follow are Alan McNeille, George Barton, Robert Gordis, James Crenshaw, Roland Murphy, and Graham Ogden.

For Alan Mc Neille (1904),[7] Qoheleth's message is that "since the work of God is inscrutable and allows universal injustice and misery, man

---

5. Wisdom literature did not receive historical critical treatment until after Pentateuchal studies. Julius Wellhausen had little interest in wisdom literature since he considered it to be late in the life of Israel.

6. Bartholomew, *Reading Ecclesiastes: Old Testament Exegesis and Hermeneutical Theory*), 81.

7. Before I discuss Mc Neille, it is helpful to place his work in context of how interpreters approached Ecclesiastes around the beginning of the 1900s. Although the unity of Ecclesiastes—excluding the epilogue—became more accepted as the century continued, the beginning of the twentieth century witnessed source criticism's application to the book. This fact is particularly evident in the work of S. Siegfried.

S. Siegfried (1898) determines that Ecclesiastes had five different authors. Two different epilogists and two different editors had a part in the final form of the book included in the biblical text (Q1, Q2, Q3, Q4, Q5, R1, R2, E1, E2). For Siegfried, Q1 represents Qoheleth who exhibits a somber tone of pessimism. The Epicurean Sadducee (Q2) recommends that individuals engage in eating, drinking, and enjoying life. Q3 is the voice in the book that speaks highly of wisdom and issues forth proverbs. Q4 is a Hasid and objected to Q1 thoughts on how God governs the world. Q5 represents the many interpolators who include maxims. A first redactor (R1) added the first v. 1:1 and 12: 8, and

can come to no conclusion about life. One can only make the most of the present."⁸ Mc Neille sees the book as "a Hebrew journal in time,"⁹ that is, ruminations of a wealthy Jew as he earnestly reflects upon the disappointing and disheartening nature of life.

In the preface of his commentary, Mc Neille states that one of his goals is to "disentangle the strands which go to form the 'three-fold' cord of the writing."¹⁰ To this end he identifies two separate voices in the text. He sees the addition of the wise men in such places as 4:5, 4:9–12, 6:7, and 6:9a. Likewise, he sees the voice of a Hasid, a member of a Jewish sect that adhered to strong piety and strict observance of ritual law, at several points in the text serving to emphasize the responsibility to fear God, piety toward God, and the certainty of God's coming judgment. Examples of where the Hasid makes additions is in 3:17 where the Hasid interjects the comment that God will judge the righteous and the wicked as a balance to Qoheleth's complaint in 3:16 that "wickedness usurps the place of judgment and righteousness." Another example would be in 3:14 where Qoheleth is ruminating and lamenting the eternal and unchangeable work of God. The Hasid does not share a sense of sadness about this fact and inserts in 3:14b that God has done this so that men would fear God.¹¹

The message of Qoheleth in Ecclesiastes, Barton (1912) contends, is that "everything is vain." Some portions of the book that especially exhibit this main conviction would be the opening passage of 1:1–11, 3:1–15, 4:3–16, and 6:10–12.¹²

Barton sees the book as a unit but recognizes the hand of two glossators at work. He identifies one of the editors as intently concerned with wisdom literature, and the other has strong resemblance to the mindset of the Pharisees. The first editor was probably drawn to the book believing it to be a composition of Solomon and a part of wisdom literature. The

---

the second redactor (R2) is responsible for the addition of 12:13, 14 to the epilogue. The epilogue itself is the result of two additions 12:9, 10 from E1 and 12:11, 12 from the same. Many considered such a source criticism reading to be somewhat radical. Bartholomew, *Reading Ecclesiastes: Old Testament Exegesis and Hermeneutical Theory*, 71.

8. Ibid., 71.

9. Mc Neille, *An Introduction to Ecclesiastes With Notes and Appendices*, 8, 9.

10. Ibid., v, vi.

11. Ibid., 24, 25.

12. Barton, *A Critical and Exegetical Commentary on the Book of Ecclesiastes*, 46–50.

second editor was consumed with the impetus that a book from the hand of Solomon should have a tone of orthodox doctrine.[13]

"Though a skeptic, he [Qoheleth] had not abandoned his belief in God."[14] Qoheleth does not view God as a tender figure intricately involved in the lives of people; rather God, for him, is an incomprehensible being. Therefore, endeavoring to grasp the works of God is vanity. The sum total of humanity's knowledge is that God has placed humanity within the grip of fate.[15]

Robert Gordis (1951) takes into account the unity of the book and addresses the cahier genre of the book, the crucial use of quotations, and Qoheleth's worldview. Prior to the release of Gordis's commentary on Ecclesiastes, the common approach of interpreters was to deny the unity of the text. In response to the suggestions of Podechard and others who detected two glossators or school at work in the book, Gordis points out that it would be unlikely that the book gained such quick notoriety for interpolations to be possible. He argues that the path including writing, popularization, and widespread interpolations would have had to see fulfillment in the time period between 275–190 B.C.E. This would have been unlikely.[16]

One benefit of the argument against the unity of the book was that it helped to explain the contradictions in the book. The removal of this hypothesis still left the contradictions unexplained, and Gordis addresses these contradictions by asserting that Qoheleth utilizes quotations in his work. Gordis argues that Qoheleth has the practice of citing maxims, drawing from his familiarity with them. Gordis sees four different types of quotation uses in the book. First, Qoheleth simply utilizes a proverbial quotation such as in 10:8. Secondly, Qoheleth often quotes an entire proverb, such as in 5:3, to help his argument but only part of that proverb will be *apropos* to his present message. Thirdly, he uses a proverb as a passage such as in 7:1–14. Fourthly, he uses proverbs to contradict each other in order to highlight his disagreement with accepted doctrines such as in 4:5–6.[17]

Gordis writes, "Ecclesiastes is not a debate, a dialogue, or a philosophical treatise. It is a cahier or notebook."[18] He sees eighteen sections apart

13. Ibid., 46.
14. Ibid., 50.
15. Ibid., 50.
16. Gordis, *Koheleth: The Man and His World*, 72.
17. Ibid., 99–108.
18. Ibid., 110.

from the epilogue and sees a few consistent statements after each section. At the end of each section, Qoheleth reiterates that humanity is ignorant of ultimate truth, everything that humanity does is vanity, and God has given humanity the task to achieve/accept happiness.[19]

Qoheleth communicates strong views on humanity, God, and humanity's imperative in this life. He does not possess the confidence that humanity could grasp life's meaning. Furthermore, he no longer held to the idea that justice would prevail in this world. He still believed in God, but his traditional views had dramatically shifted, particularly in the view of how God interacts with humanity. There is a basic message throughout the book of the vanity of all and the imperative to enjoy life. Qoheleth embraces joy as God's categorical charge, not simply in a spiritual or religious sense, but in a fully-orbed experience of life—body and mind embrace of nature and life itself.[20]

James Crenshaw (1988) summarizes Qoheleth's message by treating five main convictions present in Ecclesiastes: "(1) death cancels everything; (2) wisdom cannot achieve its goal; (3) God is unknowable; (4) the world is crooked; and (5) pleasure commends itself."[21] Crenshaw sees all of these main beliefs as a result of the fact that the author of Ecclesiastes lacks a solid confidence in the goodness of God.

After surveying the different pursuits for meaning in this life (pleasure, work, wealth, renown, and wisdom), Qoheleth determines that all of these are meaningless since death takes away any benefit that these bring. With all of the confidence placed in wisdom and its great value, the author of Ecclesiastes laments that wisdom could not bring certainty to life. Unlike the book of Job, Ecclesiastes presents God as one who not only is beyond humanity's ability to know but also is somewhat removed from personal relationship. Concerning the world, Crenshaw sees Qoheleth as viewing a dismal monotony of both the past and future days; the world is crooked and sinners sometimes prosper—*contra* the retribution theology in Proverbs. Given this entirely dismal viewpoint of life, seeking to enjoy this life is the one thing that makes this life meaningful. Yet, Qoheleth "wants to assure those who grasp for pleasure that emptiness will reign regardless of their successful use of life's opium, until death seizes its prey."[22]

19. Ibid., 110.
20. Ibid., 112–20.
21. Crenshaw, *Old Testament Wisdom: An Introduction*, 117–28.
22. Ibid., 117–28.

A Polemical Preacher of Joy

Roland Murphy (1992) exhibits a measured approach to Ecclesiastes. This approach, which could be considered a unique contribution to the discussion on Ecclesiastes, appears in his stated approach to the book and his summary of Qoheleth's message. Murphy approvingly draws from Johannes Pedersen in speaking about how commentators approach the book.

> Very different types have found their own image in Ecclesiastes, and it is remarkable that none of the interpretations mentioned is completely without some bias. There are many aspects in our book; different interpreters have highlighted what was most fitting for themselves and their age, and they understood it in their own way. But for all there was a difficulty, namely that there were also other aspects which could hardly be harmonized with their preferred view.[23]

Murphy, therefore, approaches the book carefully, cognizant of the tendencies of interpreters to focus on one or a few aspects of Qoheleth's message. With this in mind, Murphy explains the message not by choosing one aspect but by choosing nine crucial words and concepts that convey the essence of Qoheleth's message. He surveys the words: הבל, יתרון, חלק, עמל, חכמה, שמחה, fear of God, retribution, death and the Qoheleth's concept of God. The following chart[24] encapsulates his summary.

Key Word/ Concept	Summary
1. הבל	Murphy writes of the pervasiveness of הבל (vanity) in the text, "there is not, Qoheleth avows, a singled unspoiled value in this life."[A]
2. יתרון	As to יתרון (profit, advantage) Qoheleth argues that it is not to be considered as referring to an advantage in the eternal age.
3. חלק	Likewise whatever חלק (portion, lot) one would have is only received in this world.
4. עמל	Qoheleth views the עמל (toil, effort) in this life to be a negative aspect of life.
5. שמחה	Murphy acknowledges the significant presence of שמחה (joy) in the book but rejects the idea that it is the basic theme of the book.

---

23. Murphy, *Ecclesiastes*, lv.
24. Ibid., lvi–lxix.

6. חכמה	חכמה (wisdom) is a significant word in Qoheleth's message. Murphy concludes that he is certainly within the wisdom tradition but quarrels with it while maintaining its central goal: to discovery what humanity should do.
7. Fear of God	The fear of God in Ecclesiastes is a little different from other portions of the biblical text. Whereas Proverbs attaches the fear of the Lord with obeying his commandments, Qoheleth uses the fear of God to explain "that God is too dangerous for humans to deal with in a causal way."[B]
8. Retribution	"It is clear that Qoheleth denies that there is any intelligible retribution or justice in this life." [C]
9. Death	For Qoheleth, there is nothing after death and there are times when death would be more desirable than life.
10. God	"All that happens is his [God's] doing, and it is unintelligible. . . . [Murphy says] Qoheleth does not allow it to become a reason or source of consolation and security. Since one cannot know what God is doing, fear and reverence are in order."[D]

[A]. Ibid., lviii–lix.
[B]. Ibid., lxiv–lxv.
[C]. Ibid., lxvi.
[D]. Ibid., lxviii.

Graham Ogden (2007) perceives Qoheleth's pressing question to be one that wrestles with the question of what advantage people gain from all their activities in this life. The answer to this question is that there is no advantage to all of the toil in this life. How then is one to live? To this question, Qoheleth answers with a message of joy in the midst of the enigma or הבל that is this life. Ogden also sees in Qoheleth's message an implicit suggestion of an advantage in the afterlife.[25]

Ogden expounds upon Ecclesiastes concerning the crucial points of thesis and purpose in the book. He is well aware of the fact that completely different interpretations have emerged from this one book, such as a view of pessimism *contra* a view of joy. The determining factors for Ogden's conclusion and interpretation are the meaning of הבל and whether or not הבל encapsulates the writer's thesis and purpose. Many have determined that הבל has a negative meaning and, from this conclusion, determined that the book has a negative tone to it as well. Ogden launches into a detailed exposition of why he determines the word to mean enigmatic rather than vanity.

25. Ogden, *Qoheleth*, 16–17.

He also argues that הבל appears in a number of concluding statements. Notwithstanding this fact, the words and these concluding statements do not offer Qoheleth's advice. Ogden contends that this counsel arrives in restated invitations to enjoyment.[26]

Ogden argues that the book follows a question-answer-response format: an inquiry concerning humanity's יתרון, coupled with the reply to this question and the ensuing discussion. This format, for Ogden, is the framework through which the book is to be understood. The first eight chapters highlight this question-answer-response format and engulf all of the material within them. Qoheleth draws from personal experiences for the question and the answer, which is that there is no יתרון or advantage. This realization leads to the principal matter—that life should be received as a gift from God that humanity should enjoy. Following these eight chapters of question-answer-response, chapters nine to twelve exhibit a transition to discourse material detailing wisdom's worth.[27]

Modern Literary Interpretation

As the historical-critical interpretation of the book continued and grew during the twentieth century, the second half of the century also witnessed the rise of modern literary readings. Interpreters realized that while the historical critical method had value, it was not the only set of tools at the disposal of the scholar. This shift opened the pathway for canonical, structural, and dialogical readings. For many of these interpreters the structure of the book received more attention than the message (or function). I will give attention to the works of Brevard Childs, Addison Wright, James Loader, and Theodore Perry.

Brevard Childs (1979) advocated a canonical approach to Ecclesiastes. This approach seeks to take seriously the place of Ecclesiastes within the Old Testament canon while not forsaking the fruits of historical criticism. The result is that the final product of the text carried more weight than efforts of source and form criticisms. His views about the message (or function) and the shape of the book are heavily influenced by this canonical approach. One particularly significant to this approach was the fact that Childs considers the epilogue to be a vitally crucial part to understanding

---

26. Ibid., 16–17. (See 1:7; 2:24; 3:12, 22; 5:17 (18); 8:15, and 9:7–10).
27. Ibid., 16.

the book, *contra* the overwhelming conclusion of historical critical interpreters. He writes, "From the canonical perspective the crucial issue focuses on determining the effect of the epilogue on the interpretation of the book regardless of whether the addition derives from one or two editorial layers."[28]

In Childs's view the epilogue demonstrates a profound awareness of the Old Testament canon; this awareness is particularly apparent in vss. 9, 11, and 13. First, this epilogue positions Qoheleth as not merely a lone pessimistic voice but a member of the wise within the wisdom tradition. He has a significant role as he brings a corrective to the established perception of the wisdom tradition. Secondly, the epilogue establishes that the words of the wise, of which Qoheleth's words are a part, are divine and, thus, should receive attention. Thirdly, the epilogue also provides the theological rubric through which the book should receive interpretation: "fear God and keep his commandments."[29] The message (or function) of the book is viewed through canonical lens.

Addison Wright's (1968) contribution to the study of Ecclesiastes has had a significant impact. He approaches the book as a sphinx with many riddles and, thus, employs a New Criticism approach producing an analytical examination of the book's structure. For him, the riddles that the book presented included such questions as "authorship, structure, genre, message and background, . . . the reasons for its very presence in the biblical canon."[30] Admitting the many questions that the interpreter would have about the book, Wright argues that the first point of business must be to determine the underlying structure of the maze that the book forms.

He understands this underlying principle to lie outside the hypothesis of multiple authors or even the idea that the author was wavering between orthodox and unorthodox views. For Wright the structure includes three succeeding patterns that appear from 1:12—11:6. Taking these patterns as a framework, Wright argues, reveals a discernible schema to the book that brings forth a clear message.[31]

To arrive at this conclusion and to give an objective analysis of the structure of the book, Wright employs what was, at the time he wrote, a new approach, New Criticism. It was a balanced reaction to other approaches to

---

28. Childs, *Introduction to the Old Testament as Scripture*, 585.
29. Ibid., 585–87.
30. Wright, "The Riddle of the Sphinx: The Structure of the Book of Qoheleth," 313.
31. Ibid., 313.

structural analysis that tended to produce subjective outlines that do not fully engage rhetorical and literary forms within the work. Rather than focusing entirely on the thought of the work, this New Criticism that Wright applies directs attention to the form of the work. This approach notices the repetition of words and stylistic forms, such as *inclusios*, symmetry, announcements of topics, recapitulation, and other literary forms. In addition to these literary observations, the new critic pays close attention to changes in literary styles, person, mood, and numerical patterns. He then brings all of these notations to bear upon the division of the thought in the work.[32]

Wright's analysis of the structure of Ecclesiastes discovers that the book divides neatly in two divisions: 1:12- 6:9 and 6:10—11:6. The first part of the book addresses the vanity of the toil in which humanity engages; the second part addresses the inability of humanity to comprehend God's work. Wright also points out that these aforementioned patterns along with others concur with crucial points in the thought of the work: "It is a case of verbal repetitions marking out and exactly coinciding with repetitions of ideas."[33] For example, there are eight sections from 1:12—6:9 that ruminate on the vanity of human endeavors, and these investigations only appear in this portion. Chapters 7 and 8 entertain an examination of traditional wisdom on what humanity is to do; the repetition of the words "to find out" stops when this section closes. Chapters 9:1—11:6 investigate the problem of what will come after man; the repetition of "to know" ceases with this idea in this section.

Wright outlines the book in the following manner. After the title in 1:1 and the poem on toil in 1:2-11, the text delves into Qoheleth's probe into life (1:12—6:9). In this large section the author examines the pursuit of pleasure (2:1-11), wisdom and folly (2:12-17), and toil (2:18—6:9). The second half of the book (6:10—11:6) contains Qoheleth's conclusions. He concludes that humanity does not know what God has done, what humanity is to do, or what will come after humanity. The text ends with a poem on youth (11:7—12:8) followed by the epilogue (12:9-14).[34]

For James Loader (1979), there is no orderly progression of thought nor does the book contain a disconnected collection of proverbs. הבל, which Loader understands to mean emptiness or vanity, appears at both the beginning in 1:2 and 12:8. This term also appears in each chapter except

32. Ibid., 318–19.
33. Ibid., 324.
34. Ibid., 324.

chapter 10. Loader sees that "this one conviction of emptiness and senselessness is the dominant motif in the book."[35] The book does not develop an orderly presentation of thought, but does present different pericopes that exhibit a polarity within each passage. In his view, the book contains a polar structure and tension within each literary unit in order to communicate this attack on the established tradition of wisdom literature.[36]

The polarity present in many passages in Qoheleth follows a recurring pattern. Loader writes, "Their contents are structured as pole A: :pole B where God always works in such a way that a negative, unfavorable tension results (הבל)."[37] An example of a passage and the polar tensions that Loader identifies is in chapter 3:1–9. This passage outlines a series of events over which humanity does not have control. Humanity's inability to determine the events that happen to humanity is a dominant theme throughout the book. A rhetorical question with a negative tone comes after this poem, which further emphasizes the fact that humanity cannot impact humanity's outcome. "The time . . . just falls over man and therefore no labor can produce advantage. If the occasion arrives for something desirable to happen, it happens. But when something undesirable is to happen, nothing can stop it."[38] Therefore, against a traditional wisdom perspective, human effort to control חכמה is to no avail. Loader summarizes the tension in this passage as follows: the pole is life, followed by a contra-pole which speaks of abandonment and death produces the tension to this structure which states that since the individual has no security, humanity should surrender to what will happen—it is beyond humanity's control.[39]

Theodore Perry (1993) takes a dialogical approach toward Qoheleth. Although other interpreters have seen the hands of a number of editors or even also different voices in the book, Perry is unique in that he assigns these two different voices throughout the book, interacting with one another. I will touch on his understanding of the genre; his perception of genre will help to elucidate his understanding of the message or debate that takes place in the book.

Perry places Ecclesiastes under the genre labels of essay, collection, and debate. Part of the genius of the genre of the book is that it allows for the

---

35. Loader, *Polar Structures in the Book of Qoheleth*, 9.
36. Ibid., 9.
37. Ibid., 105.
38. Ibid., 32.
39. Ibid., 32–33.

A Polemical Preacher of Joy

fluid pessimistic musings as well as a *contra*-voice within the same work. As will be seen in the example below, the first chapter outlines a presentation of a view with an interwoven opposing view. The end of the first chapter emerges with the pessimistic voice, which Perry labels as K, speaks in the first person, and launches into a reflective and autobiographical essay.[40]

Yet this essay is a special kind of essay because it also incorporates other genres as well such as proverbs; the book is also an interactive collection of proverbs. The proverb is a foundational unit of wisdom literature, and it evokes a response to it. A collection of these proverbs that sometimes communicate varied and rival thoughts gives the effect of an environment of comment followed by challenge. Qoheleth, Perry argues, has sets of the proverbs from two different voices, with contrary perspectives, challenging one another, such as in 1:1–11, 3:1–8, and 7:1–12.[41]

Perry comments on how masterful Qoheleth's work is in that he personalizes the traditional wisdom genre. He does this by allowing the voice of experience to speak with all of its questions and pessimism that could interact with a difference of opinion and human experience. This form of debate allows individual experience to challenge and battle traditional conclusions. "The resulting literary dialogue has implication far beyond surface form: it implies a radical intellectual and spiritual approach, a dialogical view of truth and reality based on a willingness to consider human experience . . . as a valid basis for religious truth."[42]

The literary style of Ecclesiastes, including reflective essay, collected proverbs, and debate, can best be illustrated by looking at two passages to which Perry applies his approach: 1:4–7 and 3:2–8. Perry argues that although most would concur that the sages had a pedagogical aspect in their content, many do not fully take into account the methodology that these sages used, which included placing opposing views within a debate format. The passage in 1:4–7 provides an example of this presentation. The voice of what Perry calls "K" is the voice of the Pessimist; it appears in italicized letters below. The other voice Perry calls "P," who is the one who argues with K's pessimism, and it appears in normal type set letters.[43]

    1:4 *A generation goes, and a generation comes*
        But the earth remains forever.

40. Perry, *Dialogues with Kohelet*, 6.
41. Ibid., 6, 7.
42. Ibid., 7.
43. Ibid., 10, 11.

> 5 *The sun rises and the sun goes down,*
>   Yet it pants to return to its starting point where it rises again.
> 6 *Moreover, it goes southward but returns northward*
>   *The wind goes forth around and around!*
>   Yet it can reverse its direction. . .
> 7 *All rivers flow to the seas!*
>   But the sea is not full; And the rivers must return to their source, since they continue to flow in their destination.

Again, Perry's approach does not see one voice in Ecclesiastes or one perspective on a given subject but rather a debate between two voices. Perry points out that his approach to Ecclesiastes does not deny pessimism in the book but seeks to show that it is not the only voice. The book argues that "our existence is neither futile nor ephemeral; or rather that neither of these connotations of vanity (הבל) is necessarily pessimistic."[44]

The Message of Ecclesiastes: A Summary

With a selected survey of twentieth-century interpretation of Ecclesiastes complete, a brief summary of this history of the suggested messages in Ecclesiastes would be helpful at this point; Douglas Miller[45] provides such a summary. Some of the main suggestions have been to consider the author of the book a repentant king, an ascetic, a bitter skeptic, a realist, or a preacher of joy. Since הבל[46] is such a central portion of the message of the book, mention of this important term will also appear in the brief summary and assessment of these suggestions, which will also provide an opportunity to refer to some of the interpreters discussed above.

The suggestion that the author of Ecclesiastes, Qoheleth, is a repentant king understands Solomon to be that king. In this perspective on the book's message, Solomon confesses his shortcomings and considers his past failures and futile activity to be הבל. His purpose in unveiling his indiscretions, as well as those of others, is to persuade the reader to take a different path. This suggestion stands when parts of the book are examined,

---

44. Ibid., 46.

45. Miller, "What the Preacher Forgot: The Rhetoric of Ecclesiastes," 216–21. I acknowledge my indebtedness to Douglas Miller for his summary and assessment of these different views on the message of Ecclesiastes.

46. For a more detailed exposition of הבל see Miller, *Symbol and Rhetoric in Ecclesiastes: The Place of Hebel in Qohelet's Work*. This key word will also receive attention in chapter 5.

especially portions that speak of the wickedness and futile deeds, but does not endure in the light of all of Ecclesiastes; there are portions of the book, Miller observes, that do not fit this suggestion. The author labels certain things הבל and evil which are not in a person's control; for example, in Eccl 2:21, when a person leaves wealth to one who did not earn it. Qoheleth also brings complaint against God for such things as the lack of justice in the world in 6:1–6 in addition to the observation that the same end goes to both the wise and the fool as in 2:15–16. Possibly the strongest piece of evidence that brings this hypothesis into question is the fact that the author encourages the reader not to be too righteous in 7:15–18.[47]

Another suggestion is the ascetic view, which asserts the author to be one who tries to persuade those pursuing worldly and materialistic lives to practice self-denial in preference for the afterlife. To accomplish this goal, Qoheleth points out how the things of this world fail to produce satisfaction. In this understanding הבל speaks of that which is insignificant in the perspective of eternity. For Miller, the two major difficulties with this suggestion are that Qoheleth expresses uncertainty about life beyond the grave such as in 3:19–22 and 9:3–6. Moreover, instead of telling his readers to forsake enjoyment in this life, the author actually encourages them to enjoy this life (see 2:24–25; 3:12–13, 22).[48]

Another theory about the message of Ecclesiastes is that it is one of a bitter skeptic who is so frustrated with life and disappointed that life is not what it should be that he simply declares everything to be הבל, meaningless or absurd. The examples of meaninglessness that the author cites give the

---

47. Miller, "What the Preacher Forgot: The Rhetoric of Ecclesiastes," 216. George Barton in chronicling the history of interpretation of Ecclesiastes writes of the understanding of what were, very likely, the earliest commentaries of Ecclesiastes, the Jewish *midrashim*. The understanding of the *midrashim* was that Solomon was the author of Ecclesiastes and wrote it in his elder years to "expose the emptiness and vanity of all worldly pursuits and carnal gratifications, and to show that the happiness of man consists in fearing God and obeying his commands." Barton, *Ecclesiastes*, 19.

48. Miller, "What the Preacher Forgot: The Rhetoric of Ecclesiastes," 217. This view is present in the interpretations of Gregory Thaumaturgus and Jerome. Gregory, possibly the earliest Christian commentator, who saw Solomon as a prophetic figure utilized this writing "to show that all the affairs and pursuits of man which are undertaken in human things are vain and useless, in order to lead us to the contemplation of heavenly things." Interpreters such as Gregory of Nyssa and Jerome followed this lead and utilized the allegorical method to determine similar conclusions. Jerome considered the objective was "to show the utter vanity of every sublunary enjoyment, and hence the necessity of betaking one's self to an ascetic life, devoted entirely to the service of God." Barton, *Ecclesiastes*, 20.

reason for why he is so negative and bitter. Many in the post-Enlightenment period find this view of Qoheleth as a cynic to be appealing because this view portrays the author as one who is honest about the questions and difficulties of faith, in light of the frustrations of life. The problem with this view is that it does not adequately account for the apparent contradictions or tensions in the book: the good and the bad of life, the kindness and unpredictability of God, and other paradoxes.[49] There are simply too many positive statements in the book, particularly concerning wisdom, enjoyment, and labor, for this to be the message of Ecclesiastes. Trying to reconcile the apparent contradictions as the result of rhetorical devices has led some to posit the following two views on the message of Ecclesiastes.[50]

The realist view is another suggestion for the message of Ecclesiastes. The author is able to hold the good and unfortunate aspects of life in tension without becoming a cynic. While refusing the repentant king and ascetic views, those who hold to a realist view see that some of the statements in Ecclesiastes had a deliberate rhetorical role intended to lead the reader to a definite conclusion and response. In this view Qoheleth uses הבל to speak of the many limitations and complications that people encounter in life instead of understanding the word to mean absurd or meaningless as the pessimistic and preacher of joy views do. הבל refers to "anything that is superficial, ephemeral, insubstantial, incomprehensible, enigmatic, inconsistent, or contradictory."[51]

---

49. Some of the suggestions to explain the clear presence of these contradictions include the idea that Qoheleth held to the bitter skeptic view of life and only included positive statements of enjoyment as a means of wishful fancy. Barton posits the proposal that the contradictory statements show the presence of a later editor at work on the book of Ecclesiastes. One example of how this explanation could support the bitter skeptic view is how it explains the apparent contradiction of 2:26. The argument is that the same chapter that includes statements of the wise and the fool having the same fate (2:15, 16) and that there is no good but eating and drinking and enjoying one's self (2:24) would not include 2:26, which gives the orthodox view that God will punish the sinner and reward the good. The sentiment in 2:26 is the result of a later orthodox Jewish editor whose thinking paralleled that of the Pharisees. Ibid., 44–45.

50. Miller, "What the Preacher Forgot: The Rhetoric of Ecclesiastes," 218–19. James Crenshaw has an understanding of Ecclesiastes that somewhat fits the bitter skeptic view. (See above) Crenshaw, *Old Testament Wisdom: An Introduction*, 117–28.

51. Seow, *Ecclesiastes*, 47. In speaking about the genre of Ecclesiastes, Michael Fox has some comments that emphasize the intentional tension/contradiction that Qoheleth creates in Ecclesiastes. (His view will be discussed more in the next section on the issue of the genre of Ecclesiastes.) Fox, *A Time to Tear Down and a Time to Build*, 14–26; Fox, *Ecclesiastes*, xiii.

A Polemical Preacher of Joy

The position that I hold can be called the "preacher of joy" position, while accepting some of the emphases of the realist position. Given the fact that interpreters have written so much about Ecclesiastes and the difficulties in interpreting it, one should refrain from being overly confident about any interpretation.[52] I agree with the realist position in its point that the author uses rhetorical devices to advance his argument. Clearly the author utilizes rhetorical questions in order to lead the reader to a specific conclusion and response. The author desires the reader to accept the apparent tension in life between the way things should be and the way they are. The ultimate goal, however, is for the reader to come to the response of accepting the gift of joy despite the difficulties of life. As to the word הבל, one must not be rigid in trying to force this word with a legitimate semantic domain to always fit the meaningless or absurd rendering; the meaning can be somewhat fluid. R. Norman Whybray has some helpful thoughts to further this view.

Norman Whybray considers Qoheleth to be a preacher of joy and identifies the seven texts (2:24; 3:12, 22; 5:17; 8:15; 9:7–9; 11:9, 10; 12:1) that encourage the reader to follow after pleasure and enjoyment; these joy statements exhibit greater intensity with the progression of the book.[53]

---

52. This position does not answer all of the contradictions and questions in Ecclesiastes that interpreters have grappled with for centuries, and many of the other positions have strong points as already stated. However, it is my opinion that the preacher of joy position is the most convincing of the ones briefly surveyed in this project. With this conclusion, I proceed to demonstrate its likelihood as Qoheleth's overarching—not necessarily all-inclusive—message.

53. The increasing emphatic nature of these joy statements appears in the text. In 2:24, there is the simple statement, "There is nothing better for mortals than to eat and drink, and find enjoyment in their toil." The following two statements of joy include an assertive phrase in the beginning. "I know that there is nothing better for them than to be happy and enjoy themselves as long as they live" (3:12). Yet another assertive phrase appears in 3:22. "So I saw that there is nothing better than that all should enjoy their work . . . ." The fourth statement increases the intensity ever so slightly as 5:18 declares, "This is what I have seen to be good; it is fitting to eat and drink and find enjoyment in all the toil with which one toils under the sun the few days of the life God gives us . . . ." In 8:15, Qoheleth puts more of a personal endorsement behind his statement of joy. "So I commend enjoyment, for there is nothing better for people under the sun than to eat, drink, and enjoy themselves, for this will go with them in their toil through the days of life that God gives them under the sun." In the next cluster of joy statements, Qoheleth commands. "Go, eat your bread with enjoyment, and drink your wine with a merry heart . . . ." (9:7). "Let your garments always be white; do not let oil be lacking on your head." (9:8). "Enjoy life with the wife whom you love, all the days of your vain life that are given under the sun, because this is your portion in life and in your toil at which you toil under

These punctuating statements about joy serve as a leitmotiv, and the respective contexts for these joy statements lead to the conclusion that the ability to enjoy life is a gift from God. One needs to accept the unalterable lot that one has in life, its relative brevity, and the fact that humanity cannot tell the future. In light of and in spite of these unchangeable facts Qoheleth encourages the reader to pursue enjoyment, which is a gift from God.[54]

THE STATE OF THE QUESTION: GENRE IN ECCLESIASTES

The thesis of this work is that the author of Ecclesiastes employs, in part, what this book calls an "anti-apocalyptic genre" in Ecclesiastes, to further Qoheleth's overarching message of joy.[55] I have surveyed the state of the question concerning the message (function) of the book, and I now give a selected survey of how interpreters have wrestled with the question regarding the genre(s) of the book. This survey is important to place the following chapters in the context of scholarly ruminations. Many interpreters have posited numerous ideas on the particular genre (or genres) of Ecclesiastes. A survey of scholarship on this topic reveals the following: the diversity of opinion on the genre of Ecclesiastes, the particular approach of Tremper Longman, and the narrative approach of Michael Fox. This sampling is relevant to the rest of the work because the variance of genre-label discussion regarding Ecclesiastes demonstrates that the conversation is ripe for another suggestion, which is what I offer in chapter four.

After reviewing the genre labels for Ecclesiastes, Roland Murphy concludes, "There is no satisfactory solution to the literary form of the book."[56] A brief survey of the different genre labels that interpreters have given the book reveals the difficulty of determining the genre of Ecclesiastes. Virtually all interpreters would certainly place it under the large genre label of wisdom literature, but beyond this single note of harmony there is a multitude of suggestions.

Royal testament, diatribe, and reflection are all suggested genre labels. A royal testament is "an Egyptian Wisdom genre in which the speaker, a

---

the sun" (9:9). Whybray, "Qoheleth, Preacher of Joy," 87, 88.

54. Ibid., 87–98.

55. By "overarching message of joy" I mean that the author's prevailing communication in the book is one of joy. The function is to move the audience to joy.

56. Murphy, *Ecclesiastes*, xxxi.

king, relates his experiences to his son and gives advice applicable to him in particular."[57] Gerhard von Rad characterizes the salient aspects of the royal testament to be that "it contains a number of fairly long didactic poems or short sentences which . . . purport to be a wise man's personal experience of life."[58] Murphy disagrees with von Rad's label for Ecclesiastes since king fiction does not appear past chapter two.

A diatribe is another genre label assigned to Ecclesiastes. The Hellenistic diatribe's main characteristic is the "dialogue that the writer holds with an interlocutor, real or fictitious."[59] Crenshaw[60] offers some refutation by confining the dialogue or argument to the mind of Qoheleth. Another manner of thinking about the diatribe is in the context of a teacher and student. The teacher utilizes this form to draw attention to error and then to turn the student to the truth. In such a case the "fictitious opposition" of the student could also represent actual contrary ideas of groups.[61]

Reflection is also another genre label assigned to Qoheleth. Although there are many different kinds and stages of reflections, it is sufficient to say that a reflection "has a loose structure, begins with some of kind of observation, which is then considered from one or more points of view, leading to a conclusion."[62] Crenshaw, although he concludes that "no single genre governs everything spoken,"[63] is in favor of the reflection as the prevailing generic label. Qoheleth shares his personal experiences that have the foundation of his authority. He makes observations, reflects, and then shares that reflection; Qoheleth says, "I said in my heart," "I gave my heart," "I saw," "I know," and "there is." The continued use of the first person pronoun "I," Crenshaw writes, places the *persona* of the speaker into the center of attention. If the audience doubts the testimony of Qoheleth, the editor places the authority of Solomon's *persona* and magnitude behind Qoheleth. This, coupled with the plentiful first-hand experiences, makes these words in the genre of reflection powerful.

In addition to this reflection, diatribe, royal testament, or other genre labels, there are other literary forms used to convey the book's message.

57. Fox, *Qoheleth and His Contradictions*, xiii.
58. von Rad, *Wisdom in Israel*, 226–27.
59. Murphy, *Ecclesiastes*, xxxi.
60. Crenshaw, *Ecclesiastes, A Commentary*, 29.
61. Kreuger, *Qoheleth*, 13.
62. Murphy, *Ecclesiastes*, xxxi.
63. Crenshaw, *Ecclesiastes*, 28.

I will give attention to these before moving on to suggestions from other interpreters. Likewise, another form that one would expect in Ecclesiastes (and is present) would be the instruction. The saying, according to Murphy, uses the indicative mood to make gnomic statements based on experience. For example, Ecclesiastes 11:4 says, "One who pays heed to the wind will not sow and one who watches the clouds will never reap." The instruction has a persuasive objective and can be seen in 4:17—5:6.[64]

From the plentitude of suggested genre labels, one can easily see why Murphy said, "There is no satisfactory solution to the literary form of the book."[65] Also, Loader observes that "Qoheleth forms his reflections by making use of a variety of chokmatic Gattungen."[66] Loader observes that the author uses such literary forms such as the *tob*-saying, the comparison, the metaphor, the parable, the allegory, and the woe-saying to convey his overall message. The *tob*-saying is comparative in nature by stating "better is x than y." One such example is 4:6,[67] "Better one handful with tranquility than two handfuls with toil and chasing after wind," in the context of pointing out the meaningless, enigmatic, or absurd nature of toil motivated by envy.

The comparison is another literary technique that Loader observes in Ecclesiastes. An example would be 2:13, "I saw wisdom is better than folly, just as light is better than darkness." Yet another example would be 11:5, "As you do not know the path of the wind or how the body is formed in a mother's womb, so you do not understand the work of God, the Maker of all things" where the human ignorance of meteorological happenings and the formation of a human being in the womb is compared to (and thus makes the point of) humanity's ignorance of God's work.[68]

Closely related to the comparison is the use of the metaphor in the book. Such examples would be 3:5 and 7:26. Loader understands the mention of casting stones in 3:5 to be a metaphor for semen. The author uses a number of metaphors in 7:26 to equate women with entrapment.[69]

---

64. Murphy, *Ecclesiastes*, xxxii.

65. Ibid., xxxi.

66. Loader, *Polar Structures in the Book of Qoheleth*, 28.

67. Ibid., 21. Other examples of the *tob*-saying are: 4:3, 13; 5:4; 6:3, 9; 7:1–3, 5, 8, 11; 9:16, 18.

68. Ibid., 22. Other examples are 7:6; 9:12; 7:12.

69. Ibid., 23.

Loader also notices the presence of the parable in the book. In 9:14–15 the author uses a parable to illustrate that the disdain that the poor man receives; the fact that he is disregarded devalues the wisdom that he has.[70] Similar to the parable is the use of the allegory, and this literary form is also present in the book. Old age is spoken of allegorically in 12:3–4 with terms referring to a house setting and daily life occurrences.[71] Qoheleth also uses the woe-saying which is present in 10:16, 17. He employs a number of literary forms and genres in order to make his presentation, and it would not be unusual for him to develop new forms or hybrid genre forms within this mixture of literary forms.

Tremper Longman employs a theory and method of genre different from many other commentators and designates Ecclesiastes's genre as a "framed wisdom autobiography."[72] Differentiating his theory and method of genre from that of Gunkel, Longman considers the form critical approach to be too diachronic and prefers to utilize a more synchronic approach to genre. He, thus, proceeds with an approach that is more descriptive and reflective of the perspective of Hirsch. With Hirsch, Longman agrees that proper genre identification is essential for proper interpretation and that such proper identification is the result of a "give-and-take reading process." He also realizes that the reader's distance from the culture and time of the text and author provides an obstacle to the necessary genre identification.[73]

Fluidity is also an important consideration in this process, as the interpreter must realize that the concept of genre is, itself, fluid. "Any single piece of literature may be described with more than one genre label." The definition of genre is based upon resemblances between clusters of texts; a text may be a part of a large genre based upon a few resemblances and also be a part of a narrow genre based on many characteristics. Again, genre identification is fluid; a text can even have more than one genre label. "Genre distinctions do not fall from heaven. They are approximate ways by which we may speak of similar texts."[74] With this understanding of genre, Longman identifies Ecclesiastes as a "framed wisdom autobiography," while acknowledging the different labels such as wisdom literature or reflection that one could also apply. The real significance of Longman's findings for

---

70. Ibid., 23.
71. Ibid., 24.
72. Longman, *The Book of Ecclesiastes*, 16–17.
73. Ibid., 16–17.
74. Ibid., 16–17.

the query of this investigation is his method of genre identification: he utilizes a synchronic approach, understands it as a give-and-take process, and recognizes fluidity in the process of genre identification.

To the question of Ecclesiastes's genre, Michael Fox[75] adds a different note to the above-mentioned cacophony; he sees Ecclesiastes in the form of a narrative. He also considers the efforts of interpreters to make the rough places or contradictions in Ecclesiastes plain as counterproductive; Qoheleth intended the contradictions in the text. In order to make his point, he surveys attempts made to deal with the contradictions—attempts that, according to Fox, do not work.

There is always, Fox believes, a need for a holistic reading, such as understanding apparent contradictions by a more precise definition of terminology, but this holistic manner of reading does not warrant the attempt by some to harmonize the discords and tensions. "For example, 'I praised שׂמחה' (8:15) is said to pertain to the joy that comes from fulfilling commandments, whereas 'and שׂמחה—what does this accomplish?' (2:2) dismisses specifically pleasure that does not proceed from commandments." The text does not sustain such a distinction. Another attempt is to identify later additions to the text (especially trendy in the nineteenth and early twentieth centuries). Assigning contradictory sections to the speech of another person or group that Qoheleth is refuting is also another means of smoothing the contradictions. Detecting dialectic where Qoheleth is stating the ideas of another only to refute those ideas is another attempt at smoothing the rough places. Others simply conclude that Qoheleth's contradictions result from a soul and psyche that is truly disturbed and fragmented.[76]

Qoheleth's autobiography, according to Fox, stands within the framework of the narrator's words found in the epilogue (12:9–14). The same narrator also speaks of Qoheleth in the third person in 1:1-2; 7:27; and 12:8. Since one cannot take a single statement of Qoheleth and conclude that the statement encapsulates the teaching of the book, it is crucial for the interpreter to read Ecclesiastes as a narrative as opposed to seeing it as a collection of proverbs and sayings free-standing from the context of the whole. Qoheleth's presentation is reflective as he recounts what he was thinking when he had his experiences. Indeed at some points Qoheleth's thoughts should be understood as temporary and in the process of change,

---

75. Fox, *A Time to Tear Down, A Time to Build Up: A Rereading of Ecclesiastes*, 14.
76. Ibid., 14–26.

to be discarded at a later stage of life. He carries the reader with him as he goes through the struggles on the path to knowledge—only to conclude with a very incomplete knowledge. Fox's main critique of scholarship on the genre of Ecclesiastes is that the interpreter must not attempt to undo the contradictions but rather appreciate the struggle, frustrations, and tensions of life; this perpetual struggle is what Qoheleth desires to convey.[77]

SUMMARY

This chapter has presented a beginning discussion of function (message) and genre, both elements of the crucial setting-function-genre triad of this book; it has surveyed the interpretation of Ecclesiastes through the twentieth century. The century saw historical criticism fully engage Ecclesiastes. At the beginning of the century, the unity of Ecclesiastes was denied, but this view would shift later in the century to approach the book as a unit, with the exception of the epilogue. Some historical-critical commentators are McNeille, Barton, Gordis, Crenshaw, Murphy, and Ogden. Modern literary interpretation, realizing that historical criticism tools were not the only tools available, has brought readings of Ecclesiastes and its message through the lens of canonical (Childs), structural (Loader), and dialogical (Perry).

After centuries of interpretation and more than two centuries of historical and modern literary criticism, a consensus for the message of Ecclesiastes has not emerged. The conversation is ripe for yet another suggestion, which this book will offer. The many views of the message, throughout the centuries, largely fall within the following views: repentant king, ascetic, bitter skeptic, realist, and preacher of joy. Aside from the overall label of wisdom literature, scholarship has not reached an agreement on the genre of Ecclesiastes. This chapter examined a few of the suggestions for this genre label: royal testament, diatribe, reflection, framed wisdom autobiography, and a framed narrative. This book endeavors to contribute another suggestion to the discussion.

---

77. Fox, *Qoheleth*, xiii. ; Fox, *A Time to Tear Down and a Time to Build*, 14–26; Fox, *Ecclesiastes*, xiii.

Chapter 2

Genre: A Definition

Having surveyed the literature on the message and genre of Ecclesiastes, attention now turns to a crucial term for this book: genre. What is genre? The purpose of this chapter is to establish a definition that I will use, particularly in chapter four, to demonstrate its thesis. My thesis is that Qoheleth, in part, utilizes a hybrid genre in his work. He, in part, employs what this book will call an "anti-apocalyptic genre" in Ecclesiastes, and the presence of this genre serves to further Qoheleth's overarching message of joy.

For this chapter the works of Harry Nasuti and Eric D. Hirsch serve as foils elucidating the particular definition adopted for this work. This book argues for a definition of genre that centers upon setting and function. The discussion also benefits from the work of genre theorists outside of the field of biblical studies: David Fishelov, Carolyn Miller, John Swales, and Adena Rosmarin. The interaction with these additional genre theorists will help to trace the threads that contribute to my view of genre, which appears at the end of this chapter.

DAVID FISHELOV

The variegated nature of genre is illustrated by the abundance of analogies that genre theorists use to define and explain genre. The concept of genre eludes solely one explanation. In his book *Metaphors of Genre*, David Fishelov provides analogies to elucidate his understanding of genre; he examines literary genres using analogies of biological species, families, social institutions, and speech acts. The biological and family analogies will receive attention here. As for the biological analogy, Fishelov finds the possibility of Darwinian evolutionary ideas enlightening genre theory intriguing. With the family analogy, he explores the socio-psychological implications in a family situation as an example of how genres innovate within a tradition. Fishelov cautions that although there is a certain level of sophistication with genre theories and their use of analogies, "it [literary theory] is not yet scientific, at least not to the standards of a natural science . . ."[1] Flexibility is important with any approach and explanation of genre. Before we examine Fishelov's use of these two analogies, a look at his working definition for genre would be helpful.

Fishelov posits a working definition for genre; he considers genre to be "a combination of prototypical, representative members, and a flexible set of constitutive rules that apply to some levels of literary texts, to some individual writers, usually to more than one literary period, and to more than one language and culture."[2] Along with this working definition, Fishelov emphasizes that he refers to historical genres rather than theoretical genres. By historical, he affirms that these genres occur throughout history as opposed to just one period of time; they are not simply "atemporal classificatory schemata."[3] Also, by historical (and not theoretical), he means that these genres, in truth, do form the works of authors and writers *contra* the idea of pragmatically assigned genres.

Since he does not see genre as theoretical, Fishelov expresses disapproval of an approach that allows the critic to see or broaden the genre label subjectively in order to establish a point. In Fishelov's perspective, such an approach betrays an overly exalted view of the critic's role and does not take into consideration the varied factors involved in establishing genres. Fishelov asserts, "Critics must be more modest about their role in the constitution of literary genres . . . ."[4]

While he disapproves of an overly active role for the critic, he does argue for flexibility in the constitution of literary genre writing. He sets forth a flexible set of rules for genre but also affirms the dynamic nature of literary genre, which must permit the reality of some rules being pliable and,

---

1. Fishelov, *Metaphors of Genre: The Role of Analogies in Genre Theory*, 2, 7.
2. Ibid., 8.
3. Ibid., 10.
4. Ibid., 11.

thus, experiencing some reshaping and loosening. Yet, writers must adhere to, at least, some of the preceded norms of that particular genre tradition.[5]

Literary Genres as Biological Species

To introduce genre as biological species, Fishelov refers to a quote from Sheldon Sacks:

> Satires exist as literary fact ... as the existence of mammals is a "fact" of the physical world. Though whales suckle their young and grow hair, they have at least as many traits in common with sailfish as they do with men; our selection of the particular similarities to define a class called mammals is justified only because, when we lump whales together with elephants, hyenas, and men, we facilitate the knowledge of the biological universe, contained, for example, in Darwin's theories.[6]

Fishelov especially argues that the biological species analogy is useful in "questions of generic evolutions and interrelationship, the complex process of the emergence of new genres on the literary scene, and the decline of old ones." Admittedly there is little likelihood of hybrids in biology, since a biological hybrid would most probably be sterile. (There are some genre theorists who have reservations about using biological species analogy since literary genres exhibit a much greater flexibility than biological species.) Unlike biological hybrids, literary hybrids often reproduce prolifically; an example would be the tragicomedy, a combination of two genres that has reproduced many works. Fishelov continues, "thus hybridization in literature is not only more common than hybridization in nature; it is also more productive."[7]

Another difference between biological hybrids and literary hybrids would have to do with the relationship between the individual unit and the larger species context. In biology, the relationship between the individual unit and the biological species will and can only exhibit the group. Fishelov asserts, "In literature each of the individual units to some extent modifies and changes the group."[8] To explicate the change that occurs in the literary texts, the author draws from Darwin's ideas of natural selection.

5. Ibid., 14.
6. Sacks, *Fiction and the Shape of Belief*, 5–6.
7. Fishelov, *Metaphors of Genre: The Role of Analogies in Genre Theory*, 20.
8. Ibid., 21.

A Polemical Preacher of Joy

Fishelov agrees with Stephen Jay Gould's summary of Darwin's presentation on natural selection.[9]

> Organisms vary, and these variations are inherited (at least in part) by their offspring. Organisms produce more offspring than can possibly survive. On average offspring that vary most strongly in directions favored by the environment will survive and propagate. Favorable variation will therefore accumulate in populations by natural selection. . . . The essence of Darwin's theory lies in his contention that natural selection is the creative force of evolution—not just the executioner of the unfit. . . . Variation must be random, or at least not preferentially inclined toward adaptation. For, if variation comes prepackaged in the right direction, then selection plays no creative role, but merely eliminates the unlucky individuals who do not vary in the appropriate way. . . . Evolution is a mixture of chance and necessity—chance at the level of variation, necessity in the working of selection.

Based on the above summary of Darwin's ideas on natural selection, Fishelov makes the following conclusions. For literary genre the individual text would be similar to the individual organism; biological species would be analogous to the literary genre. Literary and cultural selection would be for genre what natural selection would be for Darwinian understanding. This approach, however, does not require a deterministic view. It would, in fact, allow for flexibility and respect the poetic license and freedom involved. The survival of new literary creations would be an example of this approach.

Only some of these new literary creations will survive. The approach to genre is not what texts will be produced but "rather what texts will receive acceptance in a cultural environment?"[10] Concerning the survival of genres, Fishelov emphasizes generic productivity and generic sterility. The crucial element in consideration of the survival of a genre is not whether a text is read but rather whether or not that new genre is reproduced. The true distinction of survival is not merely existence but also productivity or procreation, as with the biological nature.[11]

The answer to this consideration of genre survival has much to do with the value systems that oversee selection in culture (*contra* the case in nature). Within the literary environment there is a myriad of values (aesthetic, ideological, political, etc.) that coalesce to advance some literary

---

9. Ibid., 35.
10. Ibid., 36.
11. Ibid., 37.

productions and repress others. Also crucial to understanding this process is the fact that the literary environment is not static but dynamic (much more so than the natural environment). Fishelov states, "There is a dialectical relationship between the literary production and the literary environment in which the former may not only adapt itself to the latter but also contribute to reshaping it."[12]

Literary Genres as Families

Fishelov points out that the trend in modern genre theory is to emphasize "the flexible and dynamic nature of literary genres." This dominant trend, in attempting to establish a philosophical foundation for its un-dogmatic approach, introduces Ludwig Wittgenstein's concept of family resemblance into genre theory. According to this view: "Representations of a genre may then be regarded as making up a family whose septs (subdivisions) and individual members are related in various ways, without necessarily having any single feature shared in common by all."[13]

Fishelov argues that Wittgenstein's thoughts have been used or misused to present too loose a concept of genre, and Fishelov proposes a way in which Wittgenstein's concept can be used positively in the field of genre theory.[14] He writes: "I object to this formulation of the analogy on the grounds that whereas rigid concepts of genre are justifiably rejected, the alternative presented by the radical version of the family resemblance analogy seems to go too far in implying that genres are totally open and un-delineated categories."[15] Fishelov, referencing with approval the work of Morris Weitz, presents the view that each particular work will exhibit only some characteristics with another work. Delineating genre along the lines of mandatory characteristics is, therefore, not a possible proposition. For example, determining whether a text is a novel really has to do with whether or not the text in question displays certain similarities to other texts that wear the label "novel"; in such a case these similarities would justify extending the genre label to a new case.[16]

12. Ibid., 36.
13. Fowler, *Kinds of Literature: An Introduction to the Theory of Genres and Modes*, 41.
14. Fishelov, *Metaphors of Genre: The Role of Analogies in Genre Theory*, 54.
15. Ibid., 56.
16. Ibid., 57.

Writing approvingly of the work of Elenor Rosch, Fishelov[17] presents a more positive concept of family resemblance. In this assessment, when a member of the category exhibits overlapping characteristics with the larger group but exhibits the least amount of family resemblance with the larger category, that member is considered prototypical. This understanding of prototypical is borrowed from a discussion of natural language categories; it has, however, benefit for the discussion on literary genres. With this understanding—especially pertinent to the discussion of genre here—one can think of literary genres as having a "hard-core" of members that demonstrate a high degree of resemblance to the larger category or genre family. Yet there would also be, outside of this core, more "archetypical" members that do not exhibit as many overlapping characteristics. Fishelov concludes, "This approach invites us to think of genres as clubs imposing a certain number of conditions for membership, but tolerating as quasi-members those individuals who can fulfill only some of the requirements, and who do not seem to fit into any other club."[18]

Developing Definition

Drawing from Fishelov's presentation of the nature of genre the following assertion can be made: genre is flexible but this flexibility has parameters.

Genre is flexible. Instead of focusing on a rigid list of formal characteristics, the interpreter must realize that the constitutive rules that apply to genre, which would also involve characteristics present in the literary work, are subject to change according to authorial will and purpose.

Comparing literary genres to Darwin's theory of evolution of biological species, one can also state that genres are subject to evolution that results from authorial purpose (authorial setting and authorial function for the text) in conjunction with the present literary environment. This interaction can often result in the production of hybrid genres, which can exhibit the characteristics of more than one genre. Interpreters must be mindful of this phenomenon because the literary environment, like the biological sphere, is not static but dynamic.

With this possible literary phenomenon and generic mutation in mind, it is proper to consider genres as clubs with members at the core who exhibit a high degree of family resemblances along with other members

17. Ibid., 63.
18. Ibid., 63.

who are on the fringes who may, in fact, overlap with another club and thus exhibit a lesser amount of family resemblances. Again, rather than a rigid list of formal characteristics, genre is flexible.

Despite this flexibility, one must also consider some guiding parameters to genre. A genre label is not merely theoretical and a convenient creation of the critic. It must be historical in the sense that it, conceivably, must have been, or plausibly could have been, in the mind of the author. These proposed genres must have arguably formed the work of the respective authors. The critic must, therefore, maintain a modest perspective on her role with regard to assigning genre labels.

CAROLYN MILLER

In her article "Genre as Social Action," Carolyn Miller argues for a pragmatic understanding of rhetorical genre. She has two objectives in her treatment of genre. One point of interest in her approach "is to make of rhetorical genre a stable classifying concept; another is to ensure that the concept is rhetorically sound."[19]

In order to fulfill these objectives, Miller presents a pragmatic view of genre. Furthermore, and more pertinent to the goal of this present work, she argues for an understanding of genre that engages and seeks to elucidate "the way we encounter, interpret, react to, and create particular texts."[20] Contending that a valid formulation of genre must center on the intended action it seeks to achieve rather than the form in which the discourse appears, Miller explains the relationship between genre and recurrent situations as well as the hierarchical models of communication.[21] Inaugurals, eulogies, presidential state of the union addresses, and other such discourses would be examples of what Miller means.

A rhetorically sound classification of discourse concerns itself with how the discourse works; it must, therefore, examine the rhetorical experience of the individuals who both send and receive this discourse. Since this classifying principle points toward rhetorical practice, one can say that "genre represents action." It must, therefore, entail both situation and motive, considering the fact that human activity can only receive proper

---

19. Miller, "Genre as Social Action," 23.
20. Ibid., 23.
21. Ibid., 24.

interpretation within the framework of a situation and the corresponding motives.[22]

Again, what Miller proposes is, that for rhetoric, the term genre be used to speak of the "type of discourse classification, a classification based in rhetorical practice and consequently open rather than closed and organized around situated actions (that is pragmatic, rather than syntactic and semantic)."[23] She asserts that "a genre is composed of a constellation of recognizable forms bound together by an internal dynamic. . . . The dynamic 'fuses' substantive, stylistic, and situational characteristics. The fusion has the character of a rhetorical 'response' to situational demands perceived by the rhetor."[24] Moreover, since these rhetorical forms, which themselves result in genres, are stylistic and substantive responses to the demands of the social situations, "a genre becomes a complex of formal and substantive features that create a particular effect in a given situation."[25]

"Genre, in this way, becomes more than a formal entity"; Miller asserts, "it becomes pragmatic, fully rhetorical, a point of connection between intention and effect, [an] aspect of social action."[26] Every day, similar situations transpire that elicit similar responses. These similar responses are recurring forms that tend to be considered a tradition or template for any future response to future recurring situations. Presidential state of the union addresses inaugurals, eulogies, and other such discourses would be illustrations of what Miller means. These discourses exhibit a conventional form as a result of recurring in situations with comparable situational composition. Since they and the situations that require them recur so much, rhetors draw from previous experience to determine what is appropriate and not appropriate for these discourses.[27]

In conclusion, Miller's view of rhetorical genre has its foundation in rhetorical practice. This understanding is not taxonomy of genres. There is no limit to genres in a society—the number of genres derives from the societal complexity and multiplicity.[28]

22. Ibid., 24.
23. Ibid., 27.
24. Ibid., 24.
25. Ibid., 24, 25.
26. Ibid., 25.
27. Ibid., 25. She is quoting from L. Bitzer
28. The following excerpt from her article summarizes her view. 1. Genre refers to a conventional category of discourse based in large scale typification of rhetorical action;

Genre: A Definition

This understanding of genre, Miller writes, has obvious bearing on criticism and genre theory but also upon rhetorical education. Learning a genre affords more than grasping a predictability of form or understanding a means to achieving a social goal. This knowledge of genre and the workings thereof enables us to comprehend more effectively the situations and life encounters in which one finds oneself and the prospect of seeing either failure or success in acting together. Miller concludes, "As a recurrent, significant action, a genre embodies an aspect of cultural rationality."[29]

Developing Definition

From Miller's work one can think of genre as inextricably tied to function (Miller argues social action). A proper understanding of genre encompasses a pragmatic view that centers on the intended action the literary work seeks to achieve and how the discourse works. As such, a proper view of genre must go beyond mere formal considerations although genre does include form characteristics. This dynamic of intended action fuses with the stylistic and situational realities to fulfill its function. Genre is rightly tied to what it is intended to do.

Since genre is intended to achieve a social goal, the number of genres is without limit because the boundaries for genre are determined by those social situations to which genre must speak. In other words, genre continuously evolves to communicate more effectively with its setting in light of the desired function. Like Fishelov, Miller emphasizes this flexibility as she points to the connection between intention and effect.

---

as action, it acquires meaning from situation and from the social context in which that situation arose. 2. As meaningful action, genre is interpretable by means of rules; genre rules occur at a relatively high level on a hierarchy of rules for symbolic interaction. 3. Genre is distinct from form: form is the more general term used at all levels of the hierarchy. Genre is a form at one particular level that is a fusion of lower level forms and characteristic substance. 4. Genre serves as the substance of forms at higher levels; as recurrent patterns of language use, genres help constitute the substance of our cultural life. 5. A genre is a rhetorical means for mediating private intentions and social exigence; it motivates by connecting the private with the public, the singular with the recurrent. Ibid., 37.

29. Ibid., 39.

JOHN SWALES

In his book *Genre Analysis*, Swales's objective is to present a pedagogical method concerning English in research and academic endeavors. There are three central concepts in his approach: discourse community, genre, and language-learning task (attention will turn primarily to the first two). Conceding the observation that each of these key concepts and terms has some ambiguity in its meaning, the author makes an effort to infuse clarity into his usage of these terms. His ultimate goal is to show the value of genre analysis as a tool to investigate "spoken and written discourse for applied ends."[30] His goal is, therefore, thoroughly practical in that he desires to assist both native and non-native speakers to improve their proficiency in academic communication.[31] Although his ultimate goal differs from the central objective of this particular book, his thoughts on genre are apropos to this present discussion and definition of genre.

Swales establishes early in his work that he views genre as more than text(s). It is important to utilize texts for the purpose of comprehending the manner in which texts should be organized (i.e. for the sake of information, rhetorically and stylistically). Swales contends, however, that the proper understanding of genre far surpasses a mere textual treatment, a point he further develops in his work. Moreover, he asserts that a genre-focused approach is an effective means of grasping the various communicative events that transpire in the sphere of the present-day English-speaking academy.

A crucial element to understanding his formulation of genre is communicative purpose. This is the crucial thread that joins Swales's three elements of discourse community, genre, and task. Communicative purpose propels the language activities in which the discourse community engages. It is the "prototypical criterion for genre identity,"[32] and it serves as the main determinant task.

As mentioned above, discourse community and genre will receive the primary attention in this account of Swales's thoughts on genre. As such, the undertaking of defining exactly what a discourse community is would be in order. Swales defines it as the following:[33] "A cluster of ideas: that language use in a group is a form of social behavior, that discourse is a

---

30. Swales, *Genre Analysis: English in Academic and Research Settings*, 1.
31. Ibid., 9.
32. Ibid., 10.
33. Ibid., 21.

Genre: A Definition

means of maintaining and extending the group's knowledge and of initiating new members into the group, and that discourse is epistemic or constitutive of the group's knowledge." Yet this definition leaves many questions unanswered as to the nature of discourse community, so Swales presents a list of criteria to help identify what a discourse community is. The criteria are as follows:[34]

1. A discourse community has a broadly agreed set of common public goals.
2. A discourse community has mechanisms of intercommunication among its members. . . . They must realize that they are a community.
3. A discourse community uses its participatory mechanisms primarily to provide information and feedback . . . such as journals, societies, [etc.]
4. A discourse community utilizes and hence possesses one or more genres in the communicative furtherance of its aims.
5. In addition to owning genres, a discourse community has acquired some specific lexis (technical language). Example: the technical language of the discourse community.
6. A discourse community has a threshold level of members with a suitable degree of relevant content and discoursal expertise . . . survival of the community depends on a reasonable ratio between novices and experts.
7. There does not necessarily have to be an assimilation of worldview or full participation for there to be a discourse community.

For Swales each of these criteria must be present for there to be a discourse community.

Genre is also another crucial element to Swales' treatment. In order to explain his concept of genre, Swales examines what scholars have said about genre in areas such as literary studies and rhetoric, followed by a working definition of genre. In the area of literary studies, he emphasizes the flexible and evolving nature of genre as he notes that there has been a tendency to downplay a sense of stability given the fact that many scholarly works have endeavored "to show how the chosen author breaks the mould of convention and so establishes significance and originality."[35] He points

---

34. Ibid., 24–27.
35. Ibid., 36.

out that some genre theorists, such as Alastair Fowler, give detailed treatment to genre classification but also conclude that all of this classification wanes in value when considered in light of the fact that genres are continually evolving.[36] In fact, Swales reflects on the words of Tzvetan Todorov: "A new genre is always the transformation of one or several old genres: by inversion, by displacement, by combination."[37]

In the area of rhetoric, Swales seems partial to understanding genre within the context of recurring social discourse; he speaks approvingly of Carolyn Miller. He especially notes her approach of expanding the scope of genre to study the different types of discourse. Additionally, the emphasis on the genre as focused within the idea of social action that it is used to execute is also another reason for his favorable review.[38]

In light of these investigations on discourse community and genre, Swales presents his own working definition on genre. A group of communicative events with common communicative purpose serves as the substance of a genre. Within the parent discourse community there are members with the expertise to decipher these purposes, and it is these purposes that are the foundation for the genre. The impact of this foundational rationale is to give shape for the schematic construction of the discourse as well as to have some bearing on the content and style of the discourse. Communicative purpose is a crucial element that serves as a guiding force to maintain the focus of the genre and its integrity as a rhetorical action. Propelled by its inherent purpose, genre displays resemblances in "structure, style, content and intended audience." The examples of this genre will receive the description "prototypical" from the parent discourse community if there is a high degree of expectations met for this particular discourse.[39]

Developing Definition

Drawing on the work of Swales, one can assert that genre is tied not only to function but also to the intersection of function and setting. Particularly crucial to a proper construal of genre is to understand the roles of communicative purpose and discourse community. When we think of genre, we can only rightly understand it if we consider it in light of communicative

36. Ibid., 35.
37. Todorov, "The Origin of Genres," 159–70.
38. Swales, *Genre Analysis: English in Academic and Research Settings*, 42–44.
39. Ibid., 58.

purpose: what is the genre intended to do? Without this consideration, we do not have a proper understanding of genre; in fact, this consideration must supersede our deliberations about form characteristics.

Our understanding of genre must also encompass a working appreciation of discourse community. I would not concur that all of the criteria of discourse community would need to be met, but many of them would need to be met in order to understand properly the setting that intertwines with the function of the genre and its literary work. In other words, our formulation and understanding of genre needs to begin not with formal characteristics but rather, firstly, with the community that has produced it and the community to which the work is addressed and, secondly, with the communicative purpose that the work is intended to fulfill. Thirdly, in the words of Tzvetan Todorov, "A new genre is always the transformation of one or several old genres: by inversion, by displacement, by combination."[40]

ADENA ROSMARIN

In her book *The Power of Genre*, Adena Rosmarin asserts the constitutive power of genre. She begins her work with some crucial questions.[41] "My concern, in short, is with the question of genre. It is a question that has multiple phrasings. Are genres found in texts, in the reader's mind, in the author's, or in some combination thereof? Or are they not 'found' at all but, rather, devised and used? Are they 'theoretical' or 'historical'? Are they 'prescriptive' or 'descriptive'?"

Rosmarin argues for a theory of genre that "places constitutive or constructive power in the genre"; her view of genre transcends the terms historical or theoretical in favor of a framework that emphasizes genre's usefulness in explanation of a text. Genre is one of the heuristic tools at the critic's disposal. The purpose of this heuristic tool is to persuade the audience into viewing and understanding the text in a fuller way, in a manner not previously seen or understood by the reader.[42]

With genre identified as "pragmatic rather than natural, as defined rather than found, and as used rather than described,"[43] the number of genres is endless; the number expands to however many are needed. The

40. Ibid., 35.
41. Rosmarin, *The Power of Genre*, 7.
42. Ibid., 25.
43. Ibid., 25.

purpose of genre is to further the explanatory goals of the critic. This is contrary to the traditional idea that genre is discovered and thus is "a guess or hypothesis that needs to be proven."[44] Rosmarin writes, "Genre is not, as is commonly thought, a class but, rather, a classifying statement. It is therefore a text. Genre has constitutive power. There is a pragmatic end."[45] "A genre is a kind of schemata, a way of discussing a literary text in terms that link it with other texts . . . ." "Furthermore," Rosmarin continues, "our choice is never between more or less 'valid interpretations,' but between those that are more or less useful: 'what we call truth, namely a conceptual world coinciding with the external world, is merely the most expedient error.'"[46]

She uses the metaphor of a painter producing a work of art as an example of the role of the critic and her relationship with genre. She points out that art visual representation commences with a schema that receives attention and alteration for the particular audience. The hope of accuracy and an identical exactness is elusive. To assign "naturalness" to such a work of art is truly to acknowledge the successful illusion that the painter has wrought. The art that is considered the most realistic is still "wedded to types."[47]

Rosmarin acknowledges that there is conflict present with understanding the process as such. Traditionally the critic conveys the idea and process as representation—regardless of whether the subject of discussion is a painting or poetic work. This conveyance speaks as if the painter or writer were simply a copyist. In contrast, Rosmarin argues for a rhetoric visual representation that realizes that the exposition of a text or work of art would be more appropriately considered "a knowing-how rather than a knowing-that; it happens better when we talk in terms of doing rather than of seeing, of defining and justifying rather than grounding and validating." Ernst Gombrich makes the perceptive statement: "Painting is an activity, and the artist will therefore tend to see what he paints rather than paint what he sees."[48] She is more creative in her depiction than merely copying.

Gombrich writes of placing just as much value upon the critical or explanatory text as the text itself; it has a power to make the reader see

44. Ibid., 46.
45. Ibid., 46.
46. Ibid., 20.
47. Ibid., 12.
48. Ibid., 12.

what the reader was previously unable to see. Even a painting is at the most a matching. It is "always gesturing toward the not-itself and striving to convince its audience that that gesture is a grasp, visual representation is asking its audience to entertain the paradox: that the face beheld or the text read is simultaneously itself and not itself, both what it is and what it seems . . . ."[49]

Developing Definition

From Rosmarin's work one can assert that a genre label is best characterized as a heuristic tool to explain the text. Rosmarin's work furthers the understanding of genre but takes it too far. She assigns too much power to the critic and does not sufficiently consider the role of the author; authorial intention receives low priority. She does seem to have a proper understanding of the teaching/explanatory role of the genre label. It serves to help the critic explain what she has found. I would argue that the critic should attempt to consider authorial intent in this process of discovery/artistry.

HARRY NASUTI

The works of Harry Nasuti and Eric Hirsch will receive scrutiny together before I present my own definition of genre.

Another stream for the foundational understanding of genre comes from Harry Nasuti. Examining the interpretation of the psalms in history, he addresses genre's descriptive and/or constructive role as well as genre's connection to setting and function. Harry Nasuti, utilizing examples of interpretation for the Psalms, outlines his view of genre and its role in biblical interpretation.[50] Genre relates to setting and function, and the definition of genre has both a descriptive as well as constructive role in hermeneutics. Giving a brief survey of how different voices in the scholarly community have defined genre, Nasuti turns to the work of Herman Gunkel, Claus Westermann, and Walter Brueggemann. Gunkel placed texts in a certain genre if the group of texts "share[d] certain thoughts and moods, a specific linguistic form and a common setting in life," thus combining considerations of literary and sociological observations to delineate genre. The issue

---

49. Ibid., 17.

50. Nasuti, *Defining the Sacred Song: Genre, Tradition, Post-Critical Interpretation of the Psalms*, 45–56.

of setting, in terms of this task of genre definition, is where there has been dispute.

Gunkel, by his definition of genre, brought the focus away from mainly historical-setting considerations of historical criticism to include more "typical institutional settings in the ongoing life of the community."[51] In the study of the psalms, this concern resulted in attention to typical and cultic setting that made the focus broader than the close attention to specific historical events that nineteenth-century historical criticism had.

Other scholars such as Westermann and Brueggemann would cause the focus to become even broader. For Westermann, Israel's "overall relationship with God, especially as this theological stance may be distinguished from that of the ancient Near East"[52] is the setting for the psalms. Brueggemann took this generalization further than Westermann and sees the psalms through the lens of orientation, disorientation, and new orientation, taking the scope beyond institutional or theological setting to that of the existential setting of humanity. In this further broadening of the setting, Brueggemann saw the psalms in relation to their function and not only literary or structural considerations.[53]

The significant element, as Nasuti points out, of this development in scholarship is that setting and function, as connected features, are determinative for the genre in which a text receives placement. An example of how setting and function play a decisive role in the genre placement of a text would be the penitential psalms. The traditional seven penitential psalms had this classification largely because of the theological perspective in which they received consideration. More modern readings see these psalms differently because the psalms are then read in different historical

---

51. Ibid., 46. Also see Gunkel's discussion on the "Fundamental Problems of Hebrew Literary History."

52. Nasuti, *Defining the Sacred Song: Genre, Tradition, Post-Critical Interpretation of the Psalms*, 47. Likewise, Westermann writes in his work *The Living Psalms*, "The reconciling power which the psalms have so far demonstrated throughout their long history will in the future reach to the whole of endagered humanity. That God has made man in His image and likeness, so that he, as a man who realizes his human identity, can always speak to God, in sorrow and joy alike, and can trust his Creator throughout, in all and through all—to all this the psalms give unique expression." Westermann, *The Living Psalms*, vii–viii.

53. Nasuti, *Defining the Sacred Song: Genre, Tradition, Post-Critical Interpretation of the Psalms*, 48. See Breugemann's work *The Message of the Psalms* where he presents in detail his schema of orientation, disorientation, and new orientation as separate overall genre groupings for the psalms. Brueggemann, *The Message of the Psalms*, 9.

Genre: A Definition

and theological settings. Nasuti particularly points out that "once one shifts the setting, one shifts the genre" and points to the fact that, once the penitential psalms were viewed with the Augustinian reading of the book of Romans, interpreters could group them in alignment with a shared element that the historical setting of ancient Israel would not have. Placing these texts (and their use) in different settings results in different genres or subgenres of the larger Psalms genre. Nasuti continues, "in short, to engage in genre analysis is to engage in a historical enterprise."[54]

According to Nasuti, while Gunkel attempted to describe the manner in which the psalms functioned in ancient Israel, the works of Westermann and Brueggemann were more constructive than descriptive. These scholars are advocating a transition to the way these psalms are used in the modern times; their genre analysis is more prescriptive than descriptive.[55]

Texts are placed within genres based upon the fact that there are common features to the texts. The determination of these commonalities is heavily dependent on the reader (the questions and elements for which the reader searches) and her setting, "external criteria." Nasuti writes, "To view genre in such a way is to see it as essentially a means by which certain texts are read together as mutually informative . . . as a reading convention rather than as a property of the text itself. It is also to acknowledge the importance of genre in the production of meaning." Genre analysis is, therefore, a historical exercise as well as one of self-definition.[56]

The constructive view of genre, however, is not without its constraints. Nasuti identifies three constraints on it. One constraint is the canon. The fact that these biblical texts are within a larger canon of Scripture means that similar texts within the canon are placed next to the texts in question. A tradition of genre analysis within certain communities also serves as a constraint or guideline for this treatment of genre. A corollary of this constraint is the fact that the interpreter is within a community, which provides a dialogical environment where interpreters can have their interpretations and genre analysis examined and critiqued.[57]

---

54. Nasuti, *Defining the Sacred Song: Genre, Tradition, Post-Critical Interpretation of the Psalms*, 49.
55. Ibid., 50.
56. Ibid., 52–53.
57. Ibid., 54–55.

ERIC D. HIRSCH

Hirsch details the importance of genre, the process of interpretation, the importance of authorial will in deciphering genre, and the creation of new genres. Hirsch writes, "Coming to understand the meaning of an utterance is like learning the rules of a game." The challenge is to decipher which game is being played. After determining which game is being played, the interpreter must determine the rules of the game, which is difficult since there is no rulebook available. The interpreter needs to be familiar with types of utterances or "family resemblances" that span different instances. The utterance type that encompasses the entire meaning of an utterance, according to Hirsch, is a genre. Both the speaker or author and the interpreter must be careful to be familiar with the "variable and unstable norms of language but also the particular norms of a particular genre."[58]

Hirsch further defines genre by pointing to the process of interpretation. Before the interpreter begins to interpret, she has a set of generic expectations. The details of meaning that an interpreter finds are heavily influenced by the meaning expectations with which she begins this process. Expectations held by the interpreter include not only content but also "the relationship assumed to exist between the speaker and interpreter, the type of vocabulary and syntax that is to be used, the type of attitude adopted by the speaker, and the type of inexplicit meanings that go with the explicit ones."[59] These generic expectations are only revised when misunderstanding forces the interpreter to revisit her preconceptions of genre. Understanding of verbal meaning is tied to genre. The conception of genre, therefore, is not a stagnant but rather a variable concept that evolves within the process of interpretation, growing from vague and imprecise to narrower and more precise as this process advances.[60]

Intrinsic genre is also another dimension of Hirsch's view of genre. A concept of genre is both necessary for speaking and writing, as well as interpreting. This generic concept guides the speaker as he speaks words and chooses the sequence of these words. Understanding takes place when both the interpreter and the speaker, or author, operate under the same generic conception in meaning and understanding; this shared generic conception is "the intrinsic genre of utterance." More precisely, intrinsic genre "is that

---

58. Hirsch, *Validity in Interpretation*, 70–71.
59. Ibid., 72.
60. Ibid., 72–77.

sense of the whole by means of which an interpreter can correctly understand any part in its determinacy."[61] With regard to context, speaking of the narrow meaning of the part and also referring to the milieu that helps to give the proper view of the whole, "the essential component of a context is the intrinsic genre of utterance." Extrinsic genre is incorrectly guessing at the intrinsic genre.[62]

In the process of giving guidelines on dealing with implications, Hirsch emphasizes purpose (authorial will) as an important part of genre. An implication is connected to the conventions, rules, and proprieties of an intrinsic genre. Hirsch argues that the importance of an implication is determined by the purpose of the utterance; the controlling element in any utterance or any genre is purpose.

To guard against a one-sided presentation of genre, Hirsch not only focuses on intrinsic genres but also includes "provisional, heuristic type concepts" as well. He deals with the very common occurrence of the creation of a new genre, which will require an imaginative leap (as I will suggest of the presence and use of an anti-apocalyptic genre in Ecclesiastes). The formation of a new genre involves either the assimilation of two genres or extending an existing genre to suit the needs of a new context—or both. To Hirsch, "[T]he real relationship of an intrinsic genre to broader genre ideas is a historical relationship" denoting the formation of these new genres that takes place.[63]

Hirsch concludes his thoughts on genre by stressing the need to have differing interpretive methods for different texts and also stressing the necessity of authorial will for valid interpretation. The concept of genre helps to determine whether a prospective interpretation is appropriate and valid, or not. Hirsch asserts, "Valid interpretation depends on valid inference about the proprieties of the intrinsic genre."[64]

Hirsch makes a number of points that are very pertinent to the discussion of genre in this book. For him, the idea of intrinsic genre of utterance, when both the interpreter and author have the same conception of genre, is vital to understanding what is being communicated. With this point, he also realizes that proper understanding is inextricably tied to authorial will. He also realizes that making genre identifications is difficult. One is

61. Ibid., 86.
62. Ibid., 78–88.
63. Ibid., 102–11.
64. Ibid., 121.

trying to decipher which game is being played and what rules are being employed—without the benefit of a rulebook. The interpreter's conception of genre, therefore, is not stagnant but evolves within the process of interpretation, growing from vague to more precise as this process advances. Hirsch deals with the very common occurrence of the creation of a new genre, which will require an imaginative leap. Again, the formation of a new genre involves either the assimilation of two genres or extending an existing genre to suit the needs of a new context—or both.

Having looked at both Hirsch and Nasuti, it would be helpful for us to summarize Nasuti and distinguish his view from that of Hirsch. In so doing, points of my own understanding of genre will emerge. For Nasuti, genre relates to setting and function, and the definition of genre has both a descriptive as well as constructive role in hermeneutics. The issue of setting, in terms of this task of genre definition, is where genre is really debated. The significant element, as Nasuti points out, of this development in scholarship is that setting and function, as connected features, are determinative for the genre in which a text receives placement. Placing these texts (and their use) in different settings results in different genres. (This claim is a key point of distinction between Hirsch and Nasuti.) Texts are placed within genres based upon the fact that there are common features to the texts. The determination of these commonalities is heavily dependent on the reader and her setting. Although there are constraints, Nasuti views genre as not only descriptive of meaning but also constructive of meaning.

MY DEFINITION OF GENRE

Genre is flexible, anchored to authorial will, and centered on the *foci* of setting and function. Genres are better understood as clubs, in which there is a segment that exhibits a high degree of similarities to the inner core of the membership, as well as a segment of more fringe members that exhibit a lesser degree of the core membership. It is, therefore, possible for members (texts) to carry membership in more than one club (genre). This flexibility, however, is not without restraints. The chief restraints would have to do with the actual connection of the proposed genre and its historical use—rather than merely theoretical use. The proposed genre and its label must be historical in that it actually formed the communication and purpose of the author.

I agree with Hirsch that authorial will is crucially important and that it serves as an anchor for determining meaning. It is in the pursuit of determining the many times elusive authorial intent that one arrives at the intrinsic genre. Understanding that the generic expectations with which one approaches the text have much to do with the interpretation of the text, I do not see the proper role of genre as constructive, as Nasuti argues; genre is descriptive. Although the guess that the critic or interpreter posits for the text in question is a heuristic tool for explanation, genre is not a mere creation of the critic, *contra* Rosmarin. The intention of the author is a constraint on the flexibility of genre and its resultant label.

Genre is inextricably tied to function (Miller argues social action). Since genre is intended to achieve a social goal, the number of genres is without limit because the boundaries for genre are determined by those social situations to which genre must speak. It is inextricably connected to the intersection of setting and function. Identifying and understanding genre is crucially dependent on a proper grasp of the roles of communicative purpose and discourse community at work in a particular genre and its text.

Genre is flexible, anchored to authorial will, and centered on setting and function. These three characteristics of genre are vital for proper understanding of a text and its overarching genre label, especially when new genres have been formed. Interpreting the text in terms of the authorial setting and intended authorial function is vital for proper comprehension. There are times when this authorial setting and intended authorial function require the development of a new genre, which will require an imaginative leap. This new genre (or hybrid genre) encompasses either the assimilation of two genres or extending an existing genre to suit the needs of a new context—or both. This understanding of literary setting can help to distinguish when new genres (such as an anti-apocalyptic genre in Ecclesiastes) have been created for the purpose of fulfilling a new function of the text. It is with this view that I approach the question of genre in Ecclesiastes.

Chapter 3

Wisdom and Apocalyptic Genre and Thought Meld/Clash in Second Temple Judaism

The thesis of this book is that Qoheleth, in part, utilizes a hybrid genre in his work. He, in part, employs what this book will call an "anti-apocalyptic genre" in Ecclesiastes, and the presence of this genre serves to further Qoheleth's overarching message of joy. Even with a more conventional definition of genre,[1] is the idea of an anti-apocalyptic genre in a wisdom text plausible? Before I present this argument in chapter four, my intention in this chapter is to argue that the occurrence of a wisdom text exhibiting elements of an apocalyptic genre and vice-versa is evident in certain Second Temple texts. First, I will give a definition of wisdom. Secondly, I will give a definition for the apocalyptic genre. Thirdly, I will give a number of examples of works whose composition or final editing, in the case of Job, fits in the time period of the Second Temple Period and also demonstrates the melding or clashing of apocalyptic and wisdom genres/thought.

---

1. In chapter two, I presented a definition for genre that will serve in chapter four. In this chapter I use definitions for wisdom and apocalyptic that are more conventional in that they include more focus on the literary characteristics than my definition presented in chapter two. It is important to realize that these two approaches are not contradictory. My definition does not seek to jettison observations of literary characteristics but seeks to position attention on significant elements of setting and function. The definitions of wisdom and apocalyptic in this chapter do not universally ignore these elements.

Wisdom and Apocalyptic Genre and Thought Meld/Clash

WHAT IS WISDOM?

In his definition of wisdom, James Crenshaw makes three crucial distinctions: wisdom literature, wisdom tradition, and wisdom thinking. In response to the question, "What is wisdom?" I will address these three areas. I will also briefly identify the texts that are considered wisdom texts. I will address what is distinctive about wisdom thinking and its approach to reality. Additionally, I will also address the wisdom tradition: the wisdom movement, who was involved in it, the curriculum, and the pedagogy.

Ancient Near Eastern Wisdom literature focuses on issues that are common to human existence, but Israelite wisdom literature comes from a particular cultural and theological context that has as its chief credo "the fear of the Lord is the beginning of wisdom." The texts that comprise this wisdom corpus are Proverbs, Job, Ecclesiastes, Sirach, and Wisdom of Solomon.

James Crenshaw defines wisdom (or wisdom thinking) as, "the quest for self-understanding in terms of relationships with things, people and the Creator."[2] Wisdom thought is anthropocentric. Whereas the prophetic word bellows forth with the divine word from heaven, wisdom's starting point is in ruminating upon the question, "What is good for man?" Wisdom concerns itself with discovering "what is good for man," and it determines that good to be "health, honor, wealth, and length of days." The foundational idea of order, which God has established and man can search and discover, is the ground that establishes this search for the good life. Wisdom is, thus, a humanism—a theological humanism.[3]

Wisdom is chiefly concerned with order,[4] very similar to the Egyptian concept of *Ma'at*; wisdom's pursuit is thus an endeavor to find and

---

2. Crenshaw, "Prolegomenon," in *Studies in Ancient Israelite Wisdom*, 1–36. Gerhard von Rad defines wisdom more broadly by writing, "Israel understood 'wisdom' as a practical knowledge of the laws of life and of the world, based upon experience." He goes on to note that Israel's concept of wisdom would change but would always have as its foundation practical knowledge based on experience. Von Rad, *Old Testament Theology*, 1: 418. Whybray defines wisdom as an intellectual tradition. He defines it as "innate intelligence" and also writes, "Wisdom in the religious sense also is an intellectual quality which provides the key to happiness and success, to 'life' in its widest sense." Whybray, *The Intellectual Tradition in the Old Testament*, 7–8.

3. Crenshaw, "Prolegomenon," in *Studies in Ancient Israelite Wisdom*, 4–5.

4. Although von Rad's definition is not as precise as Crenshaw's, this aspect of order also appears in von Rad's understanding. He writes, "Wisdom... consisted in knowing that at the bottom of things an order is at work, silently and often in a scarcely

continue order—individual and societal order. This concept of order suggests a design or purpose. The wise man is to be an individual of propriety, knowing what to do at the right time and the right place. For this reason, there are two seemingly opposite proverbs listed in Prov 26:4–5. The sage is to ponder all aspects of a situation and make the proper response, given the particular situation. Very different from the authoritative thunder of prophecy, wisdom seeks to bring forth its message via the power of logical argument and persuasion.

This is a quest for understanding and order that is aware of its limitations. The wise man is most definitely aware of humanity's limitations, coupled with the fact that knowledge of God is often inscrutable. The reality of life experience caused the sage to realize the innumerable possibilities as well as humanity's limitations. This aspect is part of the reason why Crenshaw writes, "Wisdom is an open system although a tendency toward frozen dogma in the area of retribution certainly developed."[5]

The wisdom motto of "the fear of the Lord is the beginning of wisdom" emanates from the concept of reality, Crenshaw argues. This view of reality meant that there would be a reward for virtue and, likewise, adverse results for vice. There is, therefore, a profound element of justice associated with this creation theology. This view of automatic justice stands in some tension with the fact that God is free to do what he desires even if that is contrary to the human understanding of justice. There are some sages who choose to grapple with this tension; the books of Job and Ecclesiastes are examples of this wrestling. This is no small issue because the lack of justice, or at least the human perception, meant a possible return to chaos.[6]

The order, which serves as the foundation for wisdom thought, faces a crisis and possible reversal into chaos whenever the theology of retribution

---

noticeable way, making for a balance of events." Von Rad, *Old Testament Theology*, 1: 428.

Roland Murphy concedes studies on wisdom literature often make reference to the concept of order. He, however, is not comfortable with this assertion. For him, wisdom literature does speak of human actions and corresponding results (such as Prov 16:24; 25:14), but it would be incorrect to speak of "the existence of an order on the basis of analogies between conduct and events in nature." The sage speaks of human conduct and references nature for the purpose of shaping human conduct. Murphy, therefore, argues that it would be more proper "to speak of man's imposing an order (however provisory) upon the chaotic experiences of life." Even such a statement must be tempered with the realization that the sages knew that humanity's knowledge has limitations. Murphy, "Wisdom Theses," 187–200.

5. Crenshaw, "Prolegomenon," 23.
6. Ibid., 26.

does not seem to stand. Also at risk is confidence in the divine power and the concept that there is a reciprocal relationship between virtue and reward, as well as vice and punishment. The sage's response to this crisis is to point to creation as a defense of divine justice even when such justice is not visible to humans.[7]

Creation is a testament to the wise person that "the universe is comprehensible, and thus encourages a search for its secrets." Creation also gives the sense of order that holds all of the institutions of life together. Whenever chaos seems to prevail and divine justice appears elusive, the sage points to creation in order to defend the divine order and divine justice.[8]

The distinction of wisdom tradition includes the wisdom movement, its curriculum, and the manner and forms in which it delivers this curriculum. The nature of the wisdom movement comes into clearer focus when one considers its beginnings in ancient Israel. Gerhard von Rad has posited that the Solomonic period was revolutionary as it set new trends and a new path for the nation. This period is marked by fresh perspective on humanity and all of humanity's experiences. The nation had expanded its territory facilitating Solomon's commercial involvement with distant lands, which bore the result of economic prosperity. With this international boom, there was also a river of ideas flowing in from other nations; the prohibition against importing religious perspectives of other people groups was not observed. The royal court became, like its Egyptian counterpart, a center of international wisdom; this was a time of enlightenment.[9]

---

7. Ibid., 28–33.

8. Ibid., 34.

9. Von Rad, *The Problem of the Hexateuch and Other Essays*, 203. Crenshaw rejects Von Rad's explanation of Solomon's role on the wisdom tradition, refuting it as "legendary in character." He considers the evidence for Solomon's wisdom leadership to be inferential and the result of comparisons being made with the Egyptian court life. He writes, "While such a view of the facts may be historically probable, one must recognize that nothing demands the existence of an institution of wise men at Solomon's court." Crenshaw, "Prolegomenon," 19.

Walter Breuggemann has a plausible and effective response to those who, like Crenshaw, largely reject the idea of Solomon as the patron of wisdom. Brueggemann argues for just this idea. He does so not on historical and literary grounds but on sociological grounds; he concedes that one cannot translate literary evidence of Solomon's role into irrefutable historical evidence for Solomon's reign. Consider 1 Kgs 3–11. Interpreters consider 1 Kgs 3:3–14 to be in the genre of an inaugural dream. Many scholars, likewise, consider 1 Kgs 3:16–28 to be a "standard and recurring example of juridical cunning." 1 Kgs 10:1–13 could simply be the result of propaganda intended to bring comparisons with international royal figures and have Solomon appear as superior. Brueggemann

A Polemical Preacher of Joy

A literary revolution also marks this era. Solomon's court is filled with scribes—both Israelite and non-Israelite—resulting in a blossoming of literature. There is increased interaction with other cultures as the kingdom expands. This growth results in the institutions of wise men in Solomon's court. It is in this setting that Solomon is prolific as he composes proverbs, songs, and other poetic expressions of knowledge, including encyclopedic knowledge.[10]

Wisdom tradition embodies and propagates wisdom thinking, which is a quest for self-understanding. This is a quest that takes place on three levels: (1) nature wisdom is concerned with the mastery of the aspects of nature for the well-being of the individual, (Also included in this level is the observation of nature as it concerns humanity and the universe.) (2) juridical and practical wisdom has the concern of the human relationships

---

favors the sociological approach that considers the fact that there must have been a sociological reason for the text to appear as they did. If it is simply based on legend, there must have been a reason for the formation of the legend. This tradition, historical or not, did not occur in a vacuum. The Deuteronomist (in 1 Kgs 3–11), the compilers of the book of Proverbs, and those who were responsible for the works Ecclesiastes and Song of Solomon drew from some body of social memory. He writes, "While that memory may not be . . . available in factual terms, it seems plausible to assume that the connection between Solomon and wisdom is remembered and not invented—remembered . . . quite impressionistic and without precision." The consideration of Solomon's role in the wisdom tradition in Israel must consider the social environment during his time that demanded such a significant shift. The context of Solomon's reign required changes in politics, ideology, and technology in order to sustain the shift that had taken place. Brueggemann posits three social functions for this wisdom intelligentsia to perform in this new transformation. 1) This new wisdom movement was liberating. Developing this wisdom tradition was not only to be like Pharaoh but most likely also to provide an intellectual seedbed that would support change, "the kind of intellectual emancipation needed for a new regime eager to operate effectively, legitimately, and prestigiously as a state." (125) 2) This wisdom apparatus was necessary for the state. Through this wisdom tradition the knowledge of other nations and cultures becomes available for use and study. This availability both fulfills and incites a new energy and eagerness for new explorations. Additionally, this wisdom movement is necessary because such a movement is needed to lead to predictable patterns of order and control. 3) The wisdom movement tended to preserve the *status quos*, and this would be necessary as a new political system sought to maintain control. He, therefore, concludes that "Solomon was a patron of a wisdom that was at once emancipator and ideological. Only such a conclusion can explain the canonical memory of Solomon . . . ." (131) Brueggemann, "The Social Significance of Solomon as a Patron of Wisdom," 117–32.

10. Crenshaw disagrees with this and finds it dubious. Crenshaw, "Prolegomenon," 17.

and their propriety in a society of order, and (3) theological wisdom is concerned with theodicy.[11]

Crenshaw continues, drawing further distinctions between family/clan wisdom,[12] court wisdom, and scribal wisdom.[13] Family wisdom seeks

---

11. Crenshaw, "Determining Wisdom's Influence," 129–42.

12. The family and tribe is a possible beginning point for premonarchic wisdom tradition. Although the biblical text does not present evidence of anyone holding the title of sage in the tribe nor family, Carole Fontaine comments on the status and role of the sage. She places the role expectations of the sage in wisdom tradition—both Israelite and non-Israelite—alongside the roles executed within the family and tribe. She defines status as "a location in the social structure defined by expectations for performance by an incumbent." Role is what she defines as "the organized set of behaviors that belongs to an identifiable position." As the head of the household, the father exhibits the role of the sage, though not the title. He has the responsibility to teach his sons—both religiously and practically. This understanding of the father as sage is seen in the common verbiage used in Proverbs of "my son/your father." See Prov 1:8, 10, 15; 2:1; 3:1, 11, 21. Prov 1–9 most likely has connections with the Egyptian courtly origins, but it also reflects the family setting where teaching happens. It uses the parent/child verbiage to portray the sage/student relationship. As an example, Prov 4:1–9 shows the stream of knowledge necessary for a full life is transmitted from the father to the son in a familial setting. In addition to the role of family teacher, the father also serves the role as counselor and arbiter in disputes. The father's authority over the family is final, and this fact makes him the likely candidate to serve in this manner. Examples of the father serving in this manner appear in Genesis. The reader views Abraham as he settles disputes and gives counsel about a mate for Isaac (Gen 12:8–12, 16:6, 21:25, 24:1–9). Similarly the biblical text shows the elders with wisdom connections in Num 11:16 when God places enablement upon seventy elders so that they may assist Moses with administrative and judicial responsibilities. Fontaine, "The Sage in Family and Tribe," 155–64.

13. Andre Lemaire addresses the issue of the sage in school. The issue causes scholarly debates to erupt. In the midst of the ruminations scholars have failed to adequately consider that Israelite society exhibited a degree of diversity: people lived on farms, villages, towns, or even in the capital. The society included the poor, the rich, and individuals who would not consider themselves to be either. Occupations ranged from farmer to military to administration. One could probably find wise people in all of these different strata of society. When considering the role of the sage in the school there are certain misconceptions that one must avoid: 1) Israelite schools were not like modern schools but probably closer to "traditional Koranic and Jewish schools." (167) 2) These schools probably taught wisdom along with other subjects. 3) The presence of the school does not preclude other forms of instruction such as instruction from the home. The existence of schools in ancient Israel is likely in light of the fact that the surrounding cultures had them, i.e. Mesopotamia and Egypt. These schools were for the purpose of preparing scribes to work in the government. The evidence showing the spread of literacy in Judean kingdom around 600 B.C.E. also points to the existence of schools. From the biblical text there is proof that the First Temple Period had various types of schools. There were royal schools (1 Kgs 12:8, 10; 2 Kgs 10:1, 5, 6; 2 Chr 17:7–9). There were schools of the prophet (2 Kgs 6:1 –2; Isa 8:16), and there were also schools connected with the temple

to equip the individual with skills that would bring success in life. This kind of wisdom, uttered from the elder, encourages the type of behavior that followed wisdom and brought happiness. Court wisdom is intended to instruct "worldly manners" to those being prepared for royalty and leadership. Scribal wisdom seeks to implant religious belief in all and was universal. It, thus, employs a dialogical tone with admonitions.[14]

Wisdom literature's pedagogy employs many different forms. The numerical saying is a form present in wisdom literature. Humanity in the search for order is prone to these types of sayings.[15] Another form is the autobiographical stylization; in this form ideas appear as a personal discovery.[16] There is also the long didactic poem.[17] The dialogue is well attested in Near Eastern wisdom texts; it is very effective for presenting a perplexing problem.[18] The fable[19] and the allegory[20] endeavor to present something that is true in a figurative manner. The didactic narrative is a form that simply presents the events openly, largely without the figurative forms of speech.[21]

WHAT IS APOCALYPTIC?

The area of apocalyptic studies exhibits a cacophony of voices, many with different approaches. The works of Robert Webb and John Collins have greatly assisted me in hearing the foundational tones in this cacophony. En

---

(Isa 28: 7–13, 2 Chr 22:11). Another point that argues for the existence of schools in Israelite history and the role of sages in them is the consideration that some biblical texts seem to have been utilized as texts for schools. Such would be the case for the book of Proverbs; its employment of pedagogical approaches as well as the mnemonic devices would argue for this usage. Teaching was mostly oral, incorporating commentary on proverbs, parables, saying, and other pedagogical forms of wisdom texts. More than likely the wisdom texts and school texts originally appeared in popular wisdom. They were later collected and transmitted in the form of a school text. Lemaire writes, "The original setting of proverbs is traditional society, but the setting of written collections is the wisdom school." (175) Andre Lemaire, "The Sage in School and Temple," 165–81.

14. Crenshaw, "Determining Wisdom's Influence," 130.
15. See Prov 6:16–19; 30:21–23; 30: 29–31
16. See Prov 24:3–34; Sir 51:13–16; Sir 33:16–17
17. See Job 27:13–23; Prov 1:10–19; Prov 2:1–22
18. Numerous examples abound in the book of Job.
19. See Judg 9: 8–15; 2 Kgs 14:9; 2 Sam 12:1–4
20. See *1 En.* 85–90, Prov 5: 12–23; Eccl 12:1–6
21. Two examples would be the prose narratives of Joseph and Job.

route to a definition of apocalyptic, there are two terms that need attention: apocalyptic eschatology and apocalypticism. I will give a definition for each of these two terms followed by a definition of apocalypse.

Apocalyptic eschatology is the way that individuals or groups perceive the activity of God in relation to their daily existence. Drawing contrasts with prophetic eschatology will assist in defining the term. Apocalyptic eschatology differs from prophetic eschatology in a number of ways. Prophetic eschatology sees God working within the present situation with the present people and political systems to actuate the divine plan. Apocalyptic eschatology, however, sees deliverance and the fulfillment of God's plan coming, not from the present system and structure but from outside of the present order;[22] it sees the in-breaking of God's power exploding into the present scene of human darkness and dismay.

Any definition of apocalypticism will, of necessity, overlap with a definition of apocalyptic eschatology, since both are related with the genre of apocalypse. Apocalypticism, Paul Hanson defines, "refers to the symbolic universe in which an apocalyptic movement codifies its identity and interpretation of reality."[23] The symbolic universe comes out of a group that suffers from a sense of alienation and, thus, employs an apocalyptic eschatology to respond to their marginalization. It is, therefore, difficult to give a single exhaustive definition of apocalypticism because it is primarily focused on the response that an oppressed people give to their immediate crisis. Responses from different groups will take different forms.[24]

Although each group would have a response unique to its own situation, there are two fundamental ingredients that the apocalypticism of any group will have. Each group will have a social setting of alienation and a response from the group to this setting. This alienation is one where foundational structures of life and belief have suffered greatly and may have disintegrated. This can be the result of literal destruction or a situation where the group is no longer in positions of power. Their collective life, therefore, is in the path of encroaching chaos.[25]

---

22. Hanson, "Apocalypticism," 29–30. Christopher Rowland, however, intimates that there is no such thing as a distinct apocalyptic eschatology. Rowland, *The Open Heaven: A Study of Apocalyptic in Judaism and Early Christianity*, 29.

23. Hanson, "Apocalypticism," 30.

24. Ibid., 30.

25. Ibid., 30.

The response to this alienation, the second fundamental ingredient, is one that utilizes apocalyptic eschatology. The people look for deliverance outside of the common structure, a structure that has resulted in its alienation. Apocalyptic eschatology enables this marginalized group to preserve their sense of identity, an identity that is enveloped with the vision of ultimate vindication, which comes from the intervention of God invading the darkness of the group's present structure.[26]

Having defined the important terms of apocalyptic eschatology and apocalypticism, I will now turn to defining the genre of apocalypse. This genre poses a challenge to define to the point that some have even suggested the banishment of the term. There are four approaches to defining the genre of apocalypse: the traditionalist, literary-form, essentialist, and eclectic approaches.[27] Each of these approaches, especially the latter, gives a different facet of this genre that eludes definition.

26. Ibid., 30. Robert Webb criticizes Hanson's definition on its blend of ideology and the social phenomenon of the movements. He argues that the term apocalypticism should only be used to denote the ideology and not the social phenomenon because such ideology may be held by an individual. Moreover, he argues that this approach to the definition blurs the line of demarcation between ideology and social movements. Webb, "'Apocalyptic:' Observation on a Slippery Term," 115–26. Although I appreciate Webb's contention on this point, I agree will Hanson's definition since the alienation of the particular social circumstances is an impetus for the apocalypticism that forms and the apocalyptic eschatology that it employs.

27. Paolo Sacchi pursues another approach that has had more of an impact in scholarly circles of Europe than in North America. Sacchi's approach is unique in that he does not attempt to trace apocalyptic's roots from wisdom or the prophetic movement. He concurs that the apocalyptic form "knowledge through vision and symbolic-mythical expression" does have a connection with the substance of thought. He, however, has a point of departure in that his research goes beyond the problems concerned with form and, instead, seeks to discover the oldest work that serves as the source for later thought in apocalyptic texts. His conclusion is that The Book of Watchers fits this description of being the oldest and containing a base of thought. The Book of the Watchers, has a date well before 200 B.C.E. (Scholarship generally considers the 300 year period between 200 B.C.E and 100 C.E. to be the period when the number of Jewish apocalyptic works grew.) He suggests that it is in this work that one can find the "soul of apocalyptic" (36 n. 8). Sacchi's central concern is to wrestle with the question, "In the history of Jewish thought, are there some significant issues later found in classical apocalyptic, that is, in those works which tradition already indicates as apocalyptic?" (40). He starts from a working hypothesis of what these fundamental thought elements would be, drawing from Klaus Koch. He then attempts to trace the history of these thoughts; he does not look for isolated thoughts but thoughts as they appear in clusters. His next step is to identify the thought in the Book of the Watchers. He determines that there are three elements that serve as the foundation of thought in the book. The first is, "The conviction that evil derives from a contamination of the natural and human sphere through the action of beings

The Traditionalist Approach

The work of Klaus Koch is an example of the traditional approach to defining the apocalyptic genre. This approach includes identifying lists of literary characteristics that identify the genre. Koch lists fourteen traits that apocalyptic texts will usually display. These traits are discourse cycles between the seer and the angelic being, spiritual turmoil as the seer receives an unexpected vision or audition, paraenetic discourses which detail an eschatological ethic, pseudonymity often hiding behind a revered man of God from the past (such as Enoch), "mythical images rich in symbolism," composite literary character, imminent reversal of earthly conditions, the end as a vast cosmic catastrophe, history is divided into segments, angelic and demonic armies, the promise of salvation which will be paradisal, the throne of God from which comes the ultimate act of redemption, a mediator who has a royal role, and the word "glory" as a catchword for the final state.[28]

There are at least two criticisms of this approach. One problem with this approach is that it views the genre through the lens of apocalyptic eschatology. By doing this, the approach does not adequately consider other concerns present in these texts. Michael Stone points out that there are often lists present in these texts and that they cover a wide range of topics. "Among the subjects they comprehend are astronomy and meteorology, uranography and cosmology, the secrets of nature and Wisdom as well as other aspects of esoteric lore not easily classified in accepted categories."[29]

---

belonging to the 'in-between world.'" This contamination is the result of rebellious angels who have brought rebellion against God's established order for the cosmos. The second is "the conviction that there exists in human beings an immortal element destined . . . to live an eternally blessed life with God." The third is "that salvation cannot be effected by human beings, but must rather derive from an event in the 'in-between world.'" This salvation takes place as a result of God's will (60). Sacchi then compares these elements to those found in Jubilees, Daniel, and both the Rule of the Community and Hodayot from Qumran. He, then, arrives at two fundamental guidelines for every apocalypse: (1) the belief in immortality (whether by resurrection or immortality of the soul) and (2) the conviction that evil has its origin in a sphere above the human. Additionally, Sacchi encourages that the interpreter make a distinction between historical and cosmic apocalypses. Sacchi's work is valuable because it brings a fresh approach to the discussion. The approach of the others is more helpful for this section because they focus on the cluster of literary elements, an approach more prevalent in contemporary scholarship in North America. Sacchi, *Jewish Apocalyptic and Its History*, 17–71.

28. Koch, *The Rediscovery of Apocalyptic*, 24–33.

29. Stone, "Lists of Revealed Things in Apocalyptic Literature," 439–43.

Another problem with this approach is the fact that lists such as these, Hanson argues, cannot possibly capture the true essence of the genre.[30]

The Literary-Form Approach

A key element of the literary-form approach is the focus on the literary features more than the content of the text. The content of this group of literature is varied, but the literary form of revelation is the prevailing feature of the brand. Christopher Rowland, a chief proponent of this approach, writes that apocalyptic "is a type of religion whose distinguishing feature is a belief in direct revelation . . . through dream, vision or divine intermediary."[31] He downplays the role of apocalyptic eschatology by pointing out that the main focus of the apocalypse is to unveil "meaning and significance to man and his world by means of revelation." The purpose is to give humanity a way of understanding the world and the involvement of the Almighty in humanity's world. This knowledge, whether it be eschatological or astronomical, would enable people to have the proper perspective in this life brimming with despair.[32]

The basic meaning of the word αποκαλυπτω attests to this approach, since the word means to reveal, disclose. The book of Revelation takes its title from the noun form of this verb; the definition of the word is a foundation to the field of apocalyptic study. The chief weakness of this approach is "that the distinctiveness of the apocalypses vis-à-vis other forms of revelatory literature in the Greco-Roman world is not taken into account."[33] This approach emphasizes one feature at the expense of others.

The Essentialist Approach

E. P. Sanders has identified what he calls the essentials of an apocalypse. He argues that "the combination of revelation with the promise of restoration and reversal" are the essentials that are unique to apocalypses. The works, Sanders asserts, of Daniel, *1 Enoch*, *Jubilees*, *4 Ezra*, *2 Baruch*, the *Apocalypse of Abraham*, and frequently the *Testament of Levi* would all

30. Hanson, "Jewish Apocalyptic Against Its Near Eastern Environment," 33.

31. Rowland, *The Open Heaven: A Study of Apocalyptic in Judaism and Early Christianity*, 21.

32. Ibid., 22.

33. Collins, "Introduction," 1–2.

contain the "combination of revelation with the promise of the vindication or redemption of a group."[34] Moreover, he argues that with this generative identification, the questions of authorial intent and audience expectancy have been addressed: "the authors intended to promise restoration by God from present oppression, and the audience understood the devices being used to make that promise impressive . . . visions."[35]

Collins rightly levels a strong critique of this essentialist approach. There are two serious weaknesses to Sanders's approach. First, these essential themes of revelation and reversal can be found, not only in apocalypses but also in the entire prophetic corpus as well. One could place all of these texts, apocalyptic and prophetic, within a broader category of "revelatory literature." A definition that does not properly distinguish between the books of Amos and *1 Enoch* has deficiencies in any genre discussion. Second, it does not give proper consideration to the cosmological and mystical leanings that appear in some apocalypses—or other themes that appear in apocalypses.[36]

The Eclectic Approach: Comprehensive Diversity

The eclectic approach seems to be the most effective approach of these four. The Society of Biblical Literature Genres Project presented a definition of the genre that drew from some of the other attempts. Serving as the chairman for this endeavor, John Collins presents the study as an attempt to salvage some order from what is a chaotic cacophony of study in this area. This endeavor attempts to see if this group of texts "shares a significant cluster of traits that distinguish them from other works."[37] He considers the genre to be a heuristic tool that can serve a two-fold purpose. The identification of this genre can serve to point to those features that are recurring in this literature. It can also serve to highlight distinctive features of these texts when they differ from the other texts in the group. The identification of this genre, Collins cautions, is not intended to reduce the genre to a simplified core; nor should the interpreter expect every apocalyptic text to have all of these features.[38]

34. Sanders, "The Genre of Palestinian Jewish Apocalypses," 447–60.
35. Ibid., 459.
36. Collins, *The Apocalyptic Imagination*, 9–10.
37. Ibid., 9–10.
38. Collins, "Preface," vi.

The fruit of this investigation was a Master Paradigm, a compilation of features for apocalypses. This paradigm consists of two main sections entailing the manner of revelation and the content, thereof.[39]

Manner of Revelation
1. Medium by which the revelation is communicated
    1.1. Visual revelation in the form of:
        1.1.1. Visions, or
        1.1.2. Epiphanes (describing the apparition of the mediator)
    1.2. Auditory usually clarifies the visual by:
        1.2.1. Discourse (uninterrupted speech by mediator), or
        1.2.2. Dialogue (between mediator and recipient)
    1.3. Otherworldly journey, when the visionary travels through heaven, hell, or remote regions beyond the normally accessible world.
    1.4. Writing (revelation contained in written document)
2. Otherwordly mediator communicates revelation
3. The human recipient
    3.1. Pseudonymity
    3.2. Disposition of recipient (circumstances, emotions)
    3.3. Reaction of recipient (often awe and/or perplexity)

Content of Revelation: Temporal Axis
4. Protology (pre-history or beginning of history)
    4.1. Theogony and/or Cosmogony (origin of God/Pleroma, and/or cosmos)
    4.2. Primoridal events having paradigmatic significance
5. History, viewed as:
    5.1. Explicit recollection of the past, or
    5.2. Ex Eventu prophecy
6. Present salvation through knowledge (in Gnostic texts)

---

39. Ibid., 5–8.

Wisdom and Apocalyptic Genre and Thought Meld/Clash

7. Eschatological crisis, in the form of
    7.1. Persecution, and/or
    7.2. Other eschatological upheavals (disturbing the order of nature or history)
8. Eschatological judgment and/or destruction upon:
    8.1. The wicked, or the ignorant (Gnostic texts)
    8.2. The natural world
    8.3. Otherworldly beings
9. Eschatological salvation, may involve:
    9.1. Cosmic transformation (renewal of entire world)
    9.2. Personal salvation
        9.2.1. Resurrection in bodily form, or
        9.2.2. Other forms of afterlife (such as exaltation to heaven with angels)

Content of Revelation: Spatial Axis
10. Otherworldly elements
    10.1. Otherworldly regions (described usually in otherworldly journeys)
    10.2. Otherworldly beings (angelic or demonic)

Paraenesis
11. Paranesis (by mediator to the recipient)

Concluding Elements
12. Instruction to the recipient
13. Narrative conclusion

From this master paradigm, the group formed a comprehensive definition of the genre:[40]

> Apocalypse is a genre of revelatory literature with a narrative framework, in which a revelation is mediated by an otherworldly being to a human recipient, disclosing a transcendent reality which

---

40. Ibid., 9–10.

> is both temporal, insofar as it envisages eschatological salvation, and spatial insofar as it involves another, supernatural world.

With this definition, the group established the boundaries for the genre, making it easier to identify works that are apocalyptic. Though far from complete, this paradigm and definition afford the interpreter guidelines. A great strength to this work is that it enables an apocalypse to be distinguished from oracles, testaments, and revelatory dialogues which often contain eschatological elements but do not have within them the manner of revelation distinctive of apocalypses, as detailed by the above master paradigm.[41]

Robert Webb praises the fact that this approach combines the strengths of the others, and hence refers to it as the eclectic approach. As with the traditionalist approach, this approach gives due attention to both form and content, and it also gives the proper emphasis to the role of revelation, as the literary and essentialist approach do.[42] John Collins, who was a major architect of this definition, adds that the inner coherence of the genre paradigm is transcendence.[43]

For David Hellholm, the definition still needs further emendation because it, in the form presented above, does not give enough attention to the function of an apocalypse. To remedy this deficiency, Hellholm adds the following to the definition: "intended for a group in crisis with the purpose of exhortation and/or consolation by means of divine authority."[44] Partly as a response to this suggestion, Adela Yarbo Collins presents the following as an addition to the definition of an apocalypse: "intended to interpret present earthly circumstances in light of the supernatural world and of the

---

41. Ibid., 9–10.

42. Webb, " 'Apocalyptic:' Observation on a Slippery Term," 123.

43. Collins, "Introduction: Towards the Morphology of a Genre," 10. The manner of the revelation necessitates the engagement of an otherworldly being because the revelation is beyond the scope of human knowledge and, thus, cannot be received by a human directly. This manner of revelation already presupposes that another world exists; this world is a place with knowledge about human activities and affairs. Moreover, this world is a place of angels and demons with its own topography and geography. Apocalyptic eschatology also exhibits transcendence as it anticipates a salvation and deliverance that is beyond this world; salvation, whatever form it takes, always anticipates a human experience that radically differs from the present reality.

44. Hellhom, "The Problem of Apocalyptic Genre and the Apocalypse of John," 27.

future, and to influence both the understanding and the behavior of the audience by means of divine authority."[45]

THE NICKELSBURG CAUTION

George Nickelsburg writes of a common mindset in scholarship. There is a tendency to assume that the original authors/editors held to the contemporary "scholarly abstractions and heuristic categories." With this perspective, it is possible to think that the authors of sapiential texts were highly concerned with making sure that their texts were truly of the wisdom genre and did not exhibit some aspects of apocalyptic writings and vice versa. It is important to realize that such was not necessarily the case. These terms of apocalyptic and sapiential are scholarly attempts to carve a window into another time, place, and culture. These terms endeavor to transport contemporary audiences and interpreters back to the time of these authors and audiences. Nickelsburg gives a caution by saying, "It is imperative that the means not be construed as the end, or the window confused with the landscape."[46]

It is also easy for contemporary scholarship to over-emphasize the distinction and difference between these categories we have labeled wisdom and apocalyptic and to consider them mutually exclusive. In viewing one at the exclusion of the other, "we fail to see that in the world from which they have come to us, they were related parts of an organic whole." I suggest that we heed the Nickelsburg caution. In what follows, I endeavor to demonstrate this point: the "line of demarcation" between wisdom and apocalyptic (or at least our perceived line of demarcation between these two types of literature) is very permeable. We, therefore, see wisdom texts that exhibit apocalyptic characteristics/thought and vice versa. We also see texts that are neither wisdom nor apocalyptic showing a confluence of both wisdom and apocalyptic.

In what follows I have chosen texts from the Second Temple Period. I will argue that they exhibit a melding or clashing of apocalyptic and sapiential. I first examine the apocalyptic texts *1 Enoch*, *2 Baruch*, and *4 Ezra*. Afterward, the attention moves to the two epistles: James and Romans, followed by the wisdom texts: Wisdom of Solomon, *4QInstruction*, Job,

45. Collins, "Introduction," 7.

46. Nickelsburg, "Wisdom and Apocalypticism in Early Judaism: Some Points for Discussion," 36.

and Sirach. The examination of these texts is intended to demonstrate that each of these nine texts is an example of a confluence of apocalyptic and sapiential.

1 ENOCH[47]

1 Enoch[48] is an example of an apocalyptic text that shows evidence of wisdom influence—at least in the language, terminology, and literary forms the texts use. In this section I will highlight the expansive nature of "wisdom" in *1 Enoch* as well as the presence of some features that have parallel usages in wisdom literature texts.

The expansive and frequent use of the term/concept "wisdom" in *1 Enoch* is noteworthy. So important is *1 Enoch*'s concept of wisdom that it almost replaces the role of the Mosaic Law. With the exception of a few references, *1 Enoch* makes little mention of the Mosaic covenant and Torah.[49] The Law, and the proper interpretation thereof, appears in the text as revealed "wisdom." Using language that is common in wisdom texts, the writers of the Enochic texts present human conduct as the choice between two ways.[50] To walk on the path of uprightness is to obey the teachings or

---

47. Citations of *1Enoch* are taken from Charlesworth, *The Old Testament Pseudepigrapha*.

48. 1 Enoch is a composite text containing the work of numerous authors and time periods. J. Milik organizes the text in the following manner: 1) The Book of Watchers (1–36), 2) The Book of Similitudes (37–71), 3) The Book of Astronomical Writings (72–82), 4) the Book of Dream Visions (83–90) and 5) The Book of the Epistle of Enoch (91–107). Milik, "Problemes de la Litterature Henochique a la Lumiere des Fragments Arameens De Qumran," 333–78.

49. There is an explicit mention of the covenant in 1 En*och* 93:6 referring to the fact that God, "made a covenant for all generations and a tabernacle." One can make an argument for some other allusions in the texts. Chapters 1–5 employ some language reminiscent of the Pentateuch. Chapter 1:4 refers to Mount Sinai as the place of God's descent. Chapter 99:2 makes reference to the perversion of "the eternal covenant." It is not certain whether or not this reference speaks of the Mosaic covenant. Nickelsburg, "Enochic Wisdom: An Alternative to the Mosaic Torah?" 123–30.

50. See 91:4; 91:18–19; 92:3; 94:1–4; 99:10; 104:13; 105:2; 108:13. Chapter 91:18 reads, "Now I shall speak unto you, my children, and show you the ways of righteousness and the ways of wickedness." Verse 19 continues with, "Now listen to me, my children, and walk in the way of righteousness, and do not walk in the way of wickedness . . . ." Coughenour notes the comparisons that an interpreter can make between these verses and other wisdom texts such as Ps 1, Sir 1:28, and Jas 1:8. Coughenour, "The Woe Oracles in Ethiopic Enoch," 192–97.

commandments. Not adhering to these teachings receives the description of "straying from the right path,"[51] walking on the path(s) of wickedness and violence or perverting the truth."[52] The retribution for disobedience to these teachings, or wisdom, appears in sets of woes, which are similar to prophetic literature as well as wisdom texts such as Sirach.[53]

In *1 Enoch*, wisdom is inherently "primordial and eschatological;" four of the five portions of *1 Enoch* speak about the eschatological manner in which the Enochic wisdom is received.[54] The concept that wisdom comes from God and that its reception can take place only via revelation is foundational to *1 Enoch*'s depiction of the Law and its understanding as Wisdom. This revelation occurred when the revered seer and sage "Enoch ascended to heaven, received 'wisdom,' descended, wrote it in books, and gave these books to Methuselah and his sons for transmission to later generations."[55] It is noteworthy that this revelation comes via Enoch and not through Moses, as the Pentateuch depicts. Instead of being centered on the Mosaic Torah, the text presents sacred texts, or the Enochic texts, "embodying the divine wisdom necessary for the salvation of those who live in the last times."[56]

Wisdom, in *1 Enoch*, encompasses more than the Law; it also includes thoughts about the final judgment. These two are related because God will give rewards or judgments based upon how people responded to the divine laws. Additionally, Enoch's concept of wisdom has much to do with the structure of the cosmos. Nickelsburg, therefore, comments that "revealed wisdom is a comprehensive category that includes revelations about God's will expressed in commandments and laws, about the blessings and curses . . . and about the world in which these are enacted."[57]

Not only is it expressed as a comprehensive category, but the word "wisdom" also appears at crucial junctures in *1 Enoch*. The wisdom term parable[58] appears in chapter 1, but the word "wisdom" does not. The wis-

---

51. See 5:4; 93:9; 99:10

52. See 93:9; 99:2; 104:9

53. Nickelsburg, "Enochic Wisdom" 125. A woe section will receive treatment below.

54. See 1:2; 5:4; 37:2; 90:6; 92:1; 93:10; 100:6; 104:12–13

55. Nickelsburg, "Enochic Wisdom," 127. See 81:1—82:3; 104:12–13.

56. Ibid., 127.

57. Ibid., 128.

58. In 1:3, the text reads, "And concerning the chosen ones I speak now, and

dom similarities continue as Enoch, when he returns to the earth, records his revelations in a book that he refers to as "wisdom" (82:2-3).[59] Again wisdom terminology appears giving a frame for the Epistle in 92:1[60] and 104:12. The book of Parables takes the label, the vision of wisdom (37:1); the section commences with the words "the beginning of wisdom" (37:2-3). Chapter 42, very similar to Sir 24, contains a poem that laments the fact that wisdom is not present but iniquity, its converse, is present.

Robert Coughenour has done some work detailing the wisdom aspects of *1 Enoch*. One of his emphases with this treatment is the appearance of the woe form in Enoch. One section where these woes occur is chapters 91–105, the fifth section of *1 Enoch*. They often appear in series: chapters 94, 95, 96, 97, 98, 99, 100 followed by 103:5 and 8. These woe oracles often concern matters related to maintaining the social order. Some examples would include woes against oppression, deceit, and wickedness (94:6); individuals who construct houses based on sin (94:7), and who have placed their trust in riches, borne false witness, practice injustice, and put forth a false righteousness that does not come from the heart (96:4). Another

---

concerning them I take up my parable." Randall Argall, in his book, correctly notes that the phrase "take up a parable" is fitting because it, undoubtedly, carries a double meaning. The word parable not only appears in wisdom literature, in the sense of a proverb, but also is used to speak of obscure sayings like the oracles of Balaam in Num 24:4, 16. Both ideas are appropriate for understanding this text in *1 Enoch*; in this case the term points to eschatological information that will save the individual from the coming judgment. Argall, *1 Enoch and Sirach: A Comparative Literary and Conceptual Analysis of the Themes of Revelation, Creation and Judgment*, 19–20.

59. Chapter 82:3 reads, "And they will incline their ears to learn this wisdom, and it will be better for those who eat than good food." In this context the wisdom that is learned is the wisdom "which surpasses their thought." (*1 En.* 82:2c) This wisdom that Enoch brings is wisdom that is beyond human thought. This wisdom first came via the angels who could receive from the Tree of Wisdom. Argall, *1 Enoch and Sirach: A Comparative Literary and Conceptual Analysis of the Themes of Revelation, Creation and Judgment*, 35.

60. *1 En.* 92:1 starts abruptly with, "That which was written by Enoch the scribe . . ." and is addressed to "for all the offspring that dwell upon the earth, and to the latter generations which uphold uprightness and peace." Like 82:1-2, the author of this text considers the audience to be in the "end-time." Noteworthy is that the wisdom in both of these passages portends to be salvific. The following verses attest to this idea. *1 Enoch* 92:3a-b reads, "and the righteous one will awaken from his sleep, he shall arise and walk in the ways of righteousness." The author, here, gives the assurance that those who walk in righteousness and receive this revealed wisdom have received wisdom "that will deliver them from their troubles, even if ultimate deliverance comes only by way of resurrection." Argall, *1 Enoch and Sirach: A Comparative Literary and Conceptual Analysis of the Themes of Revelation, Creation and Judgment*, 40.

Wisdom and Apocalyptic Genre and Thought Meld/Clash

example of a woe that condemns actions against the social order is a woe that condemns those who eat blood, which Deuteronomy forbids.[61]

Certainly, the presence of these woes does not necessarily give evidence of a wisdom influence since concern for the social order was not isolated to one class; Coughenour concedes that one could consider these woes to be from a "legal, courtly, or popular setting."[62] One should note, however, that there are some aspects to these woes that point to a specific influence. The concerns of these woes such as the greedy chasing of wealth or "oppression, and injustice" would seem to have a popular tone to them, warranting Nickelsburg's suggestion that these woes come "from the same stratum of popular ethos as do the wisdom accounts."[63] In this wisdom-influenced context of *1 Enoch*, these woes serve an educative purpose. They are to teach the readers that a life marked by injustice, immorality, false witness, and other vices contrary to the social order is a life that leads to death.[64]

1 Enoch 1–5 stands as another example of the presence of wisdom influence in this apocalyptic work. Chapters 2:1—5:3 give an example of cosmic imagery. (Sir 43 is parallel to this passage.) "The works of heaven" and aspects of the earth receive attention particularly mentioning the two seasons and their results. The author points to this to demonstrate the orderliness with which God has created the earth. In light of the consistent orderliness of creation, the author, in 5:4, begins a strong denunciation of those who practice wickedness in disobedience to God. The section presents a wisdom observation on the orderliness of nature juxtaposed with a prophetic rebuke for humanity's lack of consistency with God's desires. To accomplish this odd combination, the author describes the created order by drawing from language and imagery common in the wisdom literature corpus.[65]

1 Enoch also contains a semblance of the "fear of the Lord" wisdom motto. After the woe of chapters 94–100, chapter 101 includes an encouragement for the audience to fear the Lord. *1 Enoch* 101:9 reads, "Do not the sailors of the ships fear the sea? Yet the sinners do not fear the Most High."

---

61. Coughenour, "The Woe Oracles in Ethiopic Enoch," 194.
62. Ibid., 194.
63. Nickelsburg, "Apocalyptic Message of *1 Enoch* 92–105," 309–28.
64. See 102:9, 10; 103: 15; 94:3
65. Nickelsburg, "'Enoch As Scientist, Sage, and Prophet: Content, Function, and Authorship in *1 Enoch*," 203–27.

The motto of Prov 1:9, "The fear of the Lord is the beginning of wisdom," does not appear in those exact words, yet the essence of the wisdom motto does. The idea is that the sailors are surrounded by the handiwork of the Creator, yet do not fear the Creator. In this apocalyptic text rich with wisdom allusions, the wisdom motto makes a veiled appearance.[66]

To be fair to the text on its own terms, Elizabeth Johnson notes, wisdom appears in these texts very differently from the traditional wisdom corpus. One can find mention of salvific wisdom; the Book of Similitudes is titled "vision of wisdom," and the ending of the Book of Heavenly Luminaries receives the label of revelation "wisdom." The usual wisdom concern of cosmic order appears in the Book of Watchers and the Heavenly Luminaries. The messiah receives identification with wisdom in the Book of Similitudes. Moreover, wisdom has its location in heavenly mysteries. The goal of wisdom in *1 Enoch* is not to lead one to a successful life on this earth but rather to unveil secrets of the cosmos such as "the future of the universe, cultic and calendrical specifications, and a particular slant on Torah interpretation."[67]

Even with all of the wisdom language and use of the term "wisdom," *1 Enoch*, still maintains a mindset that is very similar to other apocalypses of the Second Temple Period. What is pertinent to the purpose of this chapter is that these similarities show, yet again, that the line of demarcation between apocalyptic and sapiential thought was not stark but very permeable. So permeable was this line that one can notice that *1 Enoch*, a starkly apocalyptic work, contains wisdom language that has been immersed in apocalyptic thought.

2 BARUCH

Drawing from the insightful work of Frederick Murphy[68] on the sapiential elements in the Syriac *Apocalypse of Baruch*, I argue that *2 Baruch* is another example of a Second Temple Period text where apocalyptic and sapiential elements meld. For this examination I will point to the wisdom terminology of this apocalypse, the themes, and the wisdom mindset of the text.

---

66. Coughenour, "The Woe Oracles in Ethiopic Enoch," 196.

67. Johnson, *The Function of Apocalyptic and Wisdom Traditions in Romans 9–11*, 90–91.

68. Murphy, "Sapiential Elements in the Syriac Apocalypse of Baruch," 311–27.

Wisdom and Apocalyptic Genre and Thought Meld/Clash

2 *Baruch* exhibits sapiential themes: the inscrutable ways of God, teachings considered to be life, and the fear of the Lord. The fact that humanity is unable to understand God's ways is a staple of the wisdom perspective. This perspective has a strong presence in 2 *Baruch*, such as in 44:6 and 54:12.[69] Baruch receives much knowledge, but rather than being esoteric it is Law-centered knowledge. When the revelation knowledge has concluded, Baruch says, "Who can comprehend Your understanding, or who can recount the thoughts of Your mind?" (75:3–4). The divide between God and humanity, characteristic in wisdom, is firm in 2 *Baruch*. Although such would be the same for 4 *Ezra*, it is different in this apocalypse. There is a divide between humanity and divinity, but Ezra receives direct revelation, esoteric knowledge, that makes him one of the elite (4 *Ezra* 14:26). The wisdom theme that God's ways and knowledge are beyond humanity's reach is present in 2 *Baruch*.[70]

In wisdom literature, the sage is given instruction so that the adherents may have life. This same sapiential thought is present in 2 *Baruch*, such as in 45:2, "For, when you instruct them, you will make them alive." Such identification also appears in wisdom texts such as Sir 17:11, 45:5. Additionally, the "fear of the Lord" figures prominently in 2 *Bar*. 44:7, "For when you endure and persevere in his fear and do not forget his Law, the time again will take a turn for the better for you."

In addition to emphasizing the sapiential themes in 2 *Baruch*, F. Murphy also addresses the wisdom terminology in the book. Each of these, by itself, would not make a convincing argument, but the totality of observations points to the sapiential elements of this apocalyptic book of 2 *Baruch*.

The word חכם "wisdom" occurs a total of twenty-one times in 2 *Baruch*.[71] For this apocalyptic text, the concept of wisdom is similar to that found in Sir 24:23; wisdom has close identification with the Law, and knowledge of Law is available to all. In 2 *Baruch* a central criterion for how people receive assessment is how well individuals followed the Law, which

---

69. John Collins writes of wisdom, "Two concepts are of cardinal importance, the human sense of limit and the recognition of cosmic order." Collins, "The Biblical Precedent for Natural Theology," 46. Von Rad points to this limitation of human knowledge as an important foundation. The wise give forth wise sayings as well as speak of the limitations of their wisdom. Von Rad writes, "In fact, wisdom becomes communicative...precisely at the point where such limits are experienced." von Rad, *Wisdom in Israel*, 97.

70. Murphy, "Sapiential Elements in the Syriac Apocalypse of Baruch," 320.

71. Ibid., 314–15.

A Polemical Preacher of Joy

is the basis of wisdom. Two passages that convey this are chapters 44 and 51. Chapter 44:15 says, "They who have gained for themselves treasuries of wisdom, and stores of understanding are found with them, and from mercy they have not departed, and they have guarded the truth of the Law." Chapter 51:3 says, "Those who now have been justified in My Law. These are they who possessed understanding in their life, and these are they who planted the root of wisdom in their heart." The wicked are those who "rejected My Law, and stopped up their ears so that they might not hear wisdom or receive understanding" (51:4). Everyone has access to wisdom, which is not esoteric but has its focus upon the Law.[72]

The word חשב "think" occurs a total of twenty-nine times in 2 Baruch. Murphy categorizes the occurrences along the following lines: The divine thought resulting in creation, humanity's insufficient intelligence in comparison to God's intelligence, and Baruch's own thinking as the narrative progresses. The first portion is of particular importance. A preoccupation with creation is commonplace for wisdom texts. It is, thus, peculiar to note how many times the idea of creation appears in 2 Baruch. Referring to God's act of creation, the word ברא occurs nineteen times and עבד twenty-three times. Baruch's prayers, as well, feature the concept of creation in chapters 21, 48, and 54. The text ascribes the title "Creator" or "Maker" to God four times (14:15; 17:4; 44:4; and 48:46).[73]

The creation theme is common in wisdom texts, but outside of the wisdom texts the creation theme usually appears to stress the strength and sovereignty of God—*contra* God's intelligence. 2 Baruch emphasizes God's creation not to stress God's strength and sovereignty but God's thought, such as in 14:17, 56:3, and 4:3.[74]

There is also a clear separation in 2 Baruch between the righteous and the wicked. In fact, there is a definite portrayal of the fact that the righteous experience adversity while the wicked experience prosperity. To be sure, this dichotomy is present in apocalyptic literature as well. What is distinctly sapiential about this feature in 2 Baruch, according to Murphy,[75] is that the distinctive about the righteous is the wisdom they follow, and the distinctive about the wicked is the fact that they do not have wisdom.[76]

---

72. Ibid., 314–15.
73. Ibid., 317.
74. Ibid., 318.
75. Ibid., 231.
76. See 51:3–4; 44:14

Wisdom and Apocalyptic Genre and Thought Meld/Clash

Another sapiential feature in *2 Baruch* is the role that Baruch serves. Murphy highlights this role by contrasting it with that of *4 Ezra*. Baruch receives information from God for the purpose of teaching it to others who will, in turn, teach the larger populace. This is contrary to *4 Ezra* where the revelation that Ezra receives is not for everyone but only for the wise. In chapters 45:1–2, Baruch addresses the teachers who must continue the work, "You, therefore, admonish the people as much as you can. For this is our work. For if you instruct them, you will make them live." Baruch sees himself as one of the instructors who must teach the people in order that they may live. Furthermore, 77:1 shows that Baruch is to share this teaching with all of the people "from the greatest to the smallest." The fact that Baruch is also seen as a father by the people adds to the wisdom aspect of this text.[77]

After examining the terminology and themes, the question still remains: does *2 Baruch* demonstrate an apocalyptic or sapiential means of thinking? The comments of J. Collins are helpful in this determination. He writes, "While sapiential revelation is immanent, and is channeled through the natural human processes of thought, apocalyptic revelation is ecstatic, and conferred from outside."[78] Collins also notes that unlike wisdom texts apocalyptic texts "are written in an unequivocally mythological mode."[79] To the aforementioned question, an examination of the text will show that *2 Baruch* 21:13–17 exhibits a sapiential manner of thinking. Murphy points out that these verses do not express the revelation in the manner typical of apocalyptic literature; these verses exhibit five consecutive proverbs, which is a sapiential characteristic. The expectation that the evil of this present time will experience an ultimate crushing, in the consummation of history, is an apocalyptic expectation. *2 Baruch* 21:31–17, conversely, presents a different path to this expected end. This end will be a consummation via sapiential means (human reasoning) instead of solely special revelation, as

---

77. Murphy, "Sapiential Elements in the Syriac Apocalypse of Baruch," 322. Compare with Prov 1:8; 4:1; 6:20.

78. John Collins, "Cosmos and Salvation: Jewish Wisdom and Apocalyptic in the Hellenistic Age," 139. Crenshaw divides the wisdom manner of thinking or theologizing further into three states. The first stage sees the foundation of all thought to be the fear of the Lord. The second stage grapples with the concept of God's presence in the ordinary flow of humanity's life. The third stage, as Sirach depicts it, is to involve the Torah. All of these stages or manners of thinking in wisdom are anthropocentric. Crenshaw, "Wisdom in the OT" in *The Interpreter's Dictionary of the Bible*, Supp: 954–55.

79. Collins, "Cosmos and Salvation: Jewish Wisdom and Apocalyptic in the Hellenistic Age," 138.

is the case in apocalyptic literature.[80] One can, therefore, see that *2 Baruch* is another example of an apocalyptic text that exhibits wisdom characteristics. Again, wisdom and apocalyptic thought meld.

4 EZRA

John Collins has identified the apocalyptic features of *4 Ezra*. In his seminal article in *Semeia* 14, Collins identifies some qualities of *4 Ezra*.[81] He first identifies the manner of revelation that appears in *4 Ezra*. There are visions, discourses, an otherworldly mediator, pseudonymity, disposition of the recipient, and the reaction of the recipient.

In what follows I shall, drawing from the works of Michael Knibb[82] and Daniel Harrington, demonstrate ways in which apocalyptic and sapiential thought meld in this apocalypse of *4 Ezra*. I will address three examples, the first dialogue found in 3:1—5:20, a panoramic view of visions[83] 4,

---

80. Murphy, "Sapiential Elements in the Syriac Apocalypse of Baruch," 323-25. John Collins writes, "While sapiential revelation is immanent, and is channeled through the natural human processes of thought, apocalyptic revelation is ecstatic, and conferred from outside." Collins, "Cosmos and Salvation: Jewish Wisdom and Apocalyptic in the Hellenistic Age," 139. As stated above, Crenshaw divides the wisdom manner of thinking or theologizing further into three states and all of these stages or manners of thinking in wisdom are anthropocentric. Crenshaw, "Wisdom in the OT," 954-55.

81. See the master paradigm in Collins "Towards The Morphology of a Genre," 5-8, and Collins, "The Jewish Apocalypses," 28.

82. Knibb writes, "Thus in what follows I want to make a beginning at looking at one apocalyptic writing, *4 Ezra* . . . , and to attempt the one very limited task of considering in what sense, if at all, this particular work can be described as wisdom or as having characteristics which associate it with wisdom." Knibb, "Apocalyptic and Wisdom in *4 Ezra*," 56-74.

83. *4 Ezra* was written after the destruction of the temple and is consumed with the aftermath of this tragedy. The book has seven parts, to which Michael Stone refers as visions: Vision 1 (3:1—5:20), Vision 2 (5:21—6:34), Vision 3 (6:35—9:25), Vision 4 (9:26—10:59), Vision 5 (11–12), Vision 6 (13), and Vision 7 (14). Dialogue between the seer, named Ezra, and the angels is the main feature of the first three visions where the seer questions the divine governance of the world particularly as it relates to Israel and the rest of humanity. In the fourth vision, where the seer acquiesces and agrees with the perspective of the angel, Ezra comes across a grieving woman, consoles her, and has a profound experience as the woman is transformed into the heavenly Jerusalem. The fifth and sixth visions take on a political and messianic tone as they speak of the demise of the Roman Empire and evil nations as well as the arrival of a liberator. In the seventh vision, the revelation is given to Ezra (the twenty-four exoteric books along with the seventy esoteric books) ending with his assumption to heaven. Stone, *Fourth Ezra*, 50-51.

5, and 6, and some comments on how the text draws from Job and chapter 14.

One example of similarities of both wisdom and apocalyptic is in the first dialogue of 3:1—5:20. Questions arise that exceed the boundaries of human understanding as well as conventional wisdom. Uriel's questions to Ezra demonstrate the limitation of understanding as Uriel asks Ezra to "weigh for me the weight of fire, or measure for me a blast of wind, or call back for me the day that is past" (4:5). Ezra's understanding of these comes via divine revelation. Uriel does use the device of the parable to assist in crossing the chasm of understanding. (This parable form appears in both wisdom and apocalyptic texts.) In 4:13–21, after hearing Uriel recount the tale of the forest of trees of the plain along with the waters of the sea, Ezra admits that each should remain in the established boundary each has been given and, therefore, admits to the line of demarcation between earthly questions and heavenly ones.[84]

The schema present in the book of Daniel also appears in Visions 4, 5, and 6. Upon reception of a vision or dream, the seer requests assistance in comprehending it. Through an angelic being (or God) understanding comes to the seer unveiling how the dream or vision sheds understanding on both the present and the future. Daniel uses the word *raz* or mystery and *pesher* to speak of the solution. *4 Ezra* does not use these terms but the *raz/pesher* idea is present. From this pattern, it is evident that true wisdom is something esoteric; the seer must have a divine revelation to access it.[85]

Knibb begins his treatment of *4 Ezra* at the last chapter, 14. It is here that Ezra's role is portrayed in different ways; he has the role of both Second Moses and lawgiver. Ezra also appears as having similarities to a prophet. He gives himself to the restoration of the law. Before this can occur, he must receive inspiration to dictate the law to the five who are with him. This inspiration that takes place in vss. 38–41 is akin to Ezekiel when he delivered prophetic utterances. Ezra receives inspiration by drinking from a cup (Ezekiel received inspiration by eating a scroll; see Ezek 2:8—3:3). From this similarity it is likely that Ezra is seen as a prophet.[86] Having drunk from the cup, Ezra is now endowed with wisdom and understanding. The book, therefore, relates the apocalyptic writings using wisdom verbiage. (See vss. 45b–47.)

---

84. Harrington, "4QInstruction and 4 Ezra," 350.
85. Ibid., 352.
86. Knibb, "Apocalyptic and Wisdom in 4 Ezra," 63.

Two points are salient here. Ezra has great concern for the general population, but the apocalyptic writings are specifically for the wise; vss. 13 and 26 appear to make this differentiation. This intended audience of the wise also gives a hint as to the sociological setting of the apocalypse; this is an educated audience and not the general populace.[87] Secondly, a reading of *4 Ezra* 14:45–48 would suggests that these apocalyptic writings were either considered to be wisdom or at the very least had wisdom within them.

Other portions of *4 Ezra*, Knibb notes, attest to these two points. He observes the similarities between *4 Ezra* and the book of Job. Considering the similarities with the wisdom text of Job, both books address the similar issue of theodicy but approach it differently. In both books, there is much dialogue to process the quandary. For both, the dialogue is ineffective at solving the problem and answering the questions, which paves the way for the divine revelation addressing the issue. Knibb also notes the close parallels of *4 Ezra* 4:7–8 and Job 38:16–18. The manner in which the angel begins the speeches is also reminiscent of the beginning of the wisdom teacher.[88]

An examination of this book, and particularly chapter 14, reveals that the intended audience was for the specific group of the wise. Ezra, therefore, is not a popular book but one of learned reflection and revelation intended for the educated circle of the wise. Caution is also warranted, as the interpreter acknowledges that the author of *4 Ezra* is certainly writing for a different audience than those of the Old Testament wisdom books.[89] As demonstrated above, *4 Ezra* employs some rhetorical devices common to wisdom literature yet is still an apocalypse in the line of Daniel. The text, Harrington writes, "[p]resents apocalyptic or revealed wisdom."[90]

Now, I will address two epistles that are neither apocalyptic nor sapiential. Products of the Second Temple Period, James and Romans both exhibit a confluence of apocalyptic and sapiential. This examination furthers my argument that these two genres were not completely separate in the minds of authors of this time.

---

87. Ibid., 64.
88. See 5:32 and 7:49
89. Knibb, "Apocalyptic and Wisdom in 4 Ezra," 72.
90. Harrington, "4QInstruction and 4 Ezra," 355.

Wisdom and Apocalyptic Genre and Thought Meld/Clash

THE EPISTLE OF JAMES

The Epistle of James stands as another example of a text written in the Second Temple Period that melds together elements of wisdom thought and form with components of apocalyptic thought. In this section, I will demonstrate how James employs the Jewish wisdom tradition in his text. Secondly, I will address the apocalyptic eschatology present in the book.[91]

James's epistle shows a dependence on and development of Jewish wisdom tradition. This dependence is the root of the ethical dimension in James; this reliance on wisdom also appears in the use of literary forms such as wisdom sayings, wisdom admonitions, and beatitudes.

Wisdom sayings utilize experience and give advice based on said experiences; there are many of these wisdom sayings in the book of James. Two examples are Jas 2:13 and 3:18. "For judgment will be without mercy to anyone who has shown no mercy; mercy triumphs over judgment" (Jas 2:13). Frequently James uses wisdom sayings to strengthen an argument at the conclusion of a pericope. Such is the case in 3:18, "And a harvest of righteousness is sown in peace for those who make peace." With this concluding wisdom saying, the text bolsters the main point of the passage: wisdom brings about righteousness, exemplified by peace.[92]

Pattrick Hartin also outlines the use of wisdom admonitions in James. Wisdom admonitions summon the hearer to obey the advice given.

---

91. I acknowledge my indebtedness to the works of Patrick Hartin, Matt A. Jackson-McCabe, and Patrick Tiller for their work in this subject. After his treatment of James, Hartin concludes that James does not warrant the label of true wisdom but rather draws upon both wisdom and prophetic forms while also exhibiting elements of apocalyptic thinking. He asserts that the inclusion of apocalyptic thought does not displace his focus on providing exhortations and advice to the readers about how they are to lead their lives in the present." (Patrick Hartin, "'Who is Wise and Understanding Among You?' (James 3:13): An Analysis of Wisdom, Eschatology, and Apocalypticism in the Letter of James," 149–68.) I disagree with Hartin's conclusion that James is not true wisdom but value his contributions to the discussion, particularly his detailed list of wisdom elements in James. Jackson-McCabe, also concluding that James is better identified as a writing intended to give moral encouragement than wisdom literature, notes James's apocalyptic worldview is "distinguished primarily by the increased importance attached to supernatural agents and a world beyond this one, and by the hope for judgment and vindication beyond death," a determination with which I agree—while disagreeing with his argument against James as a wisdom writing. Jackson-McCabe, "A Letter to the Twelve Tribes in the Diaspora: Wisdom and 'Apocalyptic' Eschatology in the Letter of James," 504–17.

92. Hartin, "'Who is Wise and Understanding Among You?' (James 3:13): An Analysis of Wisdom, Eschatology, and Apocalypticism in the Letter of James," 151.

Additionally, there is often a reason given for the hearer to obey this advice. Three examples of how James uses this type of wisdom discourse are 1:2; 1:19–27; and 5:20. In 1:2 the author gives the wisdom admonition, "My brothers and sisters, whenever you face trails of any kind, consider it nothing but joy." This admonition is followed by another in 1:4, "And let endurance have its full effect, so that you may be mature and complete, lacking in nothing." A further wisdom admonition appears in 1:5, "If any of you is lacking in wisdom, ask God, who gives to all generously and ungrudgingly, and it will be given you." Yet another admonition appears in 1:6, "But ask in faith, never doubting, for the one who doubts is like a wave of the sea, driven and tossed by the wind." A number of wisdom admonitions appear in 1:19–27, and they find their base in a threefold saying, "Let everyone be quick to listen, slow to speak, slow to anger."[93] The ending of the letter contains a number of wisdom admonitions that deal with abstaining from oaths or the exhortation to pray. Moreover, James brings these to a conclusion with 5:20 "You should know that whoever brings back a sinner from wandering will save the sinner's soul from death and will cover a multitude of sins." Hartin observes that a twofold perspective is apparent in these wisdom admonitions. These admonitions stress the type of life that the hearers should live in the present. Additionally, there is a gaze to the future salvation. Hartin writes, "The worldview of wisdom has been broadened to include the eschatological dimension."[94]

The Beatitude, a form of wisdom literature, also appears in James. When compared to its appearance in the Old Testament, its appearance in the New Testament confers a blessing in the future *eschaton* rather than in this present life. Two examples of the beatitude appear in Jas 1:12 and 1:25.[95] In 1:12, "Blessed is anyone who endures temptation. Such a one has stood the test and will receive the crown of life that the Lord has promised to those who love him." The dominant tone in this verse is one of an eschatological perspective. Hartin writes, "An eschatological correlative is

---

93. Dibelius argues that proper understanding warrants recognition that these three admonitions mirror ideas found in Jewish wisdom. He highlights that v. 19b exhibits both the content and form of Jewish sapiential literature. Dibelius, *A Commentary on the Epistle of James*, 110. Sophie Laws also concurs with this comparison. Laws, *A Commentary on the Epistle of James*, 80.

94. Hartin, "'Who is Wise and Understanding Among You?' (James 3:13): An Analysis of Wisdom, Eschatology, and Apocalypticism in the Letter of James," 152.

95. Hanck, "μακαριος," 362–64.

evident here: the blessedness projected onto the future stands in opposite correlation to what is experienced in the present."[96]

Another example appears in 1:25, "But those who look into the perfect law, the law of liberty, and persevere, being not hearers who forget but doers who act—they will be blessed [μακαριος] in their doing." This verse is not in a beatitude form but μακαριος occurs in a descriptive form. The hearers' present actions will bring future blessings. In both of these examples, the promised eschatological blessing serves as the motivation for the present lifestyle. Hartin argues that an eschatological worldview has been infused into the traditional wisdom worldview.[97]

The above observations show the dependence on Jewish wisdom literature that James possesses. Matt Jackson-McCabe has commented on the apocalyptic eschatology present in James; the eschatological dimensions of James's exhortations have more affinity with Jewish apocalyptic literature than the wisdom tradition. Absent from the text are the otherworldly journeys, history divided into periods, or the dreams, visions, and revelations present in Jewish apocalyptic literature. John Collins describes the apocalyptic worldview as "distinguished primarily by the increased importance attached to supernatural agents and a world beyond this one, and by the increased judgment and vindication beyond death."[98] In James, Jackson-McCabe writes, both of these characteristics have a prominent place in the underlying worldview; he exhorts the readers in view of the imminent *parousia* of the Lord when God will judge the evil presently in the world.[99]

As to worldview, James views the cosmos as existing between two poles: good and evil. In the wisdom literature of the Old Testament the dualism is between the "wise" and the "fool." James, taking this dichotomy much further, expresses a choice between God and the world for he says in 4:4, "Do you not know that friendship with the world is enmity with God? Therefore whoever wishes to be a friend of the world becomes an enemy of God." The choice is essentially a choice between God and the devil, and

---

96. Hartin, "'Who is Wise and Understanding Among You?' (James 3:13): An Analysis of Wisdom, Eschatology, and Apocalypticism in the Letter of James," 152.

97. Ibid., 153.

98. Collins, "Wisdom, Apocalypticism and Generic Compatibility," 170.

99. Jackson-McCabe, "A Letter to the Twelve Tribes in the Diaspora: Wisdom and 'Apocalyptic' Eschatology in the Letter of James," 508.

for this reason James in 4:7 exhorts his readers to submit to God and resist the devil.[100]

The relationship between this understanding of the cosmos and human ethics emerges in James's exhortations on wisdom. He speaks of wisdom that is from above and from God; this wisdom brings about proper ethical behavior. There are those, however, who exhibit a behavior that is selfish, jealous, and divisive, and every foul deed; this behavior stems from a wisdom that is demonic (instead of from God) and earthly (instead of from above).[101] Jackson-McCabe asserts, "The world is in general a source of impurity, the avoidance of which, along with an active concern for the socially disadvantaged who suffer under the present circumstances, is at the very heart of James's conception of 'true religion.'"[102]

The solution to this cosmic quandary is in an imminent divine intervention into time and space, bringing about the ultimate triumph of good over evil. James refers to this event as the *parousia tou kuriou*. Similar to apocalyptic literature texts of this period, James considers his audience and himself to be living on the precipice of history's consummation. This event will overturn the present situation in the world: "the rich" will be abased and the "meek" will be lifted (1:9–10; 5:1). The rich will experience a "day of slaughter" (5:5) as they and their dealings are destroyed (1:11). The poor, however, will inherit the kingdom for God has chosen them.[103]

---

100. Ibid., 508.

101. Ibid., 509.

102. Ibid., 509.

103. Ibid., 510. Patrick Tiller comments further on James's teachings on the rich and poor, what Tiller refers to as an apocalyptic ethic. Tiller demonstrates that Jesus' Sermon on the Mount is the dominant background material for the ethic in the Epistle of James. For example, in James 2:5b, the author rebukes the practice of showing favoritism to the rich over the poor. Tiller argues that part of the background for this rebuke is Matt 5:3, "Blessed are the poor in spirit because the kingdom of heaven is theirs." and Luke 6:20, "Blessed are you poor because the kingdom of God is yours." Tiller concludes that the background for James rebuke in 2:5 is, "the conflation of at least two traditions: that God has chosen the poor and that he has promised that the poor will inherit the kingdom." For James, this conflation results in something further. Tiller writes, "If Jesus has pronounced the poor blessed, then one ought not to dishonor the poor (v.6), but honor them." Tiller, "The Rich and Poor in James," 170–72.

Particular to James's repudiation for the rich is how he utilizes an apocalyptic lens to view the present issue. His eschatology (as seen in Jas 5:1–6 where, in light of the coming judgment, he admonishes the rich to lament) is the basis upon which he exhorts the righteous and rebukes the ungodly, the rich. Yet eschatology is not the foundation of the thought but rather an apocalyptic division of the cosmos. James divides the world

The co-existence of sapiential and apocalyptic features, as Jackson-McCabe rightly concludes, is a noteworthy and integrated confluence in this text. James's ethical teaching comes forth immersed with an expectation of an imminent appearing of the Lord who will issue divine judgment. For James, wisdom results in the proper ethical behavior and is antithetical to the self-serving disposition of the demonic wisdom of this world. The driving force for James, like apocalyptic texts of this time, is the imminent arrival of the kingdom. In light of this reality, the primary charge to the believers is to await patiently the kingdom and be strong (5:7–8); this anticipation evokes the charge to "resist the devil" and follow after the "wisdom from above." I, therefore, add James to my list of texts that demonstrate a melding of apocalyptic and sapiential.

ROMANS

In her insightful work E. Elizabeth Johnson speaks of Paul's use of both the wisdom tradition and apocalyptic tradition in Rom 9–11. In examining Rom 11:33–36, she notes that the scholarly literature notes how Paul could be in one tradition or the other but does not entertain the possibility that he resides in both; the research points to considering Paul as a sage or as a seer but does not consider the possibility of both. She argues that Rom 9- 11 displays a wisdom and apocalyptic confluence.[104]

It must be said that Rom 9–11 is part of a letter and does not fit the description of an apocalypse or wisdom book. The style of the argument is more fitting for philosophical teachers than for sages or visionaries. Yet Johnson does recognize within it various motifs from both sapiential and

---

between "above and below" (3:5), "God and this world" (4:14), "God and the devil" (4:7; 3:15). James assails against a perspective of the cosmos that assigns right and wrong in a manner contrary to the ways of God. Ibid., 176.

Tiller concludes that in the midst of examining the otherworldly focus and phenomenon of apocalyptic texts, interpreters often miss the "this worldly" ethic that is present in these texts. Inherent in these apocalyptic texts, and also present in James, is abhorrence for the *status quos* of the present social realities, i.e., the oppressive hand of the rich upon the poor. In this epistle, James has taken Jesus' teachings and immersed them in a thoroughly apocalyptic mindset of reality, and brought forth a scathing critique of the social reality and a path of how this will change. Ibid., 178–79.

104. Johnson, *The Function of Apocalyptic and Wisdom Traditions in Romans 9–11: Rethinking the Questions*, 352–53.

apocalyptic literature.[105] I shall first address the apocalyptic elements of the text followed by the wisdom elements.

Apocalyptic Influence

Two themes that suggest apocalyptic influence are the theme of mystery and the fullness of Israel and the Gentiles. In Rom 9–11 Paul's thoughts center on the present situation and future of Israel; such is also a centerpiece in apocalypses such as *4 Ezra* and *2 Baruch*. In both of these latter books, the concern of the historical threat to Israel is assuaged by information via a revelation. For Paul this revelation that addresses his concern for Israel is described in 11:25 as a heavenly μυστήριον. What is fundamentally in question is whether or not God has rejected his people (see Rom 11:1). Paul in Rom 11:25–26 answers the question with, "Lest you be wise in your own conceits, I want you to understand this mystery, brethren. A hardening has come upon part of Israel until the full number of the Gentiles come in, and so all Israel will be saved."[106] The previously mentioned apocalypses *4 Ezra* and *2 Baruch* also face a situation where the tenuous nature of national survival brings into question if God is still committed to his elect.[107]

Paul speaks about the fullness of Israel and also of the Gentiles. In like manner both *4 Ezra* and *2 Baruch* espouse the idea of the "full number" of elect that must come before the *eschaton* sees fruition.[108] Other apocalyptic texts also express this idea that the repentance of all of Israel is a prelude to the *eschaton*.[109]

---

105. Johnson, *The Function of Apocalyptic and Wisdom Traditions in Romans 9–11: Rethinking the Questions*, 123.

106. Ibid., 124.

107. Ibid., 124. *4 Ezra* answers the questions: (*4 Ezra* 6: 25) "It shall be that whoever remains after all that I have foretold you shall be saved and shall see my salvation and the end of my world. *2 Baruch* answers the question: (*2 Baruch* 81:4) "The Most High . . . revealed to me a word that I might be comforted, and showed me visions that I might not be again sorrowful."

108. See *4 Ezra* 4: 35–37 and *2 Baruch* 23:4–5

109. Dale C. Allison, Jr. "The Background of Romans 11:11–15 in Apocalyptic and Rabbinic Literature," 229–234. Allison points to other apocalyptic passages that give the impression that the repentance of Israel is a precursor to the ultimate redemption. He points to *T. Dan.* 6:4; *T. Sim.* 6:2–7; *T. Jud.* 23:5; *As. Mos.* 1:18; *2 Bar* 78: 6–7; *Apoc. Abr.* 23:5

E. Johnson points to vocabulary in Rom 9–11 that she argues carries the influence of apocalyptic thought, both generally and specifically in Paul's writings. These words are δόξα, σώζω, ζωη, and μυστήριον.

With respect to the term δόξα, the vessels spoken of in Rom 9:23 are prepared for δόξα, or specifically the eschatological δόξα του θεου (5:2).[110] This eschatological hope is, in fact, the ultimate apocalyptic vindication that the redeemed will share with the sovereign Lord.[111]

In the respect to the term σώζω, Johnson argues that the salvation vocabulary (σώζω, σωτηρία) additionally attests to Paul's apocalyptic mindset in Rom 9–11. Salvation, for Paul, has a profoundly futuristic element to it. With the death and resurrection of Christ as the foundation for salvation, the *parousia* of the Lord is the consummation of it.[112]

With regard to the term ζωή, Paul's phrase of ζωή ἐκ νεκρων in 11:15 is evidence of his belief that the faith of (or some of) the Gentiles, the disbelief of Israel, and the fulfillment of salvation are distinctive features of the consummation of history. Although Israel's present refusal of the divine gift of salvation has meant the world's reconciliation, Israel's acceptance of the gift will result in "life from the dead."[113] Paul describes this life as ζωή αἰώνιον (see Rom 2:7; 5:21; 6:22, 23; Gal 6:8); God gives life to that which was dead. This multifaceted concept is abundantly present in Jewish apocalyptic literature, particularly in the concept of resurrection from the dead.[114]

Concerning the term μυστήριον, David Aune writes, "The term 'mystery' is virtually a technical term in early Jewish and early Christian apocalyptic and prophetic texts."[115] Johnson notes that this section of Romans mirrors thoughts expressed in *1 Enoch*.[116]

---

110. Also see 1:23; 3:7, 23; 4:20; 6:4; 11:36; 15:7

111. Johnson, *The Function of Apocalyptic and Wisdom Traditions in Romans 9–11: Rethinking the Questions*, 127. Also see Koch, *Rediscovery*, 28–32.

112. Ibid., 128.

113. Ibid.

114. Ibid.

115. David Aune further notes that Rom 11:25 is one of the two Christian oracles that use this key term to begin a clause. The other is 1 Cor 15: 51, "Behold! I tell you a mystery . . . ." Revelation 10:7, 1:20; 17:7 also portray the use of the term in the context of important prophetic declarations. The distinctive phrase, "the mystery of God hidden for ages but now revealed" (and its variations) is known as the "revelation schema." Moreover, the phrase "I know a mystery" appears three times in the Jewish apocalyptic text of *1 Enoch* to unveil a schema of events yet to come (*1 Enoch* 103:1; 104: 10, 12). Aune, *Prophecy in Early Christianity and the Ancient Mediterranean World*, 333.

116. For I know this mystery; I have read the tablets of heaven and have seen the holy

A Polemical Preacher of Joy

Wisdom Influence

The evidence of a wisdom tradition influence in Rom 9–11 is not as plentiful as the apocalyptic influence. One passages that Johnson points to as showing the influence of the sapiential tradition is 9:20–23. Additionally, she points to the fact that these three chapters, which end with a wisdom hymn, seek to answer a question of balance and order.[117]

Romans 9:20, E. Johnson argues, shows indications that Paul draws from Isa 29:16 but employs it in a manner reflective of the influence of the wisdom tradition as seen in Wis 15:7 and Sir 33:13. She argues that the first half of the verse comes from Isaiah 29:16. The point of Isa 29:16 is that the clay is subject to the sovereignty of the potter. It cannot and would not ask the potter why the potter has made it or declare that the potter did not make it.[118]

Similarly, another prophetic voice, Jer 18:1–11 also paints a similar picture to communicate that God (the potter) is free to do what God wills to do with the clay (Israel). The difference between these prophetic voices and Rom 9: 20 is that these prophetic voices do not speak of two kinds of vessels as appears in Rom 9. Two kinds of vessels and this imagery of a potter appear in the wisdom texts of Wis 15:7 and Sir 33:13.[119]

Looking at the differences between these prophetic and wisdom texts is instructive. The two prophetic texts paint a picture of the potter with one pot and emphasize that it would be ridiculous for the pot to defy the potter. The two wisdom texts address an entirely different issue and highlight the difference between two different kinds of people or vessels. Johnson, therefore, notes that what is at work here in Rom 9: 20 is Paul drawing from the prophetic text of Isa 29:16 and baptizing it the sapiential development of these two wisdom texts (Wis 15:7 and Sir 33:13) in order to further his argument. This is done to address the critical quandary of this passage; the

---

writings, and I have understood the writing in them; and they are inscribed concerning you. (*1 En.* 103:2) And now I know mystery: For . . . they will speak evil words and lie, and they will invent fictitious stories and write out my Scriptures on the basis of their own words. (*1 En.* 104:10) Again know another mystery: that to the righteous and the wise shall be given the Scriptures of joy, for truth and great wisdom. (*1 En.* 104:12)

117. Johnson, *The Function of Apocalyptic and Wisdom Traditions in Romans 9–11: Rethinking the Questions*, 131.

118. Ibid., 132.

119. Ibid.

crucial issue under consideration here is the freedom of God "to elect some and not others."[120]

This entire section of Rom 9–11 and its argumentation has the purpose of addressing a query of balance and order. It is, thus, similar to the agenda of sapiential writers. Johnson writes, "The μυστηριον which supplies the conclusion, like the heavenly secrets of the apocalypses, is part of God's wisdom."[121] There are a number of examples where wisdom literature exhibits a concern for the balance and order within this life. In like manner Paul, in this section, struggles with God's dealings with both Israel and the Gentiles, a concern for balance and order which is "cosmic, historical, and moral."[122] His repeated point is that both Jews and Gentiles are sinners who need to receive justification by faith; they, therefore, have the same status before the Almighty. The problem remains that Jews are not receiving this message but Gentiles are. The apostle, thus, finds his argument in a predicament because the tension of God showing impartiality yet also showing faithfulness to Israel must receive a response. Paul's response is that this imbalance is the result of God's master plan; God has a purpose in salvation history for both Jew and Gentile to fulfill, leading to a restoration that will take place in heaven. There is a theological necessity for the πλνρωμα of both Israel and the Gentiles for Paul's argument to be valid. For Johnson, "Rom 9–11 are driven by a concern for the integrity and consistency of God."

By themselves, these points in Johnson's argument are not completely convincing of a wisdom influence. When taken in the context of Paul's likely dependence on the wisdom tradition in other portions of Romans, however, these points have more potency. I, therefore, agree with Johnson's argument for a confluence of wisdom and apocalyptic thought in Rom 9–11.

THE BOOK OF JOB

Many characteristics in the book of Job warrant its label of wisdom literature,[123] and scholars have also noted its apocalyptic features. John

120. Ibid., 133.
121. Ibid., 137.
122. Ibid., 138.
123. Murphy, *The Tree of Life*, 33. Roland Murphy attests to the wisdom character of the book when he writes of Job, "It is a book of Israelite wisdom, and it stays within

A Polemical Preacher of Joy

Collins has written that Job "has the greatest affinities with apocalyptic."[124] Collins contends that like apocalypses, Job captures a situation where the expectation of the order seems elusive and God's speech from the whirlwind addresses this dilemma. Similarly Christopher Rowland has stated in his work that "the whole structure of Job offers an embryonic form of the later apocalypses."[125]

In his book, Timothy Johnson[126] takes the intimation of these scholars one step further and suggests that Job takes the form of a "nascent apocalypticism." He makes this argument drawing heavily from the master paradigm that the Society of Biblical Literature's Genre Project formulated in *Semeia* 14.[127] In what follows, I draw from Johnson's argument for Job as proto-apocalypse. In so doing, I will point to another text, whose final composition is possibly in the Second Temple period, which exhibits qualities of both apocalyptic thought and wisdom thought.

Timothy Johnson also utilizes the definition for an apocalypse proffered by the SBL study group, from which the master paradigm arose. Where would the divine revelation be in Job? Johnson notes that most would see the whirlwind as an example of divine revelation. The book is written in a narrative form and the revelation arrives from God—directly without a mediator. The one who receives the revelation, like in apocalypses, is indeed a human: Job. Johnson correctly notes that the only item that, at first, seems to be absent from Job would be the element of eschatological

---

the perspective of such wisdom. "Its sapiential character is shown by the many explicit references to wisdom and by the abundance of wisdom themes that appear." One can notice the several references to wisdom in the book. In chapter 28:12, 20 the question arises, "Where is wisdom found." The class of "wise men" is referred to in 34:2. Eliphaz speaks of the tradition of wisdom in 15:18. For Murphy, the wisdom themes present in the book especially warrant its wisdom literature label. The book exhibits an overt concern for creation as seen in Job 12:10–25; 36:22—37:24; and 38–41. The personification of wisdom appears in Job 28. Compare this with such a personification in Prov 1, 8, 9, Sir 24; Wis 7–9. The quandary of deciphering a theology of retribution also appears. Notice the same in Eccl 4: 1–2; 6:1–6; 8: 5–15; Sir 2: 1–6; 11: 4–6; 39:16—41:13. It gives an honest portray of life's challenges. See Job 7:1–2; 14: 1–6 (Compare with Eccl 2:17, 23; Sir 40:1–10). Murphy, *The Tree of Life*, 33–34.

124. Collins, "Cosmos and Salvation: Jewish Wisdom and Apocalyptic in the Hellenistic Age," 140.

125. Rowland, *The Open Heaven: A Study of Apocalyptic in Judaism and Early Christianity*, 206–7.

126. Johnson, *Now My Eyes See You: Unveiling an Apocalyptic Job*, 2.

127. See the master paradigm in Collins "Towards the Morphology of a Genre," 5–8.

salvation. (He does make this argument via an examination on the tradition in the interpretation of Job.)

Section One: Medium by which the Revelation is Communicated

Johnson points to three revelations in the book to demonstrate Job's fulfillment of this section of the master paradigm. First he mentions Eliphaz's vision in 4:17–21.[128] Although Eliphaz does not make a journey to another world, the text does show that the experience incorporated a number of senses. He hears a voice and feels the result of the experience with trembling, his bones shaking, and the hair of his flesh bristling, according to vss. 14–16.[129]

A second revelation would be Job 28; it serves as a theophany. The argument at this point is not as convincing although worthy of consideration. A third revelation is God's speeches from the whirlwind, the book's quintessential revelation. Visual and auditory components take the form of both discourse and dialogue.[130]

Section Two: Otherworldly Mediator Communicates Revelation

Johnson identifies Job 4:12–21 as a use of a mediator in the book of Job. Although it is not certain who the mediator is, the content of the message is discernible. Cyril S. Rodd also sees a mediator in this passage and writes, "The essential point is that what Eliphaz meets is a messenger from God with a revelation for him."[131] This phenomenon is strange for wisdom.

Section Three: The Human Recipient

John Collins has written, "In all Jewish apocalypses the human recipient is a venerable figure from the distant past, whose name is used pseudonymously."[132] Although Johnson argues that the revelation goes to

---

128. Katherine Dell has written that portions take the form of an apocalypse. Dell, *The Book of Job as Skeptical Literature*, 104.

129. Johnson, *Now My Eyes See You: Unveiling an Apocalyptic Job*, 53.

130. Ibid., 55.

131. Rodd, *The Book of Job*, 15.

132. Collins, *The Apocalyptic Imagination*, 6.

Job in each of the three narratives, the most convincing observation is that of Job 38–41, the portion known as YHWH speeches. After God speaks, Job's response is one of humbled awe and repentance (42:6).[133]

As to the subject of pseudonymity, Johnson contends that this feature also applies to the book of Job. There are some scholars who consider Job to have been an actual person[134] (but there are some who consider the character to be a fabrication for literary purposes).[135] Marvin Pope, however, asserts that "Job" was a frequent name in the second millennium B.C.E. and that there very well may have been a venerable figure who was named Job.[136] Considering that the consensus that the final form of editing is the result of later editing, Johnson concludes, "It is possible to conceive of a story that either embellishes the sufferings of an ancient legend or affixes the name of such a legend to this story."[137]

Section Four: Protology (Pre-history or Beginning of History)

Johnson points to at least three portions of Job that exhibit this characteristic: 4:17b, 28:23–28, and 38–41. In 4:17b, Eliphaz presents the query, "Can human beings be pure before their Maker?" The image of humanity at creation is the foundation of this question, and, thus, is reminiscent of humanity's primordial relationship with God. Likewise, Job 28:23–28 speaks about the primordial process in which God presents wisdom. The theophanic revelations of Job 38–41 are some of the most significant revelations of creation in the Old Testament.[138]

Section Five: History, Viewed as Explicit Recollection of the Past

Johnson notes this would not seem to apply to Job at the interpreter's first glance. Yet, all three revelations contain an element of recounting creation's beginning point. In Eliphaz's vision this recounting is from the vantage point of human-divine relationship. In Job 28, this reflection occurs in the

---

133. Johnson, *Now My Eyes See You: Unveiling an Apocalyptic Job*, 51–53.
134. Westermann, *The Structure of the Book of Job: A Form-Critical Analysis*, 6–7.
135. Murphy, *Book of Job*, 4–6.
136. Pope, *Job*, 6.
137. Johnson, *Now My Eyes See You: Unveiling an Apocalyptic Job*, 51–53.
138. Ibid., 53–55.

context of the wisdom-divine relationship. In the divine speeches of Job 38–41, this reflective view is in the theophany and the details of creation and order within it.[139]

Section Six: Present Salvation through Knowledge (as in Gnostic texts)

Although the book of Job is not a Gnostic text, Johnson does argue that the revelations in Job 28 and divine speeches give knowledge that Job did not previously possess. As a result of this knowledge, Job is able to navigate successfully the present or subsequent situation. For example, after the revelation in Job 28 that wisdom cannot be located within humans, Job is positioned to reject the rhetoric that comes from his friends. As well, after the divine speeches and the revelation thereof, Job gains new insight about God—evident in Job's admission that he did not fully understand prior to the revelation.[140]

Section Seven: Eschatological Crisis

Johnson readily admits that eschatological crisis as it appears in apocalyptic texts is not present in Job, but the book does portray a "cosmological crisis." Johnson concludes that "it is not hard to argue that the principles of 'persecution' and 'upheaval' that mark an 'eschatological crisis' are present in Job."[141]

Although different from the persecution of apocalyptic literature, Job does experience persecution. Job, unaware of its source, receives persecution from the Satan as the prologue points out the cosmic wager between God and the adversary. Job also receives persecution from his wife who counsels him to curse God and die in Job 2:9. Furthermore, the three friends and Elihu persecute Job in their accusations based on limited knowledge.[142]

Not only does Job receive this persecution but his experience amounts to a cosmic crisis for him as it results in potentially overturning the standing view of wisdom. Job has followed the path of wisdom and now experiences

---

139. Ibid., 55–56.
140. Ibid., 56.
141. Ibid., 56–57.
142. Ibid.

the upheaval of his personal history, as he has lost the people dear to him, his possessions, and his prestige. He now regrets the day of his birth (Job 3:3). This cosmic crisis also results in Job's doubt concerning his theology of retribution. That which was once a foundation and interwoven into the fabric of worldview and life has now unraveled.[143]

Section Eight: Eschatological Judgment

Again, Johnson admits that the element of eschatological judgment as it appears in apocalyptic is not readily apparent in the book of Job, yet he makes an argument. The most convincing portion of his argument has to do with the judgment that appears in the theophanic whirlwind speeches. Leo Perdue posits that the theophanic judgment is similar to that found in ANE combat myths. The Behemoth, Leviathan, and the ungodly have received judgment from God and now Job is the recipient. For Perdue, "Theophanic judgment, depicted in YHWH's coming in the whirlwind, serves as the controlling image for the two speeches."[144]

Section Nine: Eschatological Salvation

Job experiences a personal salvation in the epilogue when he receives twice as much as he had before. One must, however, state that the book of Job in MT obviously does not have an instance of eschatological salvation. This element of the paradigm does not appear in the book.[145]

Section Ten: Otherworldly Elements

Johnson shows points of intersection between the book of Job and the master paradigm particularly concerning the number of "otherworldly regions [or] beings" in the text. The first and most obvious portion that would demonstrate otherworldly elements would be in Job 1:6 where the reader faces the "heavenly beings" and "Satan." The reader is at once

---

143. Ibid., 56–57.

144. Ibid., 57–58. "The Divine warrior comes as the storm god to defeat his enemies and render judgment resulting in the repelling of threats of chaos against his rule." Perdue, *Wisdom in Revolt*, 202.

145. Johnson, *Now My Eyes See You: Unveiling an Apocalyptic Job*, 58.

transported to God's heavenly court. Johnson notes that the plotline of the book launches both from the otherworldly places and the interaction that takes place among these otherworldly beings.[146] The YHWH speeches also exhibit traits of otherworldliness, particularly when one considers the theophany and the many examples from primordial creation, the afterlife, and elements of astronomy.[147]

Johnson points to Job 38:7 and the singing of "morning stars" (בקר כוכבי) and the delight of "all heavenly beings" (כל־בני אלהים) present at the creation of the earth. Speaking of the afterlife, the text says in 38:17, "Have the gates of death been revealed (גלה) to you, or have you seen the gates of deep darkness?" The question in 38:19 inquires about the dwelling of light and darkness, both astronomical marvels.[148]

Section Eleven: Paraenesis

The best candidate for a paraenesis, which is the element that provides ethical exhortations and warning from the mediator to the recipient, is in Job 40:2. This verse is an example of an ethical admonition as it declares, "Shall a faultfinder contend with the Almighty, anyone who argues with God must respond." Although this may be the only candidate in the book of Job, this does not mortally wound Johnson's argument because Collins asserts that the paraenesis is not frequent in apocalypses, only appearing in a few Christian apocalypses.[149]

Section Twelve: Instructions to the Recipient

Johnson points to Eliphaz as the recipient of the instructions in 42:8. (These instructions appear after God's revelation and form a crucial portion of the concluding framework of the book.) There has been scholarly consternation as to why Eliphaz would be the recipient of such instruction. It is fitting, however, that Eliphaz would receive the instruction because the first revelation in the book came to him.[150]

---

146. Ibid., 59.
147. Ibid., *Job*, 60.
148. Ibid., 61.
149. Ibid., 62 and Collins "Towards the Morphology of a Genre," 5–9.
150. Johnson,, *Now My Eyes See You: Unveiling an Apocalyptic Job*, 63.

Section Thirteen: Narrative Conclusion

The narrative element of the text is without dispute; both the prologue and epilogue are in this form. John Collins writes, "There is always a narrative framework in which the manner of revelation is described."[151]

My purpose in this section is not to argue Johnson's generic label of nascent apocalypse, but rather to marshal the observations of such an argument to evidence that there is, in fact, a melding of apocalyptic and sapiential thought in the book of Job. This text, whose completion perhaps took place in the Second Temple period, is another example of apocalyptic and sapiential melding.

WISDOM OF SOLOMON

Shannon Burkes[152] argues that Wisdom of Solomon is in the form of sapiential literature but also exhibits apocalyptic views.[153] Drawing from Burkes, I will address the appearance of the concept of death in Wisdom of Solomon and how this usage points to a melding of sapiential and apocalyptic.

Burkes writes, "in spite of its suggestive title, many people have recognized that Wisdom of Solomon has a peculiarly chameleon-like quality that frustrates categorization."[154] Although the book does not fit the form of an

---

151. Ibid., 63. See the master paradigm in John Collins "Towards The Morphology of a Genre," 9.

152. Burkes, "Wisdom and Apocalypticism in the Wisdom of Solomon," 21–44.

153. Burkes addresses three main observations to support this conclusion; she addresses the book's concept of death, appearances and reality, the cosmos, epistemology, and wisdom as savior. The most convincing part of the argument is the examination of how Wisdom of Solomon treats the subject of death. The other portions of the argument could serve as supporting observations but do not exert the same convincing force. Although the focus I have chosen is the concept of death in Wisdom of Solomon, there are other noteworthy aspects to consider, as well. As in apocalyptic texts such as 1 *Enoch* and Daniel, history and eschatology are understood in the context of the cosmos. Salvation has more dependency upon understanding rather than only obedience. Individuals must understand what God has revealed via the cosmos, but angelic revelations are necessary to interpret this understanding. Wisdom of Solomon draws from the apocalyptic thought where "mysteries of God" allude to the eschatological "prize for the blameless souls," and the righteous that have died are "numbered among the sons of God" (1:22). Collins, "Cosmos and Salvation: Jewish Wisdom and Apocalyptic in the Hellensitic Age," 137.

154. Burkes, "Wisdom and Apocalypticism in the Wisdom of Solomon," 22. "There is no type of literature in the bible into which Wisdom as a whole fits." Gilbert, "Wisdom

Wisdom and Apocalyptic Genre and Thought Meld/Clash

apocalypse nor possess the supernatural mindset that such a genre would have, there are discernible points of the apocalyptic worldview present in the text. The presence of this apocalyptic worldview is accentuated by the fact that these elements differ from previous wisdom literature writings. The book, therefore, possesses distinct similarities with the apocalyptic texts in terms of its assumptions and expectations of the universe. This peculiarity, Burkes suggests, is due to the wisdom tradition experiencing a transformation. She writes, "The earlier sapiential literary form is now being used as a vehicle for apocalyptic ideas, and such reuse can create in the reader a sense of incongruity."[155]

The book's concept of death, Burke argues, is an effective entry into the apocalyptic worldview expressed in Wisdom of Solomon. Death receives the strongest attention in the first section of the book chapters 1–5.[156] It is here that the book shares the idea that death is not necessarily the retribution for sin. This sentiment stands in contrast to not only Deuteronomic theology but also Proverbs and Ezekiel.[157] The author utilizes a situation in 2:12–20 to bring out the teaching on death: the fact that a righteous individual, who has stood against his oppressors because they disobey the law, has suffered torture and death. This provides a challenge for the author because he now finds himself going against a well-established tradition that considered the sudden death of an individual to be the result of divine judgment.[158]

The author broadens the discussion from the mere fact that individuals suffer death for obeying the commandments. In four verses, the author

---

Literature," 307. Another scholar communicates this quandary differently; Lester Grabbe declares with certitude that Wisdom of Solomon is a wisdom book but then adds that by "focusing on only one or another aspect of the book, one could make a case for a variety of literary genres." He notes that the emphasis for individuals to acquire wisdom and the movement of Lady Wisdom draw from Prov 4. Additionally, Ben Sira has similarities to Wisdom of Solomon, as both are considered wisdom literature (along with Proverbs, Job, and Ecclesiastes). Grabbe, *Wisdom of Solomon*, 25.

155. Burkes, "Wisdom and Apocalypticism in the Wisdom of Solomon," 22.

156. Daniel Harrington outlines the text along three main sections: chapters 1–5 deal with righteousness and immortality, chapters 6–9 address wisdom, and chapters 10–19 address the function of wisdom in Israel's early history. Harrington, *Invitation to the Apocrypha*, 56.

157. Ezek 18:4, "Know that all lives are mine; the life of the parent as well as the life of the child is mine: it is only the person who sins that shall die." This idea already received some challenge in other portions of Scripture such as Job, Ecclesiastes, and Second Isaiah.

158. Burkes, "Wisdom and Apocalypticism in the Wisdom of Solomon," 24–25.

declares that death is not a creation of God and that God does not delight in death, for all things were made to live and are void of the poison of death. He also declares that Hades does not reside on earth and that death's presence and activity among humanity is because the ungodly summoned and formed a covenant with death (1:13–16). Moreover, 2:23–24 says that God created humanity to experience incorruption.[159]

In the struggle to balance strict monotheism alongside divine justice, Burkes argues, the author gives deference to divine justice by easing the stress on strict monotheism. This observation would be valid if one entertains the possibility that God did not create death which would mean that "death would seem to be a power independent of divine will and an outsider to creation, able to operate in the world contrary to God's own wishes for living creatures."[160]

This understanding stands *contra* Deut 32:39, "See now that I, even I, am he; there is no god besides me. I kill and I make alive; I wound and I heal; and no one can deliver from my hand." In this statement there is a monotheistic perspective on everything that happens. It is this monotheistic explanation for all events that particularly causes Job bewilderment and, thus, causes him to say, "It is all one; therefore I say, he destroys both the blameless and the wicked. When disaster brings sudden death, he mocks at the calamity of the innocent. The earth is given into the hand of the wicked; he covers the faces of its judges—if it is not he, who then is it?" (Job 9:22–24). In Job's understanding, there is a strict monotheism so whatever happens must find its root in the power of God.[161]

For the author of Wisdom, Pseudo-Solomon, death is an entity that functions *contra* the will of God; it is even personified. We see that the ungodly are able to enter into a covenant with death. This view of death bespeaks of a dualistic idea of the cosmos. On one side there is God and his creation, and on the other there is Death which works in conjunction with the devil and Hades. What is especially unique about this perspective of the cosmos, Burkes notes, is not only the fact that it is incongruent

---

159. Ibid., 26.

160. Ibid., 25–26. Yehoshua Amir understands this formulation of death to be strong enough to be a rival of God. Amir, "The Figure of Death in the 'Book of Wisdom,'" 157. The author of Wisdom of Solomon would most likely not agree with taking this formulation that far because he attests to the sole supremacy of God in 12:14 and 16:13. Yet this comment of 2:24 is contrary to the normal view presented in wisdom literature. It is odd for any kind of human suffering to be beyond the God of creation.

161. Ibid., 26.

with the wisdom tradition but also the fact that this dualistic perspective is placed in the mouth of Solomon, who is the spokesperson for the tradition. Furthermore, and especially pertinent to the objective of this chapter, this type of dualism appears in Jewish apocalyptic literature where there is an archenemy of God—usually presented as either the devil or death.[162] Burkes, therefore, justly concludes, "This part of the book has obvious similarities to apocalyptic eschatology, with its post-mortem division of righteous and unrighteous, Death/the Devil, day of judgment, and desolation of the earth by a warrior deity."[163] This argumentation is a small but noteworthy example where it is possible, plausible, and arguable to suggest that, in this text, wisdom and apocalyptic thought is present in the same book. The perceived line of demarcation between wisdom and apocalyptic is very permeable.

4QINSTRUCTION

Matthew Goff notes that, "*4QInstruction*, the longest Qumran wisdom text, demonstrates that a sapiential text from this period can combine elements from both apocalypticism and traditional wisdom."[164] He thus seeks to establish "that *4QInstruction* combines the . . . educational mindset of traditional wisdom and apocalyptic worldview."[165] In what follows, I will point to both the pedagogical approach within the text as well as examples of the melding of apocalyptic and wisdom thought.

Demonstrating the combination of apocalyptic and wisdom thought in *4QInstruction*, Goff rightly points to the pedagogy in the text. Following the sapiential tradition, especially in Proverbs, *4QInstruction* has a pedagogical tone to it as it seeks to teach ethical and prudent behavior. Goff notes, "The sapiential and apocalyptic traditions differ in terms of pedagogy in that the former provides advice regarding specific areas of ordinary life more consistently than the latter."[166]

---

162. Ibid., 26–28.

163. Ibid., 29. Perdue observes that the concept "of a devil, opposed to humanity and to divine rule, who is in control of death and is responsible for corrupting the design of God's creation of life, is an apocalyptic concept." Perdue, *Wisdom and Creation*, 300.

164. Goff, "Wisdom, Apocalypticism, and the Pedagogical Ethos of 4QInstruction," 58.

165. Ibid., 59.

166. Ibid., 60.

A Polemical Preacher of Joy

Comparing the pedagogical approaches in both *4QInstruction* and apocalyptic texts is noteworthy. The text is concerned with some of the mundane aspects of living. For example, *4QInstruction* (see 4Q416 2 ii 6–7) gives a warning about indebtedness, 4Q418 81 17: "Be very intelligent, and from all your teachers increase learning." Another example would be in 4Q416 2 ii 14–15, "Have understanding in all the ways of truth, and all the roots of iniquity perceive." There is an assumption in the text that the מבין have a thirst for learning. This stress on instruction is also present in apocalyptic literature as well. Goff points out some examples of this feature. In *1 Enoch* 82 and 105, the reader sees how Enoch is charged to teach the revelation that has come to him. Furthermore, the visions in Daniel contain an instructional impetus. Baruch in *2 Baruch* 44–45 and 76:5 likewise brings teaching to Israel.[167]

If *4QInstruction* and apocalyptic texts both have an emphasis on instruction as well as a prudent and righteous life, then what is the difference? The difference exists in the motivation. Usually in sapiential literature, Goff notes, there is a stress on such living for the sake of one's lot in this life: to live in keeping with the established order of the cosmos. In apocalyptic literature there is usually a teleological slant to the motivation. The readers are encouraged in a particular path in order that they may receive rewards and shun judgment in the life to come. One can argue that the sapiential texts that have an eschatological milieu to them, such as Wisdom of Solomon and *4QInstruction*, are examples of the apocalyptic tradition influencing these sapiential texts.[168]

Before pointing to additional examples where this wisdom text joins features of apocalyptic thought to itself, it would be helpful to point to the most important concept in the text—the רז נהיה.[169] The most important source of the מבין's wisdom is the רז נהיה. The phrase appears over twenty times in *4QInstruction*. The phrase is a combination of רז, which is Persian meaning mystery with נהיה the Niphal participle of the verb "to be." There has been discussion about how to translate the phrase. Goff translates it as "the mystery that is to be," and Harrington translates it as "the mystery that is to come." The term deals with the full scope of time and is not limited to eschatological concerns.[170] It addresses the daily aspects of life as well as

167. Ibid.
168. Ibid.
169. Ibid., 61.
170. Ibid., 61.

92

more speculative matters such as creation and the ultimate judgment. In *4QInstruction*, the מבין receives knowledge not only by receiving the רז נהיה but also by ruminating upon this revelation. Goff notes, "One could say that the רז נהיה gives the addressee the key, but the addressee still has to open the door himself. The acquisition of wisdom through the study of revealed knowledge reflects a combination of ideas from sapiential and apocalyptic traditions."[171]

The רז נהיה can give this kind of knowledge because it is intertwined with the deterministic divine plan. "One is able to understand the world," Goff continues, "by means of this mystery." The מבין can appreciate God's dominion because the מבין has received the רז נהיה, and this knowledge will spur a disposition of humble awe. The מבין's lifestyle is, therefore, to be one of righteousness and consecration as well as diligent study of the רז נהיה; wisdom comes by the continuous reflection on the revelation.[172]

Daniel J. Harrington's commentary on *4QInstruction* is helpful in noting the apocalyptic nature of this text; I am indebted to his insightful observations. In the first section (4Q417 1 i 1–13) the מבין receives encouragement to give himself to the "mystery that is to come." Again, what this phrase precisely means is somewhat elusive, but there is some inkling to its significance by what one can expect from its reception. The text speaks of how the receiver shall be aware of "the truth and iniquity, wisdom and foolishness . . . together with their punishments in all ages everlasting." Additionally the recipient is to experience a greater knowledge of God and God's glory. Harrington notes that this mystery that is to come would properly be understood as apocalyptic since it gives revelations about "God, eschatology, and ethics." This would be true even though the text does not follow the expected form of an apocalypse.[173]

In the second section 4Q417 1 I 13–18a instructs the מבין that the recompense for deeds has been placed in "a book of memorial" which is reminiscent of the heavenly tablets, which is an apocalyptic motif. The presence of the apocalyptic motif suggests a mindset that allows for such a motif. In the third section 4Q417 1 I 18b–24, the charge goes to the מבין to "gaze on the mystery that is to come" and doing this will cause one to "know the paths of everyone that lives and the number of his walking." These words are also reminiscent of apocalyptic literature, and the text

---

171. Ibid., 65.
172. Ibid., 67.
173. Harrington, *Invitation to the Apocrypha*, 345.

shows how revelation about the future has an influence on how one lives life in the present.¹⁷⁴

Dualism is present in 4Q418 69 as the text makes a distinction between the "foolish" and "elect." Harrington notes that this dualism exhibits an apocalyptic dimension because it not only focuses on the different paths for this present life but also encompasses eternal destinations. In 69 6 the "foolish-minded ones" receive admonishment that they "were fashioned by the power of God . . . to the everlasting pit shall your return be." Contrastingly, the "truly chosen ones" will be with the angels "in light everlasting . . . glory and abundance of splendor with them" (69 14).¹⁷⁵

4Q418 126 ii contains some rather bold apocalyptic thoughts. In Fragment 126 the text speaks of how God will "repay vengeance to the masters of inquiry" (6) and "raise up the head of the poor. . .in glory everlasting and peace eternal" (7–8).

Many of the teachings found in *4QInstruction* reflect a predominant concern on matters of this world. The younger, less experienced "O understanding one" receives instruction from the wise sage about matters related to money, societal interaction, and family relationships. Although the expected appeals and allusions to Scripture and common sense are present, which is usual for wisdom, there are also a number of places in the text where there is a melding between theological and eschatological sentiments as they are joined with wisdom teaching. Moreover, the framework of נהיה רז would seem to place the entire work within an apocalyptic mindset.¹⁷⁶

There is an epistemology that is more akin to that of the apocalyptic worldview than wisdom. Goff notes that "because of its reliance on

---

174. Ibid., 346.

175. Ibid.

176. Ibid., 354. F. García Martínez disagrees with the suggestion of Goff that *4QInstruction* points to both worldly and heavenly wisdom, and the רז נהיה is partly the reason for this difference of opinion. He contends that the רז נהיה gives the entire work a "'revelatory' character to all the contents of *4QInstruction*, including the worldly ones, and makes all of them heavenly wisdom." By including this secular teaching in the נהיה רז the author grants the same authority to it as the otherworldly mysteries. Martinez, therefore, regards, "*4QInstruction* as the representative of a new and different sort of Jewish wisdom, a wisdom whose authority is not grounded on human knowledge but on divine revelation." Martínez, "Wisdom at Qumran: Worldly or Heavenly?" 10, 14. Although Martinez's observation is noteworthy, I have more agreement with the presentation of Harrington that sees this רז נהיה as placing the entire text in an apocalyptic mindset. I prefer to consider this text as having been immersed in the apocalyptic mindset.

revelation, the epistemology of *4QInstruction* is much more in keeping with apocalypticism than biblical wisdom."[177] Wisdom in Proverbs is the result of humanity's examination of reflection upon the world around the individual. For apocalyptic texts such as Daniel and *1 Enoch*, wisdom comes as the result of a heavenly revelation. Dan 2:29, for example, refers to God as the "revealer of mysteries" (גלא רזיא). The presence of the word רז evidences one of the many ways that apocalyptic traditions differs from the wisdom tradition. Yet this term (and mindset) appears in this wisdom text, and, thus, stands as another example of apocalyptic and wisdom melding together in the Second Temple Period.

SIRACH

In this section I will highlight how apocalyptic and wisdom thought clash in Sirach. In this wisdom text, the author argues against key elements of apocalyptic thought. In order to demonstrate this polemic, I will focus on portions of the text where it seems likely that the author argues against apocalyptic thought, particularly as it appears in *1 Enoch*.[178]

Sirach is contemporary with the Book of the Watchers (*1 Enoch* 6–36), the Astronomical Book (*1 Enoch* 7–82), and Aramiac Levi Document; these authorial/editorial groups are likely aware of and polemical toward one another concerning foundational issues.[179] Boccaccini argues more

---

177. Goff, "Wisdom, Apocalypticism, and the Pedagogical Ethos of 4QInstruction," 63–64.

178. I am indebted to the works of Benjamin Wright III and Jeremy Corely. Jeremy Corley asks the question how the Jewish contemporaries of Ben Sira would decipher the questions of heaven and earth. There were three sources to which they looked. One source would be the traditional wisdom, believed to be contained especially in the Law of Moses (Sir 24), or they would seek out the revelations that appeared in apocalyptic writings, such as appear in portions of *1 Enoch*, or they would delve into the Greek philosophers and scientists, for example, Aristotle and Eratosthenes. In his article, Corley suggests that an examination of Sir 1:1–10 gives a spirited defense of traditional Hebrew wisdom tradition against the competing voices of Jewish apocalyptic literature and Greek science. Corley, "Wisdom Versus Apocalyptic and Science in Sir 1, 1–10," 273–74.

179. Wright, "Putting the Puzzle Together: Some Suggestions Concerning the Social Location of the Wisdom of Ben Sira," 89–113. Agreeing with Randall Argall, Wright notes that reading "Sirach and *1 Enoch* against one another has shown that they treat identical themes—revelation, creation, and judgment—and articulate them similarly. How does one, or even can one, move from literary theme to social reality?" Wright, "Putting the Puzzle Together: Some Suggestions Concerning the Social Location of the Wisdom of Ben Sira," 91. After noting the difference between Sirach and *1 Enoch*, Argall writes, "The

precisely that Ben Sira is cognizant of apocalyptic theologies and refutes them in his writing.[180]

Firmly in the wisdom tradition,[181] the author refutes some of the ideas held by apocalyptic texts of this time. Corley observes in Ben Sira an argument against the revelations contained in Jewish apocalyptic literature such as *1 Enoch*.[182] In the mind of Ben Sira, the Mosaic Law is the repository of divine wisdom, so these claims to revelation outside of the Law, made by someone like Enoch, could not be valid. Ben Sira's thoughts on the possibility of revelation outside of the Torah echo Deut 29: 28[29], "The secret things belong to the Lord our God, but the revealed things belong to us and to our children forever, to observe all the words of this law."[183]

In *1 Enoch* 13 and 14 there are three occasions when Enoch declares that his visions come to him in his sleep. Possibly against this idea, Ben Sira, in 34:1, writes of how fools "are sent winging by dreams." The passage of Sir 34:1–8 refutes the different possible methods to receive these revelations

---

two traditions go their separate ways on the common ground. . . . Such differences are the stuff of conflict. . . . [The differences] are enough to make a case that each tradition views the other among its rivals." Argall, *1 Enoch and Sirach: A Comparative Literary and Conceptual Analysis of the Themes of Revelation, Creation and Judgment*, 250.

180. Wright notes a challenge. The challenge is to "reconstruct the social situation" showing a number of groups interacting and conflicting with one another when these texts only give allusions to such polemics but never explicitly explain them. Wright, "Putting the Puzzle Together: Some Suggestions Concerning the Social Location of the Wisdom of Ben Sira," 90.

181. Ben Sira bears the label of wisdom literature for good reason. There are a number of traditional Hebrew wisdom reverberations that echo in the text. One example of such a reverberation would be Sir 1:1–10 use of Prov 8:22–31. The reader sees that Sir 1:4 statement, "Before all things wisdom was created, and prudent understanding from eternity" is a reverberation from the sounding of Prov 8:22, "YHWH created me the first of his way, the beginning of his works from of old." Furthermore, Job may serve as another echoing source, particularly in Job 28 where the text speaks of the search for wisdom. Job 28:20 reads, "But wisdom—from where does she come? And what is the place of understanding?" A similar question appears in Sir 1:6 with "The root of wisdom—to whom has it been revealed? And her subtleties—who has known?" Likewise, Corley suggests that Job 28:23, "God understands the way to her, and he knows her place," is sounded again in Sir 1:8. Corley, "Wisdom Versus Apocalyptic and Science in Sirach 1, 1–10," 273–74.

182. Argall also points to this aspect. One example would be Ben Sira's argument in 3:17–29 against esoteric teaching. Argall, *1 Enoch and Sirach: A Comparative Literary and Conceptual Analysis of the Themes of Revelation, Creation and Judgment*, 73–78.

183. Corley, "Wisdom Versus Apocalyptic and Science in Sirach 1,1–10," 275. Corley notes that there are some scholars who see in Ben Sira a polemical refutation of Greek learning and "searching into the ultimate nature of the universe and of humankind." Shekan and Di Lella, *The Wisdom of Ben Sira*, 160.

beyond what already appears in creation and the Torah. Wright argues that Ben Sira attempts to undermine the thought that such forms of revelation could contain God-given information.[184]

The author continues to refute the idea that individuals can know such information beyond the Torah or creation. Sir 1:3 queries, "Height of heaven and breadth of earth and depth of the deep—who can fathom out?" The anticipated response is that there is no human who can. *1 Enoch* 93:13–14 asks a similar question, but the anticipated response is already in *1 En.* 93:2, "I, Enoch . . . will let you know according to that which was revealed to me from the heavenly vision." Likewise there is a portion of the Book of Watchers that says, "I, Enoch, saw the vision of the end of everything alone; and none among human beings will see as I have seen" (*1 En.* 19:3). Possibly as a refutation, Ben Sira declares that God shows his wisdom to "all flesh" via creation. Yet the particular recipients of this revelation are "those who love him," Israel, according to Sir 1:10. In *1 En.* 82:2 only Enoch and his heirs are recipients of God's wisdom, and in the end-times all the elect can receive it (5:8). In fact, in *1 En.* 17:7, the patriarch says, "I saw the mountains of the dark storms of the rainy season and from where the waters of all the seas flow." For Ben Sira, wisdom alone possessed this privilege according to Sir 2: 4, 5. Moreover, Sir 1:3 intimates that God alone has knowledge of these cosmic dimensions.[185]

Sir 1:2 advances the question of who is able to enumerate the grains of sand. Corley notes that such a question is usually joined with a query about the numbering of the stars. *1 Enoch* 93:14 poses the query whether any person knows the number of the stars. (This section of *1 Enoch*, the Astronomical Book, was likely extant during the time of Ben Sira.)[186]

The question of who is able to count the number of raindrops arises in Sir 1:2.[187] This may be a polemic against thoughts such as that found in

---

184. Wright, "Putting the Puzzle Together: Some Suggestions Concerning the Social Location of the Wisdom of Ben Sira," 101. Wright correctly notes that Ben Sira does his argument a disservice because dreams and the interpretations thereof are a common occurrence in the Hebrew Bible. It is true that 34:6 allows for an exception, dreams that have been sent by the Most High. The problem with Ben Sira's argument at this point is that he does not detail how one can discern if the dream is from God or simply a reflection of the onlooker (v.3). Wright, "Putting the Puzzle Together: Some Suggestions Concerning the Social Location of the Wisdom of Ben Sira," 102.

185. Corley, "Wisdom Versus Apocalyptic and Science in Sirach 1, 1–10," 278.

186. Ibid., 279.

187. Ibid.

1 En. 26:1 where the patriarch reports, "I saw there three open gates of the heaven from where the south wind, dew, rain, and wind come forth."

These matters of revelation and human ability to know are not the only possible anti-apocalyptic thoughts contained in Ben Sira. Calendar concerns possibly incite Sir 1:2 and its reference to days.[188] Sirach 1:2 inquires who is aware of "the days of eternity," which assumes the answer to be no one. This sentiment is *contra 1 En.* 72:1 where the patriarch receives the revelation of "the nature of the years of the world unto eternity." This knowledge, that Ben Sira considers to be solely in God's possession, is what Enoch claims to have.[189]

Concerning the issue of the calendar in third century B.C.E. Judaism, Michael Stone writes, "It is difficult to overstress the importance of the calendar."[190] The solar calendar does not receive an explicit mention in the Book of Watchers, but the text seems to assume such a calendar. Argall states that in Sir 43:2–8, Ben Sira, in the larger context of creation, expresses a view on the sun and the moon that one could understand to be a refutation of a solar calendar. Ben Sira's comments that the sun "parches the earth and no one can endure its blazing heat" (43:3), "it breathes out fiery vapors" (43:4). He does not assign calendar significance to the sun. When, however, he discusses the moon, he focuses significant attention on its calendrical role, and the moon, thus, decides the seasons, festivals, and pilgrimages.[191]

In light of these considerations I, too, contend that Ben Sira is engaged in polemical arguments against the apocalyptic thought of his day, as contained in writings such as *1 Enoch*. This text, therefore, is another example of the presence of apocalyptic and wisdom thought in the same writing. The refuting tone of this wisdom text is similar to what I will argue that the author of Ecclesiastes exhibits against similar contemporary apocalyptic thoughts.

---

188. Ibid.
189. Ibid., 279.
190. Stone, "Enoch, Aramaic Levi," 166.
191. Wright, "Putting the Puzzle Together: Some Suggestions Concerning the Social Location of the Wisdom of Ben Sira," 95.

Wisdom and Apocalyptic Genre and Thought Meld/Clash

SUMMARY

This chapter has presented a definition for wisdom and apocalyptic. Wisdom is "the quest for self-understanding in terms of relationships with things, people, and the Creator."[192] Its approach to life is based upon order; individuals come to know this order via human reasoning. It has defined apocalypticism as a symbolic universe produced by a people who suffer alienation and who respond using apocalyptic eschatology. For this chapter, the genre of apocalyptic is best defined by the master paradigm and the eclectic definition mentioned above.

In order to demonstrate that apocalyptic and sapiential genre and thought melded and/or clashed in the Second Temple Period, this chapter has examined this phenomenon in nine texts. The apocalyptic texts that exhibited this reality were *1 Enoch*, *2 Baruch*, and *4 Ezra*. In one way or another each of these apocalyptic texts exhibited a strong influence of wisdom thought and/or genre within it. The two epistles, James and Romans, are neither apocalyptic nor sapiential but demonstrate a confluence of wisdom and apocalyptic. The wisdom texts, Job, Wisdom of Solomon, *4QInstruction*, and Sirach, present an influence of apocalyptic within them. *4QInstruction* presents revealed wisdom. Apocalyptic elements are strongly present in Job to the extent that Timothy Johnson considers the book a nascent apocalypse. Sirach sounds a polemical tone against the apocalyptic thought of the day.

My main purpose with this chapter has been to demonstrate this melding and/or clashing among wisdom and sapiential thought in texts of the Second Temple Period. I am more concerned with emphasizing this "mixing, melding, and clashing" of thought from these two genres, rather than focusing on the literary characteristics. From the above investigation, it becomes clear that the line of demarcation between these two genres and corresponding thought (or the "perceived line" from the perspective of twenty-first-century scholars) is, in the minds of these authors, arguably permeable.

My choice of these texts has not been to present an exhaustive list but to interact with enough texts from varied genres to advance this foundational plank in the argument of this book. The strength of this case lies not in one text whose melding of apocalyptic/sapiential overwhelms the reader but in the fact that this melding takes place in a number of different

---

192. Crenshaw, "Prolegomenon," 3.

texts. Particularly key for this book is the last example of Sirach and how the author, arguably, refutes the apocalyptic thought of his day. In what follows, I will build an argument that the author of Ecclesiastes also argues against apocalyptic thought of his day. The presence of Sirach and its anti-apocalyptic argument makes my argument in chapter four more plausible.

Chapter 4

Setting and Function of Ecclesiastes

This chapter includes three sections. The first section examines the setting of Ecclesiastes, focusing primarily on the date of the book and secondarily on considerations of the implied author and implied audience. The second section examines the function of three passages, 7:1–10, 3:10–22, and 9:1–10, as they argue against apocalyptic thought and for a disposition of joy. The third section gives an explanation for the genre label of anti-apocalyptic by drawing from and applying the definition for genre given in chapter two.

DATE (SETTING) FOR ECCLESIASTES

The central thesis of this book is that Qoheleth utilizes an anti-apocalyptic genre and that this genre serves to further his overall message of joy. For Ecclesiastes to be in polemic against the apocalyptic thought of the day, the book must be contemporary with a time of emerging (or fully-developed) apocalyptic thought. The book's dating is important to my argument for the anti-apocalyptic genre label of the passages that will be discussed. I will, therefore, recount some of the different arguments for the book's dating before narrowing the focus to the date to which I hold. This survey will serve to demonstrate the plausibility, even likelihood, of the date to which I subscribe.

A Polemical Preacher of Joy

Daniel Fredericks gives a helpful overview of the different dating views for Ecclesiastes. Scholars have examined the Qumran fragments of the book, the possibility of Greek influence, historical allusions within the text, the general tone and mood of the book, and linguistic considerations of the book in the interest of determining its date. "The words of Qoheleth, son of David, king in Jerusalem" in 1:1 historically has caused interpreters to consider Solomon to be the author of the book, which would place the date of the book in the mid-tenth century B.C.E. Early rabbis accepted Solomon as the author. This understanding would change with Luther, who began to refute the Solomonic authorship of the text. At the present time, there is general scholarly agreement that the book had its composition some time from the fourth to second century B.C.E. The language as well as other aspects of the text point to a date in the post-exilic period.[1]

Fragments of Ecclesiastes present at Qumran[2] suggest the middle of the second century B.C.E. to be the *terminus ante quem*. Charles F. Whitley suggests 152–45 B.C.E. to be a good date for its composition. This date after Ben Sira, however, is unconvincing to most scholars because it does not leave enough time for the book to have developed to canonical status in Qumran, which it apparently did have, and also because it appears that Ben Sira quotes from Qoheleth, and not vice-versa.[3]

---

1. Fredericks, *Qoheleth's Language: Re-evaluating Its Nature and Date*, 1. Fredericks himself does not hold to the date espoused in this book. His work along with that of Gleason Archer ("Linguistic Evidence for the Date of 'Ecclesiastes,'" 167–81) would be sources for contrasting views.

2. There are two fragments of Ecclesiastes found at Qumran. One, 4QQohb214, exhibits portions of Eccl 1:10–14 and is believed to be from the mid-first century B.C.E. to the early first century B.C.E. The other fragment, 4QQoha217, exhibits portions of Eccl 5:13–17; 6:3–8; 6:12—7:6; and 7:7–10, 19–20. The date for this text is believed to be from 175 B.C.E. to 150 B.C.E. Krueger, *Qoheleth: A Commentary*, 36.

3. Fredericks, *Qoheleth's Language: Re-evaluating Its Nature and Date*, 2. Charles Whitley asserts his date for the book because he contends that Qoheleth quoted from Ben Sira and not vice-versa. He examines the texts in both books used to assert Ben Sira's dependence on Qoheleth and refutes these assertions by pointing out that these texts simply have a few words that are mutually used but show no dependence. He also argues on linguistic basis that the Hebrew of Sirach seems to be earlier than Qoheleth.

Furthermore, he contends that consideration of the thought of the two books lends credence to dating Ben Sira earlier than Ecclesiastes. Largely based upon traditional Judaism, Ben Sira presents a view that is consistent with Prov 1–9 that contends that "all things are created and sustained by God and provided man accepts the dictates of Wisdom, he encounters but few difficulties in life." Qoheleth does not share this presupposition and approaches the hard questions of life based upon his own observations and experiences. Qoheleth presents a starkly unorthodox view of God and the rewards of a

Another means of determining the date of the book has been the attempt to discern Greek influence. Scholarly opinion on this influence ranges from those who see Qoheleth directly drawing from earlier Greek thinkers to those who see the author only responding to the "spirit" of Hellenism of the day. One scholar who argues that Qoheleth draws directly from the earlier Greek writers is A. H. Godbey, who believes that Qoheleth relies heavily on Ionic and Attic thinkers. This approach often lends itself to arguing for connections with specific scholars and schools of Greek thought.[4]

Others would not agree that there is such a direct indebtedness to Greek thought, but acknowledge that Qoheleth had some contact with the Hellenistic mindset. Harold Louis Ginsberg understands the elements of misogyny, admiration of youth, and the sentiment to enjoy one's money while one has the chance to be elements of the Hellenistic mindset at work in Qoheleth's teachings. Robert Balgarnie Young Scott acknowledges the fact that Qoheleth ruminates in the atmosphere of Hellenistic thought but considers the author's roots to be in (1) "skepticism native to one strain of the Near Eastern wisdom tradition and (2) in certain deeply ingrained convictions of Hebrew religion, such as the real existence of the one God, his creation of the world and man, his sovereign power over events and the awesome mystery of his Being."[5] Others, such as Franz Delitzsch, have also concluded that there are not any Hellenistic sources of thought be-

---

life of wisdom. Whitley, *Koheleth: His Language and Thought*, 122–31.

4. Fredericks, *Qoheleth's Language: Re-evaluating Its Nature and Date*, 2, 3. Harry Ranston writes of the impact of Greek thought on the book of Ecclesiastes. Two examples would be his suggestions of the dependence on the works of Theognis, the Greek poet of 540 B.C.E. and Hesiod, the Greek poet from the eighth century B.C.E. An example of the suggested Greek influence upon Qoheleth would be on the subject of loss and gain as the action and responsibility of the deity. Theognis considers the loss and advancement, contentment, and the lack of such to be the result of the deity and what the deity has done. It is believed that Qoheleth has been influenced by Theognis in such verses as 2:24, "Man can do nothing better than to eat and drink and find satisfaction in his work. This too, I see, is from the hand of God." Other possible connections of this kind would be 3:13, 9:7, and 1:5. Eccl 6:10 says, "Whatever exists has already been named, and what man is has been known; no man can contend with one who is stronger than he." It is suggested that this is a thought that Qoheleth received from Theognis when he said, "Tis not for mortals to fight with Immortals, nor to argue with them." Another suggestion of dependence is in 4:2 where Qoheleth states that the dead are more fortunate than the living. This sentiment has a strong resemblance to the thoughts expressed by Theognis. "Of all things to men on earth it is best not to be born, nor to see the beams of the piercing sun but, once born, as swiftly as may be to pass the gates of Hades and lie under a heavy heap of earth." Ranston, *Ecclesiastes and the Early Greek Wisdom Literature*, 11–62.

5. Scott, *The Way of Wisdom in the Old Testament*, 178.

hind Qoheleth's words; the author's thoughts flow from the Semitic culture, specifically Hebraic, of the time.[6]

Historical allusions in the book have also been utilized in the dating of the text. Hertzberg and Lohfink[7] have considered Qoheleth's exhortations of loyalty in 8:2 as a reference to the time of the Ptolemies and Seleucids. Those who look to historical allusions for assistance in dating the book point to 10:16, 17. They consider Ptolemy V to be the young king referred to in the text.[8]

Some scholars also seek to narrow further the dating possibilities by looking to more general aspects of the tone or mood of Qoheleth. Scholars such as Baumgartner, Gordis, and Loader point out that they do not see the tone of revolt that would have been present during the Maccabean time period and, from the absence of this revolt speech and tone, date the book earlier than the Maccabean era. Interpreters such as Barton, Gordis, Hengel, and Joseph Blenkinsopp would place the oppressive language present in the book in the Ptolemaic period. Gordis and Hengel would qualify their hypotheses in light of the fact that these observations do not necessarily point to one specific time in history.[9] The collapse of the state and foreign domination resulted in traditional wisdom clamoring for a rationalization for the situation. Otto Eissfeldt considers that this "tired philosophy" of the preacher best fits the post-exilic period. Gordis argues that the collapse of the state meant that the national concerns were no longer the focus, which would allow the emphasis to shift to "practical happiness of the individual."[10]

Attention will now turn to contemplations of the book's orthographic conventions, late Biblical Hebrew features, Aramaisms and their bearing on the determining the book's date.[11]

Choon Leong Seow considers the orthographic conventions of the book as a basis for dating it at some time from the beginning of the sixth century to the close of the third century B.C.E. The appearance of internal vowel letters suggests an exilic or postexilic date for the text, given the fact that internal vowel letters were rarely used before the sixth century. In

---

6. Fredericks, *Qoheleth's Language: Re-evaluating Its Nature and Date*, 4.
7. Lohfink, *Kohelet*, 7, 60.
8. Fredericks, *Qoheleth's Language: Re-evaluating Its Nature and Date*, 4,5.
9. Ibid., 5.
10. Ibid., 6.
11. I acknowledge my indebtedness to Choon Leong Seow for his insightful article on the date of Ecclesiastes.

comparison to pre-exilic texts of similar length, the book contains more forms with internal vowel letters. The long "i" is nearly always signified as a *yod*. The original long "u" is usually spelled with a *waw*. The masculine plural ending uniformly appears with a *waw* when that syllable is accented. These are characteristics that an exilic or postexilic text would exhibit.[12]

The book of Ecclesiastes also exhibits a number of Late Biblical Hebrew characteristics which exhibit significant differences from standard Biblical Hebrew. Franz Delitzsch as early as 1875 noted a long list of *hapax legomena* in the book and therefore concluded that the book belonged to a period after the exile, no earlier than the time of Ezra-Nehemiah.[13]

The use of שֶׁ is a distinctive feature in the book. It occurs 136 times in the Hebrew Bible; half of these occurrences appear in Ecclesiastes. Excluding Gen 6:3, this particle appears in texts that have their origin in the northern provenance or texts from a later period. This particle, a feature of northern Hebrew, found more bountiful usage in Late Biblical Hebrew, Seow argues. It appears in Qoheleth in varied usages: as a conjunction presenting a subject of an object clause or as a purpose clause (1:7; 2:13, 14, 15, 24; 3:13, 4; 5:14, 15; 8:14; 9:5; 12:9). It is this range of usage in the book that particularly presents itself as a Late Biblical Hebrew characteristic. In standard Biblical Hebrew it does on occasion appear as a relative particle but not for the function of beginning a purpose or object clause as it does in Ecclesiastes.[14]

The use of אֲנִי in the book also points to a postexilic date; the form of the first person independent pronoun that occurs in the text is always the shortened form and never the longer אָנֹכִי. It is noteworthy that the shortened form appears exclusively in the postexilic texts of Haggai, Song of Songs, Ezra, and Esther. It is also the predominant choice in Malachi, Nehemiah, Chronicles, and Daniel. The longer form appears in archaistic contexts in speeches from God seen in Mal 3:23, 1 Chr 17:1, Dan 10:11, or included in a prayer (Neh 1:6). Only the short form appears in Zech 1–8. Moreover, in Qumran and Mishnaic Hebrew documents the longer form is used solely as an archaism, appearing in biblical references.[15]

---

12. Seow, "Linguistic Evidence and the Dating of Qohelet," 643–66.

13. Keil and Delitzsch, *Ecclesiastes*, 190–97. See Delitzsch for a list and explanation of these words, the expanse of which is beyond the scope of this section.

14. Seow, "Linguistic Evidence and the Dating of Qohelet," 660.

15. Ibid., 660–61.

In pre-exilic Hebrew אֵת/אֶת־ is used to designate the definite direct object; it can also point to a personal object, usually by taking a pronominal suffix. It appears with indefinite nouns in Ecclesiastes such as אֶת־נַרְדְּךְ in 3:15; אֶת־כָּל־עָמָל in 4:4; אֶת־לֵב in 7:7. Additionally it appears in a nominative clause in 4:3. Each of these two characteristics is indicative of Late Biblical Hebrew.[16]

The feminine demonstrative זֹה used in Ecclesiastes does not commonly appear in pre-exilic Hebrew texts; זֹאת is the form that appears in these pre-exilic and exilic texts. The form that lacks the ת appears in very late texts. The Hebrew form discussed here most likely came from a dialect and was used in written communication in the post-exilic period. The occurrences of זֹה outside of Ecclesiastes take place in the setting of a speech, which would lead to the conclusion that it is a characteristic of spoken Hebrew. The book exclusively uses זֹה, and it does not use זֹאת (see 2:24; 5:15, 18; 7:23; 9:13)[17]

A number of verses show the masculine plural pronominal suffix used where the feminine plural suffix would normally be expected (2:6, 10; 10:9; 11:8; 12:1). This unexpected phenomenon is not necessarily the norm in other texts of Biblical Hebrew. Late Biblical Hebrew, however, exhibits this characteristic with regularity.[18]

In addition to these other linguistic indicators of a late date, there is also a high occurrence of Aramaisms in the book of Ecclesiastes. A sampling of the words in Ecclesiastes that have an Aramaic background would include זְמַן, כְּאֶחָד, טַחֲנָה, and כָּשֵׁר. Translated as "appointed time" זְמַן (Eccl 3:1) appears in an Aramaic document from the fifth century. Its biblical occurrences[19] are all from the postexilic period and after the fifth century. Quite possibly borrowed from Aramaic, there has been suggestion that it originally derived from Old Persian or Akkadian. Regardless of the original derivation, it can definitively be asserted that the word arrived into Late Biblical Hebrew via Aramaic after the second half of the fifth century B.C.E. Translated as "the same, equally" (11:6), כְּאֶחָד is a word that appears in Late Biblical Hebrew[20] and Mishnaic Hebrew and likely derived

---

16. Ibid., 661.
17. Ibid., 662.
18. Ibid., 662–63.
19. See Esth 9:27, 31; Neh 2:6; Sir 43:7; Ezra 5:3; 10:14; Neh 10:35; 13: 51; Dan 2:9, 16, 21; 3:7, 8; 4:33; 6: 11, 14; 7:12, 22, 25.
20. See Isa 65:25; Ezra 2:64; 3:9; 6:20; 2 Chr 5:13.

from Aramaic as well. Translated as "mill" in 12:4 טחנה occurs only in this verse. The word that is usually used for mill is רהים. There is a fifth-century Aramaic cognate for this word suggesting that it is Aramaism. Translated as "to be suitable, appropriate," כּשׁר appears in Aramaic text from the Persian period.[21]

The high frequency of Aramaisms in the book could be the result of a Jew writing in the Second Temple Period, since a prose writer would have familiarity with Aramaic. Rather than including Aramaic words, Qoheleth includes Hebrew or Hebraized parallels. Gordis writes of the high frequency of Aramaisms, "[Ecclesiastes] was written in Hebrew, by a writer who, like all his contemporaries, knew Aramaic and probably used it freely in daily life."[22] From an examination of the text, including the language of the text, he concludes that Qoheleth could not have written the book before 275 B.C.E. and was likely writing approximately 250 B.C.E.[23]

Michael Fox also sees Ecclesiastes as a later work; he suggests a date based on linguistic and political grounds. Many of the words and grammar of the book have more similarities with Rabbinic Hebrew than the pre-exilic classical biblical Hebrew. Also pointing to a date in the post-exilic time period are the numerous Aramaisms; Jews in Palestine during this time period used Aramaic even though Hebrew was the literary language. Ecclesiastes 5:7 uses the word *medinah*, "province," as the location of the reader. The "province" would denote a time when the Jews were under the rule of an empire, either Persian or Hellenistic. Fox also sees evidence of the influence of Hellenistic thought, pointing to the time when Jews would have come in contact with this thought in the third or early second centuries B.C.E. He sees the latest possible date of composition to be 180 B.C.E.; this date is the time of composition for Ben Sira, who quotes Ecclesiastes. Consideration of the fragments of Qoheleth at Qumran also leads Fox to date the book to the third century B.C.E.[24]

Leo G. Perdue provides a more precise suggestion for the date and setting for Ecclesiastes. Qoheleth, he writes, was most probably a sage in the Hellenistic period who penned Ecclesiastes during the transition from Ptolemaic to Seleucid rule of Palestine, placing the composition around 200 B.C.E. Although the Hellenistic period saw prosperity for the socially elite,

21. Gordis, *Koheleth—The Man and His World: A Study of Ecclesiastes*, 652.
22. Ibid., 61.
23. Ibid., 62.
24. Fox, *Qohelet and His Contradictions*, xiv.

including elite Jews, in the land, the ultimate power rested in the hands of the foreign rulers; one could almost consider it a colonial situation. Political and social disturbances occurred during the time of transition for Ptolemaic to Seleucid rule. Even the elite Jews who had enjoyed standing in the Ptolemaic period did not have a real voice in the present socio-political situation. Qoheleth addresses life in his people's somewhat marginalized situation. This date (circa 200 B.C.E.) and setting does appear to be the best estimation that one can make and the one to which I hold in this book.[25]

The Author and Audience

In order to accurately portray the setting of both the author and the audience it is helpful to determine the (implied) author and (implied) audience. The implied author only employs the character of Solomon for the beginning chapters in order to establish authority but does not continue with this persona after these initial chapters. Although Qoheleth gives his views on a number of different subjects, the reader does not get a portrait of who

---

25. Perdue, "Wisdom and Apocalyptic: The Case of Qoheleth," 232. Although Mark Sneed entertains the possibility of a third-century-B.C.E.-date for the book of Ecclesiastes, he does not hold to the argument espoused by Perdue concerning the unrest and dissatisfaction in the time of Ptolemaic rule. He outlines three attempts to uncover the social matrix of the book: evolutionary, historical crisis, and cultural influence approaches and why he believes them to be faulty.

The first attempt that he refutes is the evolutionary approach, which posits that the book results from what would be considered the natural progression of Jewish faith: "tradition, dogma, and then protest." Qoheleth utilizes the opportunity to refute traditional wisdom thought, similar to the book of Job. This view presupposes that there is a rigid dogmatism in traditional Hebrew wisdom, but authors such as Raymond van Leeuwen have rightly questioned and argued against the validity of such a premise. The second attempt that Sneed refutes is the historical crisis approach, which is very similar to what Perdue posits. This approach understands the book to result from a social matrix where the Jewish aristocracy has lost political power at the hands of the Ptolemaic rulers. For Sneed, this approach is weak because there is not a great deal of evidence about the Ptolemaic period, and some scholars would argue that Ptolemaic Judah was a relatively peaceful place lacking in social turmoil. The third attempt to place the book in a social matrix is the cultural influence perspective. The view attributes Qoheleth's sour tone to the reality of disorientation that takes place during the Ptolemaic period and its significant change. Qoheleth's response is the result of Hellenistic culture and its materialism, very contrary to Semitic thinking, spreading so quickly. Sneed sees this argument as circular and weak in light of the fact that materialism of this period would not have been greater than any other period. Sneed, "The Social Location of the Book of Qoheleth," 41–46.

Qoheleth is except by the pieces of hints that are in the text. "All we really know about him is that he was well-to-do if not wealthy, closely in touch with the aristocracy of wealth, and a wisdom scholar who wrote a book and one who . . . taught the people."[26]

Qoheleth's primary experience with poverty and oppression is as an observer, and his experiences seem to match those of the wealthy. In Eccl 4:1–2, Qoheleth observes the oppressed and their lot: "Again I saw all the oppressions that are practiced under the sun. Look, the tears of the oppressed—with no one to comfort them! On the side of their oppressors there was power—with no one to comfort them. And I thought the dead, who have already died, more fortunate than the living who are still alive." Also in 5:8, he refers to the oppressed poor in the third person; clearly Qoheleth does not consider himself to be among the poor. In 7:21, Qoheleth counsels against listening to the cursing of one's servants, which would suggest that he is of the social status familiar with having servants. Moreover, he does recount some experiences that only the rich would have. In 1:12—2:26, he speaks of all the wealth, achievements, and pleasures of life that he has enjoyed that still do not bring fulfillment. He worries, in 2:18–20, about leaving the fruit of his labor for a fool to inherit, and he appears to have time to search out the wisdom of the earth and "to see the business that is done on the earth" (8:16), suggesting that he is a man of means and not one of the oppressed poor. He does, however, sympathize with the struggles of his audience, which appears to be neither poor nor rich.[27]

One can also assume that Qoheleth is no longer a younger man but most likely an older, if not elderly, man. Indeed this would have to be the case for him to be considered a sage, a title that usually only the older generation could hold. Miller considers the frequent mention of death to result

---

26. Whybray, *Ecclesiastes*, 12. Offering a contrasting perspective, Sneed cautions against drawing many conclusions about the author and social location of the book. He points to the fact that wisdom literature inherently does not lend itself to sociological and historical dissection. The majority of the proverbial information in wisdom literature is of a gnomic timeless nature, intentionally. Likewise, with Qoheleth and his observations, scholars will often draw conclusions on these portions to derive autobiographical information. Sneed argues that one must exhibit some caution with these autobiographical sections because they are intended to be general stereotypical scenarios. Qoheleth, Sneed argues, does not endeavor to reveal personal information. The information that does seem personal in the first two chapters is really a literary utilization of Solomon's persona. "Like other wisdom writers, he wants his appeal to be universal." Sneed, "The Social Location of the Book of Qoheleth," 47.

27. Miller, "What the Preacher Forgot: The Rhetoric of Ecclesiastes," 215–35.

from the mindset of an older person. He speaks to the youth in 11:7–10 as one who knows of that which he speaks and writes of the elder years in 12:1–7 with a great sense of immediacy and familiarity.[28]

Qoheleth writes to an audience that is troubled with their state of affairs. They work tirelessly but do not see the full benefits thereof and are very vulnerable to circumstances beyond their control. The audience experiences hardship in this life and is motivated by envy. Qoheleth writes in 4:4, "Then I saw that all toil and all skill in work come from one person's envy of another. This also is vanity and a chasing after wind." An epitome of the situation of the implied audience is in 4:7–8: "Again, I saw vanity under the sun: the case of solitary individuals, without sons or brothers; yet there is no end to all their toil, and their eyes are never satisfied with riches. 'For whom am I toiling,' they ask, 'and depriving myself of pleasure?' This also is vanity and an unhappy business."

Although they labor diligently with no surplus, they continue to work with the mindset that they will experience this surplus one day. Qoheleth, Miller writes, sees his audience bound by a faulty view of life; they view every portion of their lives—their work, religious practice, etc.—believing that they will be able to facilitate success and stability. Their striving actually robs them of joy. Qoheleth endeavors to move his audience to another worldview that will cause them to experience both the good and the bad with a proper perspective.[29]

THE FUNCTION OF ECCLESIASTES

Perdue presupposes that Qoheleth, in Ecclesiastes, argues with a group, whether fictional or real. This is how he accounts for the many statements that appear to be contradictory; there are points where Qoheleth argues against his opponents. Some of the points of argumentation would include 2:22–23; 3:11; 3:21; 5:15–17; 7:10; 8:17; 9:5–6; and 11:8.[30]

Since Qoheleth assumes a fictional character, Solomon or a son of David, in the first two chapters and that fictional persona casts a shadow on the rest of the book, Perdue considers it plausible to suggest that Qoheleth's opponents are also fictional. These opponents could also represent ideology and/or theology dominant during the contemporary situation. Possibilities

28. Ibid., 222.
29. Ibid.
30. Perdue, "Wisdom and Apocalyptic: The Case of Qoheleth," 231.

would include traditional sages, early apocalyptic seers, and apocalyptic sages.³¹

Perdue asserts that Qoheleth is arguing against apocalyptic sages who have melded together apocalyptic thought and sapiential thought. I differ from Perdue in that I do not see the opponents as apocalyptic sages but apocalyptic seers. Qoheleth speaks against special revelation, the ability to change one's life and status, and a final judgment understanding of retribution. What is present in this text is not primarily an argument against wisdom but a further discussion of wisdom in light of the perplexities of life. I am greatly indebted to Perdue³² for his work in pointing out the elements of Ecclesiastes that argue against the beliefs of what he calls the apocalyptic sages of the time.³³ Although my identification of Qoheleth's opponents is different from his final conclusion, his presentation has been most helpful, and my following argumentation exhibits my indebtedness.

Qoheleth the sage (12:9, 10) writes in a time of social and political commotion when even those Jews who have elite status have little control of the wealth and socio-political realities of the day. It is partly this lack of power and the reality of foreign control that cause Qoheleth's audience to despair. He and apocalyptic seers each gives a response to this setting. Qoheleth gives a response emphasizing the despair and futility of the condition but also exhorting his audience to accept moments of joy when God would possibly give them in the present. The apocalyptic seers see an ultimate eschatological hope.³⁴ (Two portraits of apocalyptic seers are the books of 1 Enoch and Daniel, both apocalyptic literature.) John Collins writes of the nature of apocalyptic as a" [G]enre of revelatory literature with a narrative framework, in which a revelation is mediated by an otherworldly being to a human recipient, disclosing a transcendent reality which is both temporal, insofar as it envisages eschatological salvation, and spatial insofar as it involves another, supernatural world."³⁵

John Collins outlines the difference between apocalyptic and wisdom. Apocalyptic has a much greater emphasis on the supernatural, giving attention to agents and messengers of the supernatural and their involvement in human events and concerns. Apocalyptic anticipates a time of judgment,

---

31. Ibid., 232.
32. Ibid., 252–58.
33. Ibid., 230–31, 235.
34. Ibid., 233.
35. Collins, *The Apocalyptic Imagination*, 5.

retribution, and reward beyond the point of death. Unlike wisdom that can often have a positive view of the world, apocalyptic focuses more on the conclusion that there is a fundamental flaw with the world and life in it. As a result of this foundational observation there is an expectation that there will be an eschatological judgment that will result in reward for the righteous and retribution for the unrighteous.[36]

From Qoheleth's speech, it can be argued that he is speaking against those who subscribe to the aforementioned apocalyptic beliefs. Understanding the *setting* of Ecclesiastes, in the milieu of wisdom and apocalyptic thought, helps to recognize the *function* of this work as a polemic against certain elements of apocalyptic thought. In this section my objective is to show examples of Qoheleth's polemics against the apocalyptic thought of the apocalyptic seers. To that end, I will examine three key passages that demonstrate polemics between Qoheleth and apocalyptic seers: 7:1–10; 3:10–22; and 9:1–10. I will highlight how each of these passages functions in the larger literary context of the book and suggest how it functions in the social context of the time, its argumentation against contemporary apocalyptic thought of the time.

In order to highlight how these passages function in the literary context of the book, the outline of the book according to Seow is helpful.[37]

i. Part 1

1. Reflection: Everything is Ephemeral and Unreliable

    a. 1:2–11, Preface

    b. 1:12—2.26, Nothing is Ultimately Reliable

    c. 3:1–22, Everything is in the Hand of God

    d. 4:1–16, Relative Good is Not Good Enough

2. Ethics: Coping with Uncertainty

    a. 5:1–7, Attitude Before God

    b. 5:8—6.9, Enjoyment, Not Greed

ii. Part 2

1. Reflection: Everything is Elusive

    a. 6:10—7:14, No One Knows What Is Good

---

36. Collins, "Wisdom, Apocalypticism and Generic Compatibility," 166–85.
37. Seow, *Ecclesiastes*, 46–47.

      b. 7:15–29, Righteousness and Wisdom are Elusive

      c. 8:1–17, It's an Arbitrary World

  2. Ethics: Coping with Risks and Death

      a. 9:1–10, Carpe Diem

      b. 9:11—10:15, The World is Full of Risks

      c. 10:16—11:6, Living with Risks

      d. 11:7—12:8, Conclusion

III. 12:9–13a, Epilogue

IV. 12:13b–14, Additional Material

Ecclesiastes 7:1–10:[38] Qoheleth Rejects a Theology of Despair[39]

Nestled within the first section of the second half of the book, which deals with the elusive nature of life, 7:1-10 accentuates life's enigmatic and

---

[38]. I will provide exegetical comments via the footnotes in order to allow the text of the page to focus on the polemical function of the text. Most commentators treat 7:1–14 as a distinct unit. Longman considers vv. 13–14 to be concluding thoughts to the section. My comments in the text will regard 7:1–10 as a unit.

[39]. Proverbs constitute the first twelve vss. of 7:1–14 using the "better-than" pattern. Tremper Longman sees a connection between 7:1–14 and the question that appears in Eccl 6:12, "For who knows what is good for mortals while they live the few days of their vain life, which they pass like a shadow? For who can tell them what will be after them under the sun?" Longman sees this section in 7:1–14 to be a response to this question. He sees the question as a means for Qoheleth to communicate that, in fact, there is nothing that is completely good but that there are some things that are better than others. To that end, these better-than expressions appear. Some of these sayings would be congruent with expectations of wisdom literature such as the expressions in 1a, 5a, and 9 while others would be unexpected and incongruent with what the audience would expect from a sage such as 1b, 2, 3, and 11. Longman, *Ecclesiastes*, 179.

    Seow, for the most part, agrees with this reading but differs at the intended point of conclusion. He sees 7:1–12 as an answer to the question asked in 6:10–12 about what is טוב. The sayings about טוב and their placement so close to the question do give a response. Seow thinks that they all sound like traditional wisdom on what is good for humanity, but at the end of these sayings one must wonder what really is good. The issues of life appear in typical dialectical pattern: "fame and luxury (v. 1a), birth and death (v. 1b), funeral and wedding (v. 2), merriment and sadness (v. 3), mourning and pleasure (v. 4), rebuke and praise (v. 5), the wise and the fool (vv. 6–7), beginning and end (v. 8), patience and arrogance (v. 8)" The end result is that the reader concludes that no one knows what is good for humanity—not even the sage. The sayings each contain a morsel of truth, but in the end all of them are "vanity" according to v. 6. Seow, *Ecclesiastes* 242, 43.

paradoxical nature. It emphasizes the limitations on humanity's knowledge. In 7:11–12, the text returns to the exaltation of wisdom. 7:13–14 emphasizes that since one does not know, one should consider God in both the good and the bad.[40] Following this section, the next passage 7:15–29 continues to portray the many perplexing and elusive paradoxes in life. This recurring emphasis is an important plank in the author's message.

Eccl 7:1–10

> A good name is better than precious ointment,[41] and the day of death, than the day of birth.[42] 2 It is better to go to the house of

---

40. Whybray points out that although commentators see this section as a unit (7:1–14) many find it difficult to see any cohesion in this section. He points out that the text ends in v. 14 with the conclusion that humanity cannot know anything that will come after him which most likely echoes the words of 6:12. Whybray writes, "But if this is their aim to provide a reasoned argument to support this conclusion, it must be confessed that they go about this in a very roundabout way." This statement derives from the miscellaneous nature of the proverbs in this section, as Whybray reads this text.

Admitting to the futile efforts of many to see a note of progression, Whybray does admit to a sense of cohesion to the unit, partly by the repetition of words such as good (eleven times), wise/wisdom (six times), heart (five times); fool (four times); sorrow/anger (three times) and laughter and house of mourning (two times each). This observation indeed does grant a just reading to the text and the fact that there is a cohesive communication of thought in this passage.

Whybray's reading does not go far enough to see what Qoheleth is doing to argue against the apocalyptic thought of the time.

41. V.1a utilizes a chiastic structure that emphasizes the comparison of name and ointment. With blatant alliteration the text reads: שֵׁם טוֹב מִשֶּׁמֶן טוֹב שֵׁם. This could convey the concept of reputation, which does not necessarily have to be a good reputation (see Gen 6:4; 11:4, and Ezek 16: 14) but generally would. In fact, this stich bears a stunning resemblance to the thought of Prov 22:1a, "A good name is to be chosen rather than great riches." Fox, *A Time to Tear Down and A Time to Build Up,* 251. Crenshaw highlights the importance of this comparison between a good name and oil in pointing to a parallel verse in Song of Songs, Song 1:3, "our anointing oils are fragrant, your name is perfume poured out; therefore the maidens love you." Like the author of Song of Songs, Qoheleth makes this popular connection. Thinking of fragrance or stench easily leads one to bring the comparison of a pleasing perfume or ointment. Crenshaw, *Ecclesiastes,* 133.

The decision to compare name to שֶׁמֶן is both a syntactical and contextual one. The choice strengthens the alliteration and syntax of the verse, but it also fits the culture of the time. Ointment or oil played a highly valued role in society on joyful occasions (see Pss 45:8; 133, and Amos 6:6). Longman, *Ecclesiastes,* 182.

42. The challenge of v. 1b that perplexes commentators is to discern the connection between v. 1b with v. 1a. Murphy takes slight exception to the interpretation of scholars such as A. Lauha and Franz Delitzsch who think that v. 1b is simply another example of Qoheleth's intense disdain for life. Rather than such a pessimistic interpretation, Murphy

mourning than to go to the house of feasting; for this is the end of everyone, and the living will lay it to heart.[43] 3 Sorrow is better than laughter, for by sadness of countenance the heart is made glad.[44] 4 The heart of the wise is in the house of mourning; but the heart of fools is in the house of mirth.[45] 5 It is better to hear the rebuke of the wise than to hear the song of fools. 6 For like the

---

prefers a reading that sees v. 1b as bringing moderation to the previous stich: it is only through the vantage point of death that one can speak of a good reputation. When a child is born, she has an entire life ahead of her; when that life is complete, then, and only then, can a bystander speak of the individual's good reputation. Qoheleth in this moderation maintains the satirical tone of his work as if to convey the idea that one can, indeed, speak of a good reputation, but only after the point of death. Murphy, *Ecclesiastes*, 63.

43. Without accepting that there is a dialogue taking place in this passage, the interpreter can assert that Qoheleth is here furthering the preference of death over life. He, in this point, wants his audience to see life from the vantage point of death; he wants his audience to avoid the frivolity of life that is without this sobering reality. To that end, he suggests that the audience go to a בית אבל rather than a בית שמחה. Attending the funeral that takes place in a בית אבל will serve to sober the individual to live life in light of this point of death. This interpretation poses a challenge of harmonization with the idea of joy and carpe diem that appears in 2:24–26. To this, commentators bring an interpretation to consider the opposite tensions: the pleasure spoken of in this passage, the house of rejoicing, takes place in frivolous frame of mind but the joy that is commended takes place in the light of the fear of the Lord, as spoken of in the epilogue. Longman, *Ecclesiastes*, 183.

44. This is a better-than proverb with an accompanying motive clause. The latter portion of this proverb is particularly enigmatic. In 3a, the reader encounters כעס משחק טוב. These words are troublesome because in 1:18 כעס is connected with wisdom, and laughter receives a connection with madness in 2:2. The text emphasizes the somber reality of life. The advantage of wisdom over folly leads the thought to the conclusion that sorrow is better than laughter. Crenshaw goes further to show a connection between this sentiment and the thought of Ps 90:12, "So teach us to number our days that we may get a heart of wisdom," Revised Standard Version. Crenshaw, 134.

The motive clause of the proverbs is particularly enigmatic because פנים ייטב לב כי־ברע could be translated as the New English Bible renders it, "A sad face may go with a cheerful heart." In this rendering, which Whybray agrees with, the verse is seen as recasting the first half with the suggestion that there is a difference between what appears on the outside and what is actually the case on the inside. Whybray, *Ecclesiastes*, 114. Given the context of the text, it more than likely speaks of the fact that sorrow is the result of a more somberly honest examination of real life. Wise ruminations will result in a sad countenance. Murphy, *Ecclesiastes*, 64.

45. Krueger points out that these verses bolster the argument of 1b–3 by distinguishing those who follow the counsel of the first three verses as the wise and contrasting them from the fools. As the wise mourn, pleasure is the object of the fools in v. 4. The wise bring a rebuke but the fool goes along singing songs in v. 5. The fools and their frivolity bring destruction upon themselves as their temporary laughter is compared to a crackling of thorns in v. 6. Krueger, *Qoheleth*, 136.

> crackling of thorns under a pot, so is the laughter of fools; this also is vanity.[46] 7 Surely oppression makes the wise foolish, and a bribe corrupts the heart. 8 Better is the end of a thing than its beginning; the patient in spirit are better than the proud in spirit. 9 Do not be quick to anger, for anger lodges in the bosom of fools. 10 Do not say, "Why were the former days better than these?" For it is not from wisdom that you ask this. (NRSV)

Qoheleth's purpose, Perdue argues, in 7:1–10 is to refute a theology of despair, which is held by the apocalyptic seers, and stress that adopting such a theology is an inappropriate response in light of humanity's limited ability to know. The proper response in light of this limitation would be a resignation to this perplexing reality.[47]

One indicator leading to this conclusion of anti-apocalyptic authorial intent would be the fact that 7:1–4 is incongruent with what has already been said about joy in 2:24–26 and 3:12–13. In these earlier verses, joy and the activities such as eating, drinking, and enjoying one's work were considered gifts of God, but now in 7:1–4 those who partake in these enjoyments are fools. What is the reason for this shift? Perdue concludes that Qoheleth is citing and refuting a theology of despair resulting from the present situation of hardship and oppression. It is likely that these theologians of despair had an apocalyptic view that was despondent over the situation of the present.[48] The words of 7:10 epitomize their sentiment as Qoheleth

---

46. The text provides an effective wordplay at this point. "Thistles provide quick flames, little heat, and a lot of unpleasant noise. The singing of fools was equally as cacophonous." Crenshaw, *Ecclesiastes*, 135.

47. Perdue, "Wisdom and Apocalyptic: The Case of Qoheleth," 245, 46.

48. Murphy considers this unit, and the larger section of chapters 7 to 8, as Qoheleth disputing with traditional wisdom. He considers chapters 7 and 10 to be two of the more difficult chapters in the book. They exhibit tightly-framed aphorisms but leave the reader questioning what the relationship between these sayings is. Looking at the progression of sayings, Murphy concludes that there is a dialogue with traditional wisdom in chapters 7 and 8, a dialogue where Qoheleth desires to bring changes to this wisdom. He agrees with Addison Wright in seeing the dialogue to flow along the lines of the questions/comments emphasizing the difficulty of finding out. Like Wright, Murphy outlines the passage as follows: vv. 1–6 convey a dismal perspective of life but these considerations are cancelled out in 6b as being vanity, vv. 7–12 additional contest the sentiments of vv. 1–6. Murphy, *Ecclesiastes*, 61, 62.

Michael Fox points out the weakness of the idea that Qoheleth disputes traditional wisdom because the choice of what is a disputation of traditional wisdom thought and what is Qoheleth's actual thought is largely subjectively random. Offering what he considers to be a more accurate reading, Fox contends that the text, in the first four verses, does not denounce the occurrence of feasting and celebration. He is not intending to

rehearses the words of the theologians of despair in order to refute their concepts with, "Do not say, 'Why were the old days better than these?' For it is not wise to ask such questions." The opponents may have considered time as progressively getting worse and more dire with each passing period of time. Qoheleth, however, does not emphasize life as getting worse and worse but rather focuses on death as the apogee of life; death is, therefore, better than the beginning. God intends for humanity to "suffer in ignorance and darkness only to die in the blackness of oblivion and to be erased from human memory."[49]

In 7:7–9, the polemical nature of Qoheleth's words becomes even clearer, according to Perdue. After v. 7, where the author makes the observation about extortion and bribery having a deleterious effect on the individual, he asserts in vss. 8, 9 that pessimism is not the way of the wise. There are two better-than sayings that follow. "Better is the end of a thing than its beginning; the patient in spirit are better than the proud in spirit." Additionally, another statement exalting the path of wisdom follows in v. 9. "Do not be quick to anger, for anger lodges in the bosom of fools." The one who is truly wise recognizes that the individual was born to experience the suffering that leads to death. With this in mind, the wise course of action for the wise is to taste of joy if and when one can do so.[50]

The opponents, Perdue continues, were those who had a view of this present situation as direr than that of the past and that this situation is so bleak that a wise person or sage could not possibly rejoice. The wise course of action is to go to the house of mourning, a truly pessimistic point of view. Qoheleth's response does not deny the bleak and devastating nature

---

commend sadness as a lifestyle but rather wants his audience to realize the importance of possessing an acute awareness of one's mortality to the point that even when one does partake of feasting that one does so with the stark awareness of mortality. To live life as if death does not exist or await one is to live like a fool. Yet even in this reading, Fox admits that Qoheleth is inconsistent on this because in 5:19 Qoheleth recommends *simhah*. Fox attributes this inconsistency to frustration, Eccl 7:23–24, "All this I have tested by wisdom; I said, 'I will be wise,' but it was far from me." Qoheleth, by expressing this frustration, conveys a foundational point: "man (even the wisest) is hopelessly ignorant, and when he can discover some truths . . . their validity is shaky and they clash with other things he knows." Fox, *A Time to Tear Down and A Time to Build Up*, 251. While Fox's observations have much validity, they do not give proper observation of the setting and function of the anti-apocalyptic.

49. Perdue, "Wisdom and Apocalyptic: The Case of Qoheleth," 246.

50. Ibid., 246.

of the situation but contends that the prescription of his opponents is not good. His suggestion is to seek to enjoy this present life now.[51]

Ecclesiastes 3:10–15: Qoheleth Rejects Key Apocalyptic Thoughts

The passage of 3:10–22 follows a section where the author emphasizes that everything is unreliable. Chapter 3 asserts, *contra* the unreliability of everything such as wisdom, toil, and pleasures, that time is in the hand of God (3:1–9), appropriately ending with v. 9 asking, "What gain have the workers from their toil?" Quite the contrary to the apocalyptic seers who purport to know what the Deity has determined and, thus, to be able to move toil to success, this poem furthers the conclusion that human events do not fall into a cosmic order of time and are unknowable to people.[52]

Chapter 3:10–22 demonstrates Qoheleth's anti-apocalyptic message. The opponents of whom Qoheleth speaks adhere to apocalyptic beliefs such as "the final judgment of the righteous and the wicked, the immortality of the righteous, the knowledge of God and divine action, and the holistic structure of time and events." Qoheleth argues against their emphasis on "the justice of God, earthly retribution, moral dualism (the wicked and the righteous), and the understanding of the correlation of time and event for a successful outcome."[53] The author particularly refutes the beliefs of the apocalyptic seers with regard to humanity's ability to know the time and

---

51. Ibid. My suggestion for polemics against the apocalyptic seers has further precedence in the writings of Theodore Perry; he suggests an even more polemical tone to the book. In the book, he notes a spirited debate between two characters: "those of P the Presenter and K or Kohelet . . . K as the man of experience and P as the man of faith." Perry *Dialogues With Kohelet: The Book of Ecclesiastes*, 125, 26. The italicized letters are from K. The following has been applied to the NRSV translation: "A good name is better than precious ointment, *and the day of death, than the day of birth.* 2 It is better to go to the house of mourning than to go to the house of feasting; for this is the end of everyone, and the living will lay it to heart. 3 Sorrow is better than laughter, *for by sadness of countenance the heart is made glad.* 4 *The heart of the wise is in the house of mourning;* but the heart of fools is in the house of mirth. 5 It is better to hear the rebuke of the wise than to hear the song of fools. 6 For like the crackling of thorns under a pot, so is the laughter of fools; *this also is vanity.* 7 Surely *oppression makes the wise foolish,* and a bribe corrupts the heart. 8 Better is the end of a thing than its beginning; the patient in spirit are better than the proud in spirit. 9 *Do not be quick to anger, for anger lodges in the bosom of fools.* 10 Do not say, 'Why were the former days better than these?' For it is not from wisdom that you ask this."

52. Perdue, "Wisdom and Apocalyptic: The Case of Qoheleth," 252, 53.

53. Ibid., 247.

Setting and Function of Ecclesiastes

structure of the cosmos, the belief that God is going to reshape the world because of its corruption, and the afterlife. Ecclesiastes 3:10–15:

> 10 I have seen the business[54] that God has given to everyone to be busy with. 11 He has made everything suitable for its time;[55] moreover he has put a sense of past and future into their minds, yet they cannot find out what God has done from the beginning to the end.[56] 12 I know that there is nothing better for them than to

---

54. This verse continues what started in v. 9. At the conclusion of the poem, the message of God's established periods of time is clear. In the following verses, Qoheleth gives his response to this reflection. He starts with a reflection ראיתי (see also 3:16; 4:1, 4, 7; 6:11; 7:15; 8:10; 9:11, 13). In 1:13, Qoheleth spoke of the ענין that God has given individuals, but the connotation is expressly negative. In that context the evil business that God has given individuals referred to the futile task of endeavoring to understand what takes place in the world, but here the business is spoken of in reference to the God-directed times. Murphy, *Ecclesiastes*, 35.

55. This statement את־הכל עשה יפה בעתו encases two crucial statements: (1) "God made everything and (2) Everything is beautiful in its time." Kreuger translates this verb with a continuous, imperfective understanding: "God makes everything." The New Revised Standard Version translates the verb as a perfect tense verse. Whybray, however, asserts that "it is more probable that the perfect tense is used here in the Hebrew to express a general truth and should be rendered by the present tense." Such an idea is also attested with the same verb עשה in verses such as Isa 44:24 and Isa 45:7. Qoheleth here refers to the truth that God not only creates but also causes to be over time. The second assertion refers to the fact that God has made everything beautiful. It is, thus, congruent with the declarations in Gen 1 (see vv. 4, 10, 12, 18, 21, 25, and 31) which all refer to the creation as good טוב. The use of the word for beautiful here should not, Krueger asserts, be seen as less affirmative than the declarations in Genesis 1. Qoheleth refers to God's beautiful creation in this verse in such a way as to "expand its frame of reference to creation in its entire temporal extent." Krueger, *Qoheleth*, 85–86; Whybray, 72.

56. Verse 11b גם את־העלם נתן בלבם demonstrates the stark contrast between divine and human understanding of reality. "Distant time" העלם has been placed in the mind of humanity. This translation of distant time is arguable in light of the manner in which the word appears in the previous verses such as 1:4, 10; 2:16; 3:14; 9:6; and 12:5 where the term most likely speaks of "an idea of distant time that extends far beyond the life of an individual human being in the direction of either past or future or both." Even though this distant time has been placed in the mind of humanity, humanity cannot know what God has done from the beginning to the end; they lack the ability to grasp it. Humanity can know that God has worked but cannot not know in what way that creation is beautiful or the complexities of that creation. Creation, therefore, remains an enigma. "People cannot completely comprehend the work of God—if only because, first of all, it goes way beyond the temporal horizon of their possibilities of experience." Krueger also concludes that this 11b lays the foundation to question the idea that God unveils to individuals knowledge of what God has done in the past or what God will do in the future. Such beliefs existed in the prophetic literature of the time. Is 46:10 declares that God tells the end from the beginning. Similarly, numerous prophetic texts spoke of what was to

119

be happy and enjoy themselves as long as they live;⁵⁷ 13 moreover, it is God's gift that all should eat and drink and take pleasure in all their toil.⁵⁸ 14 I know that whatever God does endures forever; nothing can be added to it, nor anything taken from it; God has done this, so that all should stand in awe before him.⁵⁹ 15 That

---

come in the future. This verse sees these claims as questionable. Krueger, *Qoheleth*, 86.

57. This verse is the logical conclusion of the previous ones. Given the fact that the larger issues of life are incomprehensible and beyond humanity's grasp, it would make sense for the individual to shift her gaze to the smaller goals. The ultimate meaning of life and the world is beyond reach, so one should seek to enjoy the lesser and more sense-oriented pleasures in this life. In his charge, Qoheleth gives yet another variation of his *carpe diem* that is present in 2:24. Rather than a statement of exuberant enthusiasm, this statement is one of resignation. "In brief, Qoheleth advises his hearers to give up trying to fathom God's way in the world. Rather, enjoy the present." Longman, *Ecclesiastes*, 122.

58. Linked with the previous verse by וגם, this verse continues the charge to enjoy life that began in the previous verse. Qoheleth now brings greater specification concerning the enjoyment: eating, drinking, and enjoying work, which all echo 2:24. For Qoheleth the best that the individual can do, in light of not being able to understand the larger questions of life, is to enjoy this present life realizing that even this is a gift of God. This enjoyment can only be realized at the permission of God.

With the statement שיאכל ושתה וראה טוב בכל־עמלו the reader sees that which Qoheleth encourages the daily pleasures of life. In 2:24 Qoheleth places his charge of enjoyment in a very qualified manner, saying that there is nothing better. Longman, *Ecclesiastes*, 109, 122.

59. The first assertion in response to the poem of 3:1–8 came in v. 12; the second assertion appears in v. 14. Qoheleth, here, emphasizes that humanity does not have the ability to change God's manner and deeds. If one's fortune in life is undesirable, one cannot change that. In light of the immutability of God and his manner of working, Qoheleth asserts that this has all been the plan of God in order to instill a fear of God in people. (RSV) Crenshaw, *Ecclesiastes*, 99. The work of God is in the realm of the לעולם. The work of God carries the attribute of permanence. The extent of this permanence is illustrated in 14b where the phrase has antecedents in Deut 4:1–2 and 13. (להוסיף וממנו אין לגרע אין עליו) Similar language is used to speak of not adding or taking away from the Law. It is with this similar force that Qoheleth emphasizes that nothing can change what God has already done. The purpose of this immutability of God's deeds is that humanity may fear God. This emphasis on the purpose can be seen in the fact that the verbal form takes the particle. "According to Qoheleth, one is caught between the nearness of a God who fixes times and the mystery of a God whose work is unintelligible; in this situation fear of that God is the proper response." Murphy, *Ecclesiastes*, 35.

Whybray has a different understanding of the nature of the fear that God and God's immutable deeds evoked from individuals. He sees this fear before God שיראו מלפניו to be similar to the way that the fear of the Lord is used in other portions of wisdom literature. He adds that the use of מלפניו "before him," referring to God, as possibly useful for inspiring a greater sense of awe to the concept. This concept of fear the Lord is quite similar to that of 5:1 and "his meaning is that God rightly demands 'fear' from men in the sense of recognition of his essential difference from his creatures." Whybray,

which is, already has been; that which is to be, already is; and God seeks out what has gone by.⁶⁰

Qoheleth argues⁶¹ against the tenets of apocalyptic texts that the seer could, by divine revelation, know the times and deeds that only God controls. The apocalyptic seers consider it possible for humanity to know these things concerning the character and deeds of God, but Qoheleth considers all of this knowledge to be cloaked in a perpetual enigma. Moreover, the

---

Ecclesiastes, 75.

Longman has some considerations. It is true that the fear of God has a certain aspect of piety in verses such as Prov 1:7, but that is not precisely what Qoheleth means in this verse. To conclude that the phrase means the same concept here is to fail to consider the context of the phrase in this verse as well as in others such as 5:6; 7:18; 8:12. "Qoheleth believes that God acts the way that he does to frighten people into submission, not to arouse a sense of respectful awe in his power and might." Longman, *Ecclesiastes*, 124.

60. Having described the immutable action of God with the word עולם he now reinforces this comment with a repetition of the thought of 1:9. Whereas there Qoheleth speaks about the characteristic of nature with its repetitious circular cycle of events, here he speaks about the enigmatic unchangeability of God's work. He does this utilizing a "backward/forward" characterization in 15a; the past and the present are open before God and are at the sovereign disposition of the divinity." Crenshaw, *Ecclesiastes*, 35.

In 15a, Qoheleth emphasizes, "God's works overtake humanity's feeble efforts, and nothing substantially new can interrupt the awesome course of events that God has ordained. The question of 15b centers on what commentators do with יבקש את־נרדף. In light of the fact that these two verbs are almost synonymous, Fox argues that the sentence communicates, "God seeks what has already been sought which repeats and reinforces that there is nothing new under the sun." God does things that have already been done. Fox, *A Time to Tear Down and A Time to Build Up*, 213, 14.

61. Perdue, "Wisdom and Apocalyptic: The Case of Qoheleth," 252, 54. There is scholarly precedent to see Ecclesiastes as an argument between two factions. Perry's argument for it goes further than the one presented in this work. Perry, *Dialogues with Kohelet*, 89–93. The italicized letters are from K. The following has been applied to the NRSV translation.

10 I have seen the business that God has given to everyone to be busy with.

11 He has made everything suitable for its time; moreover *he has put a sense of past and future into their minds*, yet they cannot find out what God has done from the beginning to the end.

12 *I know that there is nothing better for them than to be happy and enjoy themselves as long as they live;*

13 moreover, it is God's gift that all should eat and drink and take pleasure in all their toil.

14 I know that whatever God does endures forever; *nothing can be added to it*, nor anything taken from it; God has done this, so that all should stand in awe before him.

15 *That which is, already has been; that which is to be, already is;* and God seeks out what has gone by.

author does not agree that humans could, through their deeds, change their destiny. This information is inaccessible because God is distant and beyond humanity's ability to know (see 5:1, 2).

He refutes the apocalyptic motifs by demonstrating that God has both placed within humanity the desire to search and know this life as well as the inability to search successfully. He writes in v. 10 how God has ordained humanity to ponder the unattainable; this is the consuming business that God has given humanity. Along with bestowing on humanity this business, God has also placed in the heart of humanity a sense of both the past and the future. Humanity can know that God has worked but they cannot know in what way God has worked. With this thought, Qoheleth has effectively extinguished any hope that God reveals God's will to individuals via special revelation. Such a notion is contrary to the nature of what God has done. Furthermore, Qoheleth also stresses that the past and the present are at the disposal of God; it is God who can seek out what has already been. Verse 14 reveals the reason for this God-inspired futile search; God desires to inspire a sense of fear and awe within humanity. Humanity's ignorance, *contra* the message of the apocalyptic seers, is what leads to the correct disposition to the Divine.[62] Since humans cannot know this time and the structure of the cosmos or the deeds that only God controls, people cannot utilize this information to become successful or gain profit from their labor.

In light of this perennial and futile search, what is humanity to do? Rather than trying to change life through unique revelation via a seer, humanity is simply to enjoy the journey that God has given. "There is nothing better for them than to be happy and enjoy themselves as long as they live." This is a statement of resignation in light of the impervious realities of life. Qoheleth further stresses the importance of his exhortation by defining this enjoyment via the simple staples of life: eat, drink, and take pleasure in work.

Ecclesiastes 3:16–22: Qoheleth Rejects Key Apocalyptic Thoughts

> 16 Moreover I saw under the sun that in the place of justice, wickedness was there, and in the place of righteousness, wickedness was there as well.[63] 17 I said in my heart, God will judge the

---

62. Perdue, "Wisdom and Apocalyptic: The Case of Qoheleth," 252, 54

63. This unit is comprised of the following: "an observation (v.16), . . . two comments (17, 18–21) and . . . a conclusion (22) (I saw . . . I said . . . I said . . . So I saw)." This

righteous and the wicked, for he has appointed a time for every matter, and for every work.⁶⁴ 18 I said in my heart with regard to

---

similar pattern appears in Eccl 2:13-25; 7:25-27; 8:14. Eaton, *Ecclesiastes: An Introduction and Commentary*, 83.

In this verse, Qoheleth refutes, according to Crenshaw, the idea that a judicial system guarantees just retribution to evil doers and protection for just citizens. The arbitrariness of the justice of God would be more bearable if one were convinced of God's favorable disposition to humanity. Qoheleth is not convinced of this favorable disposition, so the unpredictable nature of divine justice is all the more vexing. In fact, Qoheleth comments on observations that contradict the concept of God's favorable disposition to individuals. In the place where he would expect justice, he instead finds wickedness. Although (apocalyptic) thought would suggest God's ultimate justice, Qoheleth is of the opinion that all of this disappointment is intentionally placed by God to demonstrate that humans are really no different than the animals. "Since the future lies hidden from the eyes of the living, human beings can only rejoice in their work and its benefits." Crenshaw, *Ecclesiastes*, 101-2.

To be clear, Qoheleth does not say that the courts are void of justice but simply points to the courts as yet another perplexing example of life's arenas where there is a disconcerting inconsistency that baffles all attempts of explanation. Whybray, *Ecclesiastes*, 77.

64. This verse has been a challenge for interpreters. Barton considers this verse to be a gloss added by a pious editor. The concept of a vindication for the righteous is not congruent with the context. Barton, therefore, considers it a later addition. Barton, *The Book of Ecclesiastes*, 108.

Both Gordis and Whybray consider this verse to be legitimately part of the original text. Gordis considers this verse authentic commenting that the post-exilic age saw the rise of proto-Pharasaic groups that subscribed to a belief in the afterlife and judgment in the life to come. Judging from the context, Qoheleth quotes this belief only to deride it in a skeptical tone. Gordis, *Koheleth*, 225.

Whybray goes to great lengths to explain this verse as consistent with the context, arguing that Qoheleth is reinterpreting divine judgment. The first half of the verse addressing the wicked is consistent with ancient Israelite doctrine: God will judge the wicked. Referring to ישׁפט, Whybray notes that this word does not have to refer to retribution but rather speaks of rendering a judicial decision. This world, not the world to come, is the context for this judgment, which shall occur in the present or future time. Whybray asserts that it is not arguable to contend that Qoheleth is, here, arguing for this judgment to take place after death since such a belief would not be common and appeared late in the Old Testament and also the fact that Qoheleth seems to argue against such a belief in other verses. Qoheleth here contends that though it may seem that the wicked go unpunished for their deeds in this life that they will indeed receive their just punishment and the righteous their just reward in this life. The second half of the verse points to the concept of the time, appointed time. Yes, these occasions of miscarried justice take place, but there is an appointed time in this life when divine justice will prevail. Whybray, *Ecclesiastes*, 77.

The interpretation of Tremper Longman may possibly be the most responsible treatment—in part. He simply acknowledges that this is a tension in the text that shows that Qoheleth is wrestling with traditional views regarding divine justice. "Qoheleth asserts his belief in divine retribution but does not allow a time for it, and he goes on in the next

human beings that God is testing them to show that they are but animals.[65] 19 For the fate of humans and the fate of animals is the same; as one dies, so dies the other. They all have the same breath, and humans have no advantage over the animals; for all is vanity.[66] 20 All go to one place; all are from the dust, and all turn to dust again.[67] 21 Who knows whether the human spirit goes upward and the spirit of animals goes downward to the earth?[68] 22 So I saw that there is nothing better than that all should enjoy their work, for that is their lot; who can bring them to see what will be after them?[69]

---

few verses to cast doubt on the concept of divine retribution itself." Longman, *Ecclesiastes*, 127–28.

65. This, also, is a troublesome verse for interpreters. The crux of this verse, considering the context of the previous two verses of this unit, vv. 16 and 17, is that the miscarriage of justice in the judicial system as well as religious affairs is the tool of God to show humans that they are like animals. Barton, *The Book of Ecclesiastes*, 108.

66. The substantiation of Qoheleth's claim in v. 18 of how both humans and animals are alike appears in this verse. They are both alike in the fact that they both die. This core concern of death reappears throughout the book. If both the animal and the human die and have the same מקרה, then there is no advantage to the human. With this statement Qoheleth lays an axe to the root of belief in the afterlife. Longman, *Ecclesiastes*, 129.

67. *Contra* Whybray who sees this verse as also speaking of *Sheol*, I believe that Qoheleth, here, further specifies what he said in the previous verse. This verse echoes the thoughts of Gen 3:19. While Qoheleth affirms his belief in Sheol in 9:10, in this verse he speaks of humanity returning to the dust from which humanity has come. This thought of returning to dust also appears in Job 10:9; 34:15; Pss 104:29; 146:4 and Sir 40:11. (Murphy, *Ecclesiastes*, 37). Barton also adds the important note that Qoheleth speaks of the whole being—not simply the body. Barton, *The Book of Ecclesiastes*, 109.

68. Krueger points out that interpreters have considered this verse to be arguing against the idea of an individual afterlife. On closer scrutiny, it would appear that this verse actually goes further than that; the verse disputes the very premise of such a belief. It calls into serious question "that human beings, in distinction from animals, have something like a personal 'life spirit' whose individuality is maintained after death." Krueger, *Qoheleth*, 93.

Jewish writings around the time of Ecclesiastes also held to an idea of the breath of life as being connected with the soul of a person (see *1 Enoch* 1–36). Later Judaism did differentiate the divine breath as being separate from the dead soul (see *4 Ezra* 7:78). Krueger, *Qoheleth*, 94.

This verse does not contradict 12:7 where the text speaks of dust returning to the earth and the life spirit going to God.

69. The insight of Krueger is especially helpful at this point: "Whereas 'King Qoheleth,' through the insight that he as 'wise man' is subject to contingency and death just like the 'fool' (2:12–16), comes to the point of hating life (2:17), for the wise man Qoheleth the knowledge that as a human being he will fare no better than the animals (3:19–21) only confirms his estimation of pleasure as the 'highest' and 'only good' (cf.

Qoheleth concurs with the understanding that there is injustice in the human experience—especially in light of living under foreign rule—but refutes the view held by apocalyptic seers that there will be a day of judgment on the deeds of humanity. He argues against this view by pointing to the perplexing ubiquity of injustice—even in unexpected places—and then using this perplexity, with which the audience would agree, as a pedagogical tool that both points to God and dispels the notion of a final judgment. In v. 16, he notes that wickedness was in the place of justice as well as righteousness. As Crenshaw remarks, this reality, and the arbitrary nature of God's expected justice, is compounded by the fact that the individual is not certain of God's favor. There is no guarantee of justice, now or ever. Although v. 17 appears to stand in contrast to what is communicated in v. 16, the larger context affirms the message of v. 16 refuting the expectation of final judgment; such judgment is not even reliable in this life.[70] Qoheleth does not see hope that will come as a result of the eschatological judgment and new creation that God will bring—as the apocalyptic seers do; the situation will not get better.[71]

Qoheleth also argues[72] against a belief in the afterlife. He disagrees with the apocalyptic seers, as well as some earlier biblical writings, by

---

vv. 12-13). Even if the special effort in his work does not lead reliability to a 'gain' (3:9), a person can still receive pleasure in his work as his 'portion' (cf. v.13).... The insight into the unpredictability of the future, which brought the 'king' despair in regard to his successor (2:12, 18), [cannot] change anything, for human beings are referred by God to the present time as an opportunity for action and for enjoyment (3:1–8,11). Therefore, they should seize the available possibilities for pleasure and not push enjoyment into an uncertain future—whether in or after life." Krueger, *Qoheleth*, 94.

70. Perdue understands the presence of v. 17 in the text, speaking about judgment that God will bring on both the righteous and the wicked based upon their deeds, to be the later addition of an apocalyptic sage. He writes that the followers of these apocalyptic sages (later redactors around the time of Ben Sira, after 180 B.C.E.) appear in 3:17 and 12:14. Perdue, "Wisdom and Apocalyptic: The Case of Qoheleth," 253.

71. Ibid., 256.

72. Perry goes further than I do in suggesting the polemical/dialogical nature of the passage. Perry's argument for it goes further than the one presented in this work. The italicized letters are from K. Perry, *Dialogues with Kohelet*, 137–144. The following has been applied to the NRSV translation.

16 *Moreover I saw under the sun that in the place of justice, wickedness was there, and in the place of righteousness, wickedness was there as well.*

17 I said in my heart, God will judge the righteous and the wicked, for he has appointed a time for every matter, and for every work.

18 *I said in my heart with regard to human beings that God is testing them to show that they are but animals.*

stating in 3:19 that both the animal and the human have the same fate; there is no advantage to humanity and neither remains nor is remembered. v. 18 serves as the bridge between these two polemical emphases; it stresses the fact that God tests humans to demonstrate to them that they are like animals. The perennial injustice of this world and the futility of religious activity serve the didactic purpose that humanity, though it may feel superior, is no better than the animals—as with justice, so also in death. Verses 19 and 20 particularly emphasize this sameness of humans and animals. Verse 19 declares that both humans and animals have the same breath. Verse 20 uses the strong parallelism of "all": all go to one place, all are from the dust, and all turn to dust again. Not only does this, along with v. 21, nullify the hope of the afterlife but it questions the foundation of the afterlife: that there is a difference between humanity and animals. Having disorientated this primary presupposition, Qoheleth goes further with a poignant rhetorical question, "Who knows whether the human spirit goes upward and the spirit of animals goes downward to the earth?" Through an equating comparison of humanity and animals and an effective rhetorical question,[73] Qoheleth seems to refute (or at least strongly question) the apocalyptic tenet of an afterlife.

Considering that both the stalwart hopes of this marginalized population, divine justice and the afterlife, have been refuted, what is an individual to do? For Qoheleth the answer is to enjoy this life, for this life, and all the injustice that it carries, is one's lot. In v. 22, Qoheleth ably ties together this message with the use of the rhetorical question, "who can bring them to see what will be after them?" Here the author is emphasizing that humanity does not know what the future holds (it cannot even understand the present with all of its intricate mysteries), so Qoheleth points to the portion that humans have in this life: enjoy life if and when they are able to do so.[74]

---

19 *For the fate of humans and the fate of animals is the same; as one dies, so dies the other. They all have the same breath, and humans have no advantage over the animals; for all is vanity.*

20 *All go to one place; all are from the dust, and all turn to dust again.*

21 *Who knows whether the human spirit goes upward and the spirit of animals goes downward to the earth?*

22 *So I saw that there is nothing better than that all should enjoy their work, for that is their lot; who can bring them to see what will be after them?*

73. See chapter five for a discussion on the role of rhetorical questions in Ecclesiastes.

74. Rasiah Sugirtharajah, from a post-colonial interpretation, sees similarities between Qoheleth's perspective and that of one acquiescent to the force of a colonizing force. For Sugirtharajah, Qoheleth seeks to preserve the *status quo* of societal power

Ecclesiastes 9:1–10: Qoheleth Further Rejects Key Apocalyptic Thoughts

Ecclesiastes 9:1–10 follows a section (8:1–17) that deals with the arbitrary nature of this world. It is followed by a passage that furthers the observation that the world is full of risks. Seow sees this passage as a portion of the ethics section in part 2 of Ecclesiastes. It gives a reasonable response in light of the fact that everything is so elusive. *Contra* the apocalyptic thought of the day, the author encourages his audience not to seek the deliverance of the afterlife; there is one fate to all. Instead, he encourages them to seize upon the day at hand because so much of life is uncertain and elusive. His readers are to grasp the opportunity of this day—with joy. Eccl 9:1–10:

> 1 All this I laid to heart,[75] examining it all, how the righteous and the wise and their deeds are in the hand of God;[76] whether it is love

---

structures. One should simply accept one's lot in life, be compliant to the ruling structure and present perplexing reality. Sugirthirajah, *Postcolonial Criticism and Biblical Interpretation*, 80–81. Although Sugirtharajah does not use this term, in one regard he too concludes that Ecclesiastes is anti-apocalyptic.

75. There is discussion with regard to the כִּי. Those who see this verse as concluding the previous section see it as causal and thus translate it as, "For I have taken all this to my heart." (see NASB) Such a reading is not necessary because 8:17 forms an inclusion with the question posed in 8:1, "Who is wise?" 8:17 brings the answer with, "no one is wise." Seow, *Ecclesiastes*, 297. The reader need not read this verse as a conclusion to the previous section, *contra* Gordis. It is therefore emphatic instead of causal. Murphy, *Ecclesiastes*, 90.

76. Uncertainty veils the meaning of בְּיַד הָאֱלֹהִים. Does Qoheleth refer to the benevolent and protective hand of God, such as in Psalm 31:6, or does he simply convey the fact of God's overarching superintendence? Krueger, noting the interpretation of D. Michel, entertains the possibility that these words are beginning to refute the idea that there is an afterlife reward for the good deeds done in this life. Krueger, *Qoheleth*, 167. One can argue that the context of the argument would argue for the fact that the phrase in question refers not to the benevolence of God but God's sheer power that contains the righteous and all their works—their works, dependent on the power or hand of God, which have no reward after death.

A Polemical Preacher of Joy

or hate[77] one does not know. Everything[78] that confronts them 2 is vanity, since the same fate[79] comes to all, to the righteous and the wicked, to the good and the evil, to the clean and the unclean, to those who sacrifice and those who do not sacrifice. As are the good, so are the sinners; those who swear are like those who shun an oath. 3 This is an evil[80] in all that happens under the sun, that the same fate comes to everyone. Moreover, the hearts of all are full of evil; madness is in their hearts while they live, and after that they go to the dead. 4 But whoever is joined with all the living has

---

77. This phrase גַּם־אַהֲבָה גַּם־שִׂנְאָה also poses difficulty to the interpreter. Whybray writes that it is unclear whether this phrase speaks of the quandary as to whether God loves or hates people or if it speaks of the fact that the human passion of love and hate are beyond the knowledge and control of humanity. Whybray reads it as being a *merismus* that speaks of "the whole range of items" within these two spectrums. Whybray, *Ecclesiastes*, 140. One could argue that the phrase refers to the fact that humanity does not know whether God hates or loves humanity—and not only the extremities of love or hate but everything in between. Humanity cannot know anything about the plan of God for humanity's life—save that humanity will die. Duane Garrett rightly takes the words to their logical conclusion: No one can coerce a blessing from God [via wisdom or the pursuit of wisdom] because no one knows whether God hates or loves humanity. Garrett, *Proverbs, Ecclesiastes, Song of Solomon*, 330. I feel that Garrett overstates this point when he says that no one can know whether God hates or loves humanity.

78. This phrase הַכֹּל לִפְנֵיהֶם also carries a sense of ambiguity. The Septuagint adds the first three words of verse two to this phrase. Qoheleth's message is that everything before humanity is uncertain; the future is uncertain and anything may take place. Gordis, *Koheleth: The Man and His World*, 290.

79. By using the phrase מִקְרֶה אֶחָד Qoheleth emphasizes the universality of this one fate, death. מִקְרֶה refers to that which is chance. The term refers to the end result that comes to each one, regardless of ethical code or standing in life. It is not intended to counter the Old Testament understanding of the sovereignty of God, as if a concept of fate could overpower the will of God. The use of the term, rather, intends to counter the concept that some kind of independent deed or course of deeds that the righteous engage in can alter such an end. The phrase is followed by examples of the righteous who do good works and the wicked who are guilty of judgment. What happens to both of these vastly different groups is exactly the same. Leuopold, *Ecclesiastes*, 209.

80. With זֶה רָע Qoheleth assigns a value description to this reality of one fate coming to all—regardless of their life choices and lifestyle. With this statement, he effectively nullifies any attempt at theodicy. What God does may not always seem to be good but God is always good. The text also emphasizes that all of the heart of humanity is toward evil. Kreuger, *Qoheleth*, 170. Murphy points out the contrast of this statement with the sages such as in Prov 21:18; 5:5; 7:27 which all state that folly results in the path to death. To the contrary, Qoheleth states that all roads lead to death. Murphy, *Ecclesiastes*, 90.

hope,[81] for a living dog is better than a dead lion.[82] 5 The living know that they will die, but the dead know nothing; they have no more reward, and even the memory of them is lost.[83] 6 Their love and their hate and their envy have already perished;[84] never again will they have any share[85] in all that happens under the sun. 7 Go, eat your bread with enjoyment, and drink your wine with a merry

---

81. Many commentators contend that this verse is an example of irony, but there is a logical progression of thought from v. 3. This verse posits the questions of advantage that the living have over the dead. In this verse, Qoheleth asserts that life is still much better and desirable than death—no matter how arduous life can be. Life is preferable because there remains the possibility to enjoy as vv. 7–10 emphasize; there are no such possibilities in death as vss. 5–6 convey. Whybray, *Ecclesiastes*, 142.

The word בטחון in 2 Kgs 18:19 and Isa 36:4 conveys the meaning of trust and security. It, however, in later Hebrew developed the meaning of "faith in God, especially under adversity." Gordis, *Koheleth: The Man and His World*, 294.

82. The dog in the ancient near east was the most disdained animal while the lion was considered to be the king of the beasts. "Death reduces the kingly lion to a level below that of a living dog because it reduces him to a state of nothingness." Barton, *The Book of Ecclesiastes*, 160.

83. This verse exhibits conspicuous irony. The ultimate advantage that the living have over the dead is that the living are cognizant of the end—death. Although there is the possibility of enjoyment, this verse places the advantage of life in balance. There is, after all, one fate for all.

The phrase ואין־עוד להם שׂכר כי נשכח זכרם added to this message is the play on words that 5b contains. The word play to describe the dead rests on שׂכר (recompense) and זכרם (remembrance)e. The beginning of the book, 1:3 and 1:11, already purported that this life is absent of both of these. Murphy, *Ecclesiastes*, 92.

84. In this verse, Qoheleth further specifies the advantage of life over death. He highlights three emotions: love, hate, and jealousy. These three emotions span the entire spectrum, love and hate, as well as an emotion that may be considered to be located on neither end of the spectrum. Yet, all three of these emotions exhibit certain intensity. For Qoheleth, it is better to experience negative emotions and passions rather than to be among the dead who can experience nothing at all. "On the other hand, the relative advantage of life is really double-edged sword: To live is to love, yes, but it is also to hate and envy, not an unmixed blessing." Longman, *Ecclesiastes*, 229.

Commenting on the statement גם אהבתם גם־שׂנאתם גם־קנאתם כבר אבדה, Crenshaw observes that "the effect of the three particles and the pronominal endings attached to the three nouns for affections is deadening." Crenshaw, *Ecclesiastes*, 162.

85. The text, in other portions, such as 2:10, 21; 3:22; 5:17, 18; 9:9; 11:2, has already pointed out that one's portion or חלק is in this life. Death is a chilling halt to all of the portion or share, whether positive or negative, that one experiences in this life.

A Polemical Preacher of Joy

heart;[86] for God has long ago approved what you do.[87] 8 Let your garments always be white; do not let oil be lacking on your head.[88] 9 Enjoy life[89] with the wife whom you love, all the days of your vain life that are given you under the sun, because that is your portion in life and in your toil at which you toil under the sun. 10 Whatever your hand finds to do, do with your might; for there is no work or thought or knowledge or wisdom in Sheol, to which you are going.[90] (NRSV)

Apocalyptic thought presented the hope that the imminent future would bring both divine intervention on behalf of the righteous and an eschatological judgment upon evil. In 9:1–3, Perdue argues, Qoheleth refutes

---

86. Qoheleth's previous comments on joy have had an exhortation tone, but in v. 7 the sentiment takes on imperative force. The three imperatives in the verse אכל, לך, and ושתה carry a greater sense of urgency, an urgency heightened from ruminations upon the pervasive power of death able to even quench and kill the basic human passions and emotions. Crenshaw, *Ecclesiastes*, 162.

Bread and wine were common staples in the diet and the Psalms (Pss 104: 14–15) presents bread and wine to symbolize joy. Murphy, *Ecclesiastes*, 92.

87. The statement כי כבר רצה האלהים את־מעשיך is noteworthy. Previously Qoheleth considers joy to be a gift from the Almighty, but in 7b he goes even further to show that humanity's enjoyment is not simply something that God will allow, but it is something that God desires—for those God has chosen. כבר רצה is translated by Fox as a future perfect with the force of "has already favored. . . .In other words, the sentence does not imply that God has at some time in the past chosen you as one who will enjoy life, but if and when you do so, that will be. . .a sign of divine approbation of your pleasures." Fox, *A Time to Tear Down and a Time to Build Up*, 294.

88. Continuing his fervent charge, Qoheleth specifies how his readers are to engage in joy. They are to seize vigorously the opportunity to experience the good that life affords. Pietistic commentators look at the words of white garment and immediately think of purity. There is precedence for such an interpretation. Yet there is also precedence for white to appear in connection with rejoicing and celebration. See 2 Chr 5: 2; Esth 8:12. Likewise the comment concerning oil on the head would be *apropos* of a hot climate because in such a climate oil on the head would keep the skin moisturized. The white clothes would be worn to reflect the heat instead of absorbing heat. Oil also has connection with joy and rejoicing. See Psalm 23:5; 45:7; Prov 27:9; Amos 6:6. Longman, 231 and Barton, *The Book of Ecclesiastes*, 163.

89. The literal rendering of ראה חיים is "see life." ראה, however, can also convey the idea of experience such as see famine (Jer 5:12), see good (Job 7:7) and also in chapter 8:16 (see sleep). Each of these conveys the idea of experience.

90. כל אשר תמצא ידך לעשות בכחך עשה Qoheleth's point continues what he began in the previous verse. "Enjoy a woman as long as that is possible [v.9], and do zealously whatever you can." There is a coming of a time of death and a place of non-existence when neither will be a possibility. Qoheleth considers Sheol to be the place of non-existence. Crenshaw, *Ecclesiastes*, 163.

Setting and Function of Ecclesiastes

this false expectation by emphasizing that the same fate belongs to both those who follow the path of wisdom and those who follow the path of folly. Both groups will experience the dark reality of death and oblivion. (See also 2:14–16.) Consequently, Qoheleth rebuffs the belief that humans, through their wise living and ethics, have any ability to change or direct their fate, in this life or the false hope of the afterlife; the same fate awaits all.[91]

Apocalyptic seers expressed the belief that God unveils his plans to a select few seers. To this belief, Qoheleth expresses disdain as he emphasizes in 9: 4–6 that humans cannot know anything, apart from the certain fact that they will die.[92] This inability to know God, God's movement in the world, and humanity's proper conduct, in that order, is the result of the fact that God has placed העלם in the human heart. God has, in fact, designed

---

91. Perdue, "Wisdom and Apocalyptic: The Case of Qoheleth," 253, 256. Perry goes further than I do in suggesting a dialogical/polemical aspect to Qoheleth. Perry's argument for it goes further than the one presented in this work. The italicized letters are from K. The following has been applied to the NRSV translation. Perry, *Dialogues with Kohelet*, 137–43.

1 All this I laid to heart, examining it all, how the righteous and the wise and their deeds are in the hand of God; *whether it is love or hate one does not know. Everything that confronts them*

2 *is vanity,* since the same fate comes to all, to the righteous and the wicked, to the good and the evil, to the clean and the unclean, to those who sacrifice and those who do not sacrifice. As are the good, so are the sinners; those who swear are like those who shun an oath.

3 *This is an evil in all that happens under the sun, that the same fate comes to everyone.* Moreover, the hearts of all are full of evil; madness is in their hearts while they live, and after that they go to the dead.

4 But whoever is joined with all the living has hope, *for a living dog is better than a dead lion.*

5 The living know that they will die, *but the dead know nothing*; they have no more reward, *and even the memory of them is lost.*

6 *Their love and their hate and their envy have already perished; never again will they have any share in all that happens under the sun.*

7 Go, eat your bread with enjoyment, and drink your wine with a merry heart; for God has long ago approved what you do.

8 Let your garments always be white; do not let oil be lacking on your head.

9 Enjoy life with the wife whom you love, all the days of your vain life that are given you under the sun, because that is your portion in life and in your toil at which you toil under the sun.

10 Whatever your hand finds to do, do with your might; *for there is no work or thought or knowledge or wisdom in Sheol, to which you are going.* NRSV

92. Perdue, "Wisdom and Apocalyptic: The Case of Qoheleth," 254.

the human situation to exhibit a lack of permanency in this life or hope thereof in the future.[93]

Chapter 9:1–3 demonstrates how Qoheleth specifically refutes the tenets of apocalyptic texts. He attacks the roots of apocalyptic thought by emphasizing the lack of control that humanity has over life's experiences, the ephemeral nature of everything in humanity's experience, and the lack of differentiation between the wise and the righteous in the final fate. He points out in v.1 that all of the deeds of the righteous and the wise are in the hand, or control, of God. Far from the idea that one can manipulate one's future through adhering to a teaching or special revelation, the message of Qoheleth is that all of the deeds and the results thereof reside in the control of God—not humanity. Moreover, humanity, so distant from having special knowledge or revelation, does not really know whether God loves or hates the people of creation. With this foundational element in question, humanity has no hope of knowing whether the Almighty works for or against the individual who is on this ephemeral journey riddled with questions. Further dismantling the apocalyptic thought, Qoheleth utters the hallmark of his work, "everything is ephemeral (or vanity)." Humanity cannot possibly receive special revelation on how this life will unfold, much less about the dubious concept of an afterlife, because the ephemeral nature of existence itself will not allow it.

What happens to the vastly different groups of the righteous and the unrighteous is exactly the same. Qoheleth argues against the hopes of eschatological judgment; all reach the same fate following a life with hearts filled with madness—death. Qoheleth admits that this is an evil. This statement removes the idea that a specially selected seer or pious individual can escape the universal fate that all experience. Lifestyle does not matter; all die the same death.

Having deconstructed the false expectations given by the apocalyptic seers, Qoheleth now endeavors to rebuild a proper hope. He endeavors to direct the reader to the present and the value of this present life. To this end, he emphasizes in vv. 4–6 that the living have an advantage over the dead. He strongly emphasizes this point with an astounding comparison. Such a final and nullifying reality is death that it can take the king of the beast, the lion, and place it below the most despised animal, the dog. The living dog is better than a dead lion. The reader is not to crave a deliverance from this life for the reward of the afterlife; the living has the advantage. This

93. Ibid.

advantage, however, must be weighed in the balance of the entire human situation. The living know something that the dead do not know, and it is the only informational advantage they have over the dead. The living know that they will die. Those who have experienced death have ceased to experience the passions, albeit mixed, of life. The dead know nothing, and they feel nothing; they no longer exist. The fundamental paradigm is different from that of the apocalyptic seers. This is a corrective to the false expectations of apocalyptic thought. The dead are without hope, but the living have a hope—possibly a hope that one's fortune will change.

Contrary to the expectation of a divine in-breaking of eschatological judgment, Qoheleth presents a life of ephemeral reality leading to the universal fate of forgotten non-existence. The response to this transitory and enigmatic existence is what Qoehelth emphasizes in 9:7–10—joy. In these verses Qoheleth gives his most forceful exhortation or command to enjoy this life. He wants his audience to orientate their lives in light of the untimely certainty of death.[94] He argues that humanity's portion חלק is to enjoy their present situation and the activities therein, when they can.[95] Ultimately he ends with the charge for the reader to engage this life because there is nothing to do in Sheol.[96]

ANTI-APOCALYPTIC GENRE LABEL

Having examined the setting and function of three passages from Ecclesiastes, one may still ask the question "Is the anti-apocalyptic genre label a plausible and defensible suggestion?" This section will address this query by building upon the definition of genre given in chapter two. In it I will apply the findings of genre theorists to demonstrate further the plausibility of the anti-apocalyptic genre label proposed, for the three passages, in this work.

A consideration of the setting and function of the text suggests that Qoheleth speaks to a time when he and his audience are experiencing a

---

94. Ogden, *Qoheleth*, 167.

95. Perdue, "Wisdom and Apocalyptic: The Case of Qoheleth," 253.

96. Ogden concurs with the reading that there is a strong emphasis on seizing wisdom in this section, as well as the entire book. His reading of the text would be enhanced by the understanding of apocalyptic thought as an interlocutor in this passage. The understanding that Qoheleth is arguing against apocalyptic thought helps to properly cast the first six verses.

relatively marginalized existence under foreign or colonial occupation. He desires to turn his audience away from the grandiose expectations of the apocalyptic eschatology of his day and to cause them to deal with the perpetual struggles and contradictions of this present life. He desires that they shift their longing gaze away from the afterlife, away from anticipated special revelation that will help them to make sense of their situation and possibly advance in status—whether in this life or in that to come—and away from a search for fair and just retribution. He focuses their attention on this absurd, meaningless, vain life and encourages them to enjoy it—if and when God will grant that opportunity. This message, in the passages examined in this book, is antithetical to the apocalyptic sentiment present in other writings of this time. How does a proper understanding of genre assist in making this determination?

In his work *Validity in Interpretation*, Hirsch writes, "Valid interpretation is always governed by a valid inference about genre.... Every disagreement about an interpretation is usually a disagreement about genre ...."[97] This book has proposed that Qoheleth, in part, employs a hybrid genre in his work. He, in part, employs an "anti-apocalyptic genre" in Ecclesiastes, and the presence of this genre serves to further Qoheleth's overarching message of joy. Recognizing the presence of an anti-apocalyptic genre within the tapestry of Ecclesiastes will assist the interpreter in understanding Qoheleth's message. The purpose of this section is to explicate further what is meant by this term anti-apocalyptic genre and its use in the book of Ecclesiastes. To that end, I will build upon my stated definition for genre and the findings of genre theorists as discussed in chapter two, but one must first consider the difficulty of the task.

Arriving at a genre label has many difficulties since the interpreter, always mindful to adhere to the pursuit of authorial intent, is separated from the author by time and culture. Genre identification, Hirsch asserts, is often elusive; it is likened to a game where the interpreter must not only try to decipher the game being played but also determine the rules of the game—without the benefit of a rulebook. She cannot go back into the minds of Qoheleth and the original audience to know fully what the mutual understandings were between them in the text. The pursuit of such a guess is imperative, however, for "valid interpretation is always governed by a valid inference about genre."[98]

---

97. Hirsch, *Validity in Interpretation*, 98.
98. Ibid., 113.

Assigning a genre label to Ecclesiastes must also take into consideration the methodology, although not the conclusion, of Tremper Longman. "Genre distinctions do not fall from heaven. They are approximate ways by which we may speak of similar texts."[99] Interpreters must keep the fluidity of this process in mind since a text can have more than one genre label. A noteworthy observation from the scholarly community is that there is hardly agreement on the genre of Ecclesiastes beyond the fact that it stands within the tradition of wisdom literature. This cacophony of genre labels must caution us against strident assignments of any overall generic label. Further caution is warranted in light of the fact that there can also be new genres or unique hybrid creations created, by the author's leap of imagination, for new situations. Any "new" genre label should, therefore, receive a generous hearing.[100]

As stated above, genre is flexible, anchored to authorial will, and centered on the *foci* of setting and function. In this section I will draw from the genre theorists presented in chapter two[101] to explain my suggestion of the anti-apocalyptic genre of the passages treated above. First, I will give a rationale for the name of the genre label—anti-apocalyptic. Secondly, I will give further explanation of why I affirm the flexibility of genre. Thirdly, I will explain my understanding of genre as being tied to (social) function. Lastly, I will suggest how recognizing this anti-apocalyptic genre impacts the interpretation process.

---

99. Longman, *Ecclesiastes*, 16–17. Chandler agrees with Jane Feuer in her writing of genre in television and asserts that a genre in actuality is an abstract formulation and not an empirical reality. For that reason, "One theorist's genre may be another's sub-genre or even super-genre." Although I would certainly see there being parameters, these sentiments do rightly express the difficulty of the task. Chandler, "An Introduction to Genre Theory," 7.

100. Additionally, Daniel Chandler writing of genre theory writes, "Like most of our everyday knowledge, genre knowledge is typically tacit and would be difficult for most readers to articulate as any kind of detailed and coherent framework...readers learn genres gradually, usually through unconscious familiarization." Chandler, *An Introduction to Genre Theory*, 7.

101. Adena Rosmarin, David Fishelov, Carolyn Miller, Harry Nasuti, and Eric D. Miller

A Polemical Preacher of Joy

Application of Rosmarin

The anti-apocalyptic genre label is an explanatory heuristic tool, which is anchored in authorial will. Adapting from Rosmarin's work,[102] I would assert that a genre label is best characterized as a heuristic tool to explain the text and what an interpreter has discovered about the text and its author-intended function. Although Rosmarin assigns too much power to the critic and does not sufficiently consider the role of the author, she does seem to have a proper understanding of the instructional/explanatory role of the genre label. It serves to help the critic explain what she has found.

This heuristic tool helps to explain what has been found when the interpreter examines the cross section between author-audience setting and the possible author-intended function. I have demonstrated through the discussion of the social and political setting and the suggested function of the text that I see Qoheleth arguing against the apocalyptic thought of his day. (I, therefore, argue that this genre is in the mind of the author in that Qoheleth intends to argue against apocalyptic thought when he questions the afterlife and dispels the notion of humanity's ability to know, beyond the natural observations.) The label anti-apocalyptic emerges as a tool to explain what the author is doing with his work.[103] The credibility of this suggestion, *contra* the theory of Rosmarin, lies not in the authority of the twenty-first-century reader but in the plausibility that this anti-apocalyptic genre is in the mind of the writer and his audience that are rightly interpreting him. Moreover, I would argue that without this heuristic tool or genre label as part of the discussion, much of the meaning of Ecclesiastes is lost in the cacophony of divergent debates concerning the meaning of the text. Again, this label is not applied to the entire book but only to the passages discussed above.

The designation of the anti-apocalyptic genre label, heuristic tool, is similar to the painter producing a work of art. The interpreter, like the painter, sees the image, or genre, in the text and endeavors to paint it, assign an appropriate label. Whereas Rosmarin suggests a more creative role of the critic, I see the interpreter's genre label distinction as an attempt to closely copy, or paint, what is seen. The hope of accuracy and an identical

---

102. Ibid., 7–46.

103. Adding to this assertion must be the realization of the difficulty in naming a genre. Chandler writes, "While we have names for countless genres in many media, some theorists have argued that there are also many genres (and sub-genres) for which we have no names." Chandler, *An Introduction to Genre Theory*, 1.

exactness is elusive, yet the attempt to give a near exact representation of the image that the author originally "painted" in the text is vital for understanding.[104] Such an attempt is the anti-apocalyptic genre label suggested here.

Application of Fishelov

Based on Fishelov's presentation of the nature of genre, the following assertion can emerge: genre is flexible. Rather than a rigid list of formal characteristics, the interpreter must realize that the constitutive rules that apply to genre, which would also involve characteristics present in the literary work, are subject to change according to authorial will and purpose. When one approaches a genre discussion of Ecclesiastes, one must approach it with the understanding that genre is flexible. The interpreter can, therefore, entertain the appearance of the proposed hybrid genre, anti-apocalyptic. When the interpreter considers the genres of wisdom literature and apocalyptic literature, in as much as one can refer to these groups of literature as genres, one must approach such a discussion not by merely chronicling the formal characteristics of wisdom literature or apocalyptic literature but by considering their respective intended social functions that the respective authors of these texts intended to accomplish with these texts.

Comparing literary genres to Darwin's theory of evolution of biological species,[105] one can also state, in agreement with Fishelov, that genres are subject to evolution that results from authorial purpose in conjunction with the present literary environment. "There is a dialectical relationship between the literary production and the literary environment in which the former may not only adapt itself to the latter but also contribute to reshaping it."[106] This interaction can often result in the production of hybrid genres, which can exhibit the characteristics of more than one genre. Interpreters of the book of Ecclesiastes must be mindful of this phenomenon because the literary environment of a transitional socio-political reality, like the biological sphere, is not static but dynamic. This dynamic social and literary environment possesses the burgeoning literary and rhetorical

---

104. Rosmarin, *The Power of Genre*, 12.
105. Fishelov, *Metaphors of Genre: The Role of Analogies in Genre Theory*, 20, 21.
106. Ibid., 36.

energy to develop and re-invent means of addressing the contemporary context.[107]

With the possibility of this literary phenomenon and generic mutation in mind, it is proper to consider genres as clubs with members at the core that exhibit a high degree of family resemblances along with other members that are on the fringes that may in fact overlap with another club and thus exhibit a lesser amount of family resemblances.[108] It is possible for a text to have family resemblances with wisdom literature and yet resemblance with apocalyptic because genre, rather than a rigid list of formal characteristics, is flexible. I would argue that in the above-mentioned passages Ecclesiastes exhibits a clear resemblance with wisdom literature but also a resemblance with apocalyptic in that the text intentionally argues against some basic tenants of the message that apocalyptic seers would bring. See above discussions on 7:1–10; 3:10–22; and 9:1–10.

Yet even with flexibility there are some guiding parameters to the discussion of genre. A genre label is not merely theoretical and a convenient creation of the critic. These proposed genres must have possibly formed the work of the respective authors. It is, therefore, plausible to propose that Qoheleth, in his socio-political transitional reality, brings forth a writing that contains some traces of this anti-apocalyptic genre in it.

Application of Carolyn Miller

Another foundational plank for the anti-apocalyptic genre designation is Carolyn Miller's emphasis on social function. "Whether through discourse communities or some other social frame, genre must respond dynamically to human behavior and social changes."[109] Genre is not merely the collec-

---

107. Chandler includes an example of a case from contemporary times that would demonstrate such development. He writes, "Despite the importance of the distinction between fictional and non-fictional genres, it is important to note the existence of various hybrid forms (such as docudrama, 'faction' and so on). Even within genres acknowledged as factual (such as news reports and documentaries) 'stories' are told—the purposes of factual genres in the mass media include entertaining as well as informing." Chandler, *An Introduction to Genre Theory*, 12.

108. Additionally "Texts often exhibit the conventions of more than one genre. . . . Hybrid genres abound . . . the multiple purposes of journalism often lead to generically heterogeneous texts . . . mixed-genre texts are far from uncommon." "Traditionally, genres (particularly literary genres) tended to be regarded as fixed forms, but contemporary theory emphasizes that both their forms and functions are dynamic." Ibid., 2, 3.

109. Devitt, "Generalizing about Genre: New Conceptions of an Old Concept,"

tion of formal characteristics but is intended to fulfill a task. As seen in the aforementioned passages in Ecclesiastes, my formulation of genre is not solely focused on the form characteristics of the text, such as the genre's use of better-than sayings, repetition, or recurring phrases. These points do have valid significance, yet to confine the understanding of genre to only these considerations is to restrain needlessly the reader's understanding. It is this liberating notion that Miller presents.[110] My discussion of the anti-apocalyptic genre of the text seeks to engage the consideration of what Qoheleth wants his audience to do. In other words, what is the social function that Qoheleth seeks to fulfill, to evoke from his audience, with his text? At punctuating moments throughout his work, for example, he emphasizes joy and the pursuit of joy.[111]

Miller asserts, "Genre represents action." It must, therefore, entail both situation and motive considering the fact that human activity can receive proper interpretation only within the framework of a situation and the corresponding motives.[112] In order to demonstrate this point, attention has been given to the setting of both the implied author and implied audience. Qoheleth attempts to get his audience to turn away from the ideas of the apocalyptic seers and turn to accepting the divine gift of joy that God gives—if and when it comes. "Genre, in this way, becomes more than a

---

573–86.

110. Miller, "Genre as Social Action," 151–67.

111. The increasing emphatic nature of these joy statements appear in the text. In 2:24, there is the simple statement, "There is nothing better for mortals than to eat and drink, and find enjoyment in their toil." The following two statements of joy include an assertive phrase in the beginning. "I know that there is nothing better for them than to be happy and enjoy themselves as long as they live." (3:12) Yet another assertive phrase appears in 3:22. "So I saw that there is nothing better than that all should enjoy their work . . . ." The fourth statement increases the intensity ever so slightly as 5:18 declares, "This is what I have seen to be good; it is fitting to eat and drink and find enjoyment in all the toil with which one toils under the sun the few days of the life God gives us . . . ." In 8:15, Qoheleth puts more of a personal endorsement behind his statement of joy. "So I commend enjoyment, for there is nothing better for people under the sun than to eat, drink, and enjoy themselves, for this will go with them in their toil through the days of life that God gives them under the sun." In the next cluster of joy statements, Qoheleth commands. "Go, eat your bread with enjoyment, and drink your wine with a merry heart . . . ." (9:7). "Let your garments always be white; do not let oil be lacking on your head" (9:8). "Enjoy life with the wife whom you love, all the days of your vain life that are given under the sun, because this is your portion in life and in your toil at which you toil under the sun" (9:9). Whybray, "Qoheleth, Preacher of Joy," 87–88.

112. Miller, "Genre as Social Action," 24.

formal entity; it becomes pragmatic, fully rhetorical, a point of connection between intention and effect, an aspect of social action."[113]

To illustrate this understanding of genre and how I am applying it to Ecclesiastes, I will adapt from the article by Carolyn Miller[114] using the rhetorical genre of eulogy and bring comparisons to the occurrence of an anti-apocalyptic genre present in Ecclesiastes. A eulogy is a speech or writing given to praise another person, often times occurring at a funeral or memorial event. From a rhetorical genre theory perspective, there are three potential means of classifying this genre. It could be classified according to rhetorical substance (semantics), form (syntactic), or rhetorical action performed (semantics). The eulogy is a genre that intends to bring about a result; it is a genre that is defined by its intended purpose. It is rightly classified according to the rhetorical action it is intended to perform. Likewise, steadfast to purpose, the portions of Ecclesiastes examined above have been classified or scrutinized not primarily according to their semantics or syntactical characteristics but rather the rhetorical/social action they perform and evoke, which is to reject the false hope of apocalyptic thought, and engage this enigmatic life with joy—if and when God gives it.

Eulogies occur with such frequency that they can be considered recurring situations. As a result, there is a tradition concerning it that serves as a guideline to the genre, its form, and intended purpose, i.e., the eulogy is usually not used to denigrate an individual. There is a fusion of form and substance rooted on this situation. "Each has its characteristic substance: the elements (exhortation and dissuasion, accusation and defense, praise and blame) and aims (expedience, justice, and honor). Each has its appropriate forms (time or tense, proofs, and style)."[115] The eulogy has its own substance of expression of adoration and praise for a deceased individual as well as the aim of honor. Even if fluid in its form, the eulogy would still stay true to its purpose. The eulogy is, thus, a fusion of the substance and form. Likewise the portions in Ecclesiastes, and specifically the passages examined in this work, also have characteristic substance in terms of the literary characteristics similar to that of wisdom literature, yet the aim is related to the polemics against apocalyptic thought. This anti-apocalyptic genre, in the passages examined above, is the result of a fusion of substance and form within context, a social and literary context.

113. Ibid., 25.
114. Ibid., 151–67.
115. Ibid., 151–67.

Further bolstering the plausibility of this anti-apocalyptic genre label is the realization that there is no limit to genres in a society; the number of genres derives from the societal complexity and multiplicity.[116] In the words of Tzvetan Todorov, "A new genre is always the transformation of one or several old genres: by inversion, by displacement, by combination."[117] Amy Devitt furthers this perspective as she writes, "Individuals may . . . combine different genres or may violate the norms of an existing genre, thereby confirming that genre's existence and potentially changing it."[118]

The eulogy, particularly when given at a funeral, is a genre that is largely defined around the *foci* of setting and function. The anti-apocalyptic genre present in Ecclesiastes is defined around these *foci* as well.

Application of Nasuti and Hirsch

From Nasuti I have adapted the language of setting and function as *foci* points for genre. Whereas Nasuti relates setting and function to the reader/interpreter of any time period, I speak of setting and function with regard to the author (and the author's audience) and the author's intended function for the text. This adaptation is congruent with the genre theories of Miller and Swales. With this conception of genre in consideration, the heuristic genre label of anti-apocalyptic to describe portions of Ecclesiastes is not only plausible but also necessary in order to understand, more fully, the text.[119]

Hirsch details the process of interpretation, which includes consideration of authorial will in deciphering genre and in recognizing the creation of new genres. Hirsch writes, "Coming to understand the meaning of an

---

116. Ibid., 37. The genre theory considerations of John Swales also serve to bolster this formulation and application of genre to the aforementioned passages in Ecclesiastes. Our formulation and understanding of genre need to begin not with formal characteristics but rather, firstly, with the community that has produced it and the community to which the work is addressed and, secondly, the communicative purpose that the work is intended to fulfill. Thirdly, in the words of Tzvetan Todorov, "A new genre is always the transformation of one or several old genres: by inversion, by displacement, by combination." Swales, *Genre Analysis: English in Academic and Research Settings*, 35.

117. Todorov, "The Origin of Genres," 159–70. One may suggest that Qoheleth extends a genre in that he uses a text with functional and formal characteristics of wisdom literature to argue against apocalyptic thought.

118. Devitt, "Generalizing about Genre: New Conceptions of an Old Concept," 580.

119. Nasuti, *Defining the Sacred Song: Genre, Tradition, Post-Critical Interpretation of the Psalms*, 45–56.

utterance is like learning the rules of a game." Understanding Ecclesiastes, or the meaning of an utterance, shares similarities with learning the rules of a game. As stated above, the challenge for the interpreter is to decipher which game is being played and then determine the rules of the game, without a rulebook. The interpreter needs to be familiar with types of utterances or "family resemblances" present in Ecclesiastes. The utterance type that encompasses the entire meaning of an utterance, according to Hirsch, is a genre. Both the speaker or author and the interpreter must be careful to be familiar with the "variable and unstable norms of language but also the particular norms of a particular genre."[120]

Understanding the process of interpretation is important in coming to a proper understanding of Ecclesiastes and the appearance of an anti-apocalyptic genre within it. Before the interpreter approaches Eccl 7:1–10, 3:10–22, and 9:1–10, she has a set of generic expectations. She expects to encounter wisdom literature with its various conventions. Initially, she focuses on the formal characteristics (the usual formulation of genre). The details of meaning that she finds are heavily influenced by the meaning and genre expectations with which she begins this process. Then, however, she encounters the many contradictions or tensions in the text of Ecclesiastes such as 7:1–4 where what is considered to be a gift of God earlier in the book is now considered unacceptable. What is she to do with these points of contention? Her genre expectations face these testing points when she encounters such unorthodox statements such as chapter 3:20 that question the afterlife. Her genre expectations are tested; she determines that something must be revised. With the proper understanding of genre as detailed above, she begins to approach the text not with the primary concern of its formal characteristics but rather with the understanding that genre is flexible, anchored to authorial will, and centered around the *foci* of setting and function. She focuses on the question of the author's setting and what the author is intending to do with the text, the response he wishes to evoke from the audience (function). As to the formal characteristics, she realizes that they are flexible because genres are always evolving. Now, the interpreter's perception of genre, therefore, is not a stagnant one but rather a variable concept that evolves within the process of interpretation, growing from vague and imprecise to narrower and more precise as this process

---

120. Hirsch, *Validity in Interpretation*, 70–71.

advances.¹²¹ There is also a degree of trial and error to genre destination in that new postulations arise as old postulations are proven wrong.

This process includes the search for what Hirsch calls the intrinsic genre, which is one dimension of Hirsch's view of genre. Understanding takes place when both the interpreter and the speaker, or author, operate under the same generic conception in meaning and understanding; this shared generic conception is "the intrinsic genre of utterance." More precisely, intrinsic genre "is that sense of the whole by means of which an interpreter can correctly understand any part in its determinacy."¹²² An understanding of setting and function and how this particular text relates to this intersection is an important part of deciphering the intrinsic genre.

This process of interpretation includes not only intrinsic genres but also the very common occurrence of the creation of a new genre, which will require an imaginative leap. Such a creative imaginative leap would be the presence and use of an anti-apocalyptic genre in Ecclesiastes. The formation of a new genre, according to Hirsch, involves either the assimilation of two genres or extending an existing genre to suit the needs of a new context—or both.¹²³

Hirsch argues, "The growth of new genres is founded on this quantum principle that governs all learning and thinking: by an imaginative leap the unknown is assimilated to the known, and something genuinely new is realized."¹²⁴ He provides two examples of the two ways in which this new growth occurs: amalgamation or extension. One example of an extension resulting in a new genre is the greeting used when an English-speaking individual answers the telephone. She says, "Hello," while Italian counterparts say, "Pronto." Both communicate to the person on the other end of the telephone connection that the speaker has picked up the phone and is ready to listen. The difference between the two greetings is that "Hello" was already a salutation used in common conversation. Saying "Hello" in this situation is thus an extension of a genre to a new situation, resulting in a new genre created. An example of an amalgamation would be what Picasso did when "he turned a toy car into the head of a baboon. To make such an

---

121. Ibid., 72–77.

122. Ibid., 86. Hirsch further explains, "An extrinsic genre is a wrong guess, an intrinsic genre a correct one. One of the main tasks of interpretation can be summarized as the critical rejection of extrinsic genres in search for the intrinsic genre of a text." Ibid., 88–89.

123. Ibid., 105.

124. Ibid.

analogy is not merely to equate two known types—baboon and car—but to create a new one—the car-baboon."[125] Hirsch contends that when an author creates a new genre, he generally does both amalgamation and extension. To this I would suggest that Qoheleth has brought forth an amalgamation in terms of the fact that these texts discussed above do in fact bring teaching that would be expected in wisdom literature but also bring teaching that would be germane to arguing against apocalyptic thought. In so doing he extends the genre to a new purpose. The interpreter, at the beginning, does not factor this possibility into her initial anticipations when she approaches the text.

The process of understanding begins with certain genre expectations. After the interpreter's generic expectations have been disappointed due to numerous contradictions, she begins to postulate the possibility that what has taken place in the text is the author's imaginative leap as he has melded into the text an anti-apocalyptic genre in these specific passages. In this case she begins to discern how Qoheleth uses the literary/formal characteristics of wisdom literature primarily to refute the teachings of apocalyptic literature.[126] The concept of genre presented here and substantiated by interaction with contemporary genre theorists helps to determine whether a prospective interpretation is appropriate and valid, or not. Again, "valid interpretation depends on valid inference about the proprieties of the intrinsic genre [along with the consideration of the author's ability to take an imaginative leap]."[127]

Foundational to this discussion of the anti-apocalyptic genre label for the Eccl 7:1–10, 3:10–22, and 9:1–10 have been the following: genre is flexible, anchored to authorial will, and centered on the *foci* of setting and function. This heuristic genre label is plausible because it is, as are all genre labels, the interpreter's attempt to paint the author's intended meaning. Further bolstering the plausibility of the proposed genre label is the possible literary phenomenon of generic mutation. Moreover, this approach to genre, consistent with contemporary genre theorists, has served to emphasize that social function is the main concern of genre. I have considered the question: what is the social function that Qoheleth seeks to fulfill, evoke from his audience, with his text? From these considerations I would suggest

---

125. Ibid.
126. Ibid., 102–11.
127. Ibid., 121.

that the genre label is not only plausible but necessary as the interpreter navigates the process of interpretation.

SUMMARY

This chapter has examined the setting and function of Ecclesiastes. This examination has proposed that the proper genre label for the passages discussed above is anti-apocalyptic. After a survey of the considerations of dating and implied author and audience, the date proposed for the text is circa 200 B.C.E., a time of power transition between Ptolemaic and Seleucid power. An examination of 7:1–10, 3:10–22, and 9:1–10 has demonstrated how the author refutes key apocalyptic teachings. The plausibility of the anti-apocalyptic genre label has been demonstrated through an application of the work of the genre theorists presented in chapter two.

The application of these genre theorists' ideas has further demonstrated the definition of genre given in chapter two: genre is flexible, anchored to authorial will, and centered on the *foci* of setting and function. The anti-apocalyptic genre label is an important heuristic tool, anchored to authorial will. These texts examined here have a resemblance with wisdom literature but also resemble apocalyptic, in that these texts question apocalyptic teaching; genre is flexible and is intended to accomplish a task.

Chapter 5

The Rhetorical Strategy of Ecclesiastes

This work has argued that Qoheleth, in part, employs an anti-apocalyptic genre and that this genre advances the overarching message of joy. The anti-apocalyptic genre, however, is only one portion of Qoheleth's rhetorical tactic in Ecclesiastes. To demonstrate a panoramic view of this approach, this chapter discusses the intertwined five-pronged rhetorical strategy employed in the book. These five prongs are rhetorical questions, ethos, destabilization, the anti-apocalyptic genre usage, and re-stabilization.[1]

THE RHETORICAL QUESTION IN ECCLESIASTES[2]

The first of the five prongs is the rhetorical question. In this section, I will address the overall role of the rhetorical question in Ecclesiastes and draw conclusions on how these questions serve the book's message. Drawing from Raymond E. Johnson in his dissertation *The Rhetorical Question as*

---

1. Douglas Miller identifies threefold rhetorical strategy in Ecclesiastes: ethos, destabilization, and re-stabilization. Douglas Miller, "What the Preacher Forgot: The Rhetoric of Ecclesiastes," 216–21. I would argue that a fuller treatment of the rhetorical strategy would also include two additional prongs: rhetorical questions and the anti-apocalyptic usage.

2. I acknowledge my indebtedness to Raymond E. Johnson for his insightful work on the use of rhetorical questions in Ecclesiastes. Johnson, "The Rhetorical Question as a Literary Device in Ecclesiastes."

The Rhetorical Strategy of Ecclesiastes

a Literary Device in Ecclesiastes, the main functions of rhetorical questions that receive attention in this section are the disputational and psychological functions. Rhetorical questions, serving a disputational or polemical role, in Ecclesiastes do not function in an accusatory manner but do bolster consensus with the reader and persuade. Since there are no accusations in Ecclesiastes, it is mainly through the disputational or polemical nature of some of the rhetorical questions that one can determine what Qoheleth is disputing. One primary way that Ecclesiastes uses rhetorical questions to build consensus is with the double question, which appears in 2:25 and 6:8, 12. In 2:25, the double questions serve to reinforce the consensus already established in 2:24. In 2:24, Qoheleth writes, "There is nothing better for mortals than to eat and drink, and find enjoyment in their toil. This also, I saw, is from the hand of God." He follows this assertion with the double questions in v. 25, "for apart from him who can eat or who can have enjoyment."[3] By reinforcing the statement in v. 24 with these rhetorical questions, the author hopes to draw the audience further into unanimity with the statement.[4]

The questions of 6:8 aims to bring consensus through repeating an already established thought that began earlier in the text concerning the profitless-ness of toil. "For what advantage have the wise over fools? And what do the poor have who know how to conduct themselves before the living?" These questions bring a conclusion to the words of 5:10 stating that money and those who love it will not have great gain. Chapter 6:12 gives the third set of double questions. "For who knows what is good for mortals while they live the few days of their vain life, which they pass like a shadow? For who can tell them what will be after them under the sun?" (Eccl 6:12).[5]

---

3. This verse provides a challenge for interpreters with regard to the word *mimeni* or *memenu*. Interpreters, like Michael v. Fox, recommend that the Septuagint, the Peshitta, be followed with its rendering of *mimenu*, "from him" for this would make more sense than the other reading of "from me." Roland Murphy points out that if the verse is read with the "from me" that it is speaking of the king who surpasses all in terms of pleasures and enjoyment. With the reading with *mimenu* the text reinforces the understanding that apart from God no one can have enjoyment. The most productive thing that a person can do is to take enjoyment from the life that is given, for both the good and the worry are from the hand of God (7:14). This commitment to enjoyment is not from the Epicureans but rather from Hebrew monotheism believing that God has indeed set the path for this life. Fox, *The JPS Commentary: Ecclesiastes*, 18,19; Murphy, *Ecclesiastes*, 26; Longman, *Ecclesiastes*, 108–9.

4. Johnson, "The Rhetorical Question as a Literary Device in Ecclesiastes," 211.

5. Barton, *Ecclesiastes*, 137.

This set of double questions introduces two themes that receive further development in the second half of the book: the question of what is good and the limitation of humanity's capacity to know. One can understand these questions to be negative assertions as they emphasize the fact that no one really knows what is good for humanity—in light of the fact that humanity is not aware of the future. Humanity is like a shadow, thus the words in v. 12b, "For who can tell them what will be after them under the sun?" Here Qoheleth expresses the fact that human life is as transitory and uncertain as the shadow. Although such a thought appears in 3:22, it appears that this set of double questions serves to further a consensus/thesis.[6]

Rhetorical questions in Ecclesiastes also serve a specifically persuasive function in Qoheleth's argument. They serve as pivotal persuasive devices as they introduce, amplify, or conclude an argument. In the achievement of this goal, these questions emphasize to the reader the critical portions of Qoheleth's argument. An example of this function is the set of questions that set up a contention in the text. Ecclesiastes 1:3 is an example as it asks, "What do people gain from all the toil at which they toil under the sun?" In 3:9, "What gain have the workers from their toil?" Again, 5:11, "When goods increase, those who eat them increase; and what gain has their owner but to see them with his eyes?"[7]

Another way in which rhetorical questions bolster the persuasiveness of an argument in Ecclesiastes is to enlarge further a previous assertion. Two examples of such rhetorical questions are 6:6 and 2:24–25 (treated above). In chapter 6, the text speaks of the frustration of desires. Qoheleth has seen individuals who have wealth, possessions, and honor but do not have the ability to enjoy them; this is vanity. In v. 6, Qoheleth issues the equalizing factor to this disparity in life—death, "Even though he should live a thousand years twice over, yet enjoy no good—do not all go to one place?"[8] This statement at this pivotal moment in this section emphasizes a central point of the book—death equalizes the disparities in this life.[9]

---

6. Johnson, "The Rhetorical Question as a Literary Device in Ecclesiastes," 212.

7. Another question of this nature is 6:12.

8. Qoheleth, Crenshaw argues, here contradicts traditional wisdom teaching with this line of thought and rhetorical question. Whereas traditional wisdom literature places much value on the blessing of long life, Qoheleth seemingly contradicts this coveted blessing by focusing on the ultimate end of death. In line with the other portions of the Hebrew Bible (Prov 30:16; Isa 5:14; Hab 2:5) Qoheleth believes *Sheol* is never satisfied. Crenshaw, *Ecclesiastes*, 127–28.

9. Johnson, "The Rhetorical Question as a Literary Device in Ecclesiastes," 215–16.

The Rhetorical Strategy of Ecclesiastes

Rhetorical questions can also serve to conclude strongly or anticipate the conclusion of an argument. For example, "What gain" (or "What profit") questions such as those in 2:22, 5:16, and 6:8 (treated above) many times introduce and conclude the same section. In so doing, they set the subject matter within the context of understanding the profitless-ness of human toil and life. Other questions such as those in 3:22 and 10:14 prepare the reader for the conclusion, thus increasing the chance that the reader will agree with the conclusion.[10]

Another especially important role of the rhetorical question in Ecclesiastes is the psychological impact on the reader. These questions impact the mood of the reader, and they also affect the audience in terms of contact and victimization as well as reconstructing the norms. Ecclesiastes highlights the ironies of life such as an individual having wealth and possessions and not being able to enjoy them, and these ironies have a tendency to create a negative or pessimistic mood in the reader. An example of such a negative leaning is in 5:16, 17: "This also is a grievous ill: just as they came, so shall they go; and what gain do they have from toiling from the wind? Besides, all their days they eat in darkness, in much vexation and sickness and resentment." The negative tone that the reader often receives from the text is also aided by the fact that rhetorical questions in Ecclesiastes are often negative sentences or sentences that expect a negative response.[11]

---

10. Ibid., 217–18. Another function that rhetorical questions serve in Ecclesiastes is that of structural demarcation. Admitting that the determination of structure in Ecclesiastes has been a long-term difficulty, Johnson proceeds to elaborate on some plausible ways that the rhetorical questions in Ecclesiastes serve to show sections in Ecclesiastes. One such way is with what he calls "What profit" questions. One can see four usual characteristics in the "what profit" sections: (1) "an introductory "What profit" question, (2) a poetic composition (3) an extended 'I-Narrative' (4) a concluding "What profit" question." (5) the concluding "what profit" question will have some reference to vanity either before it or after it." Such sections are found in 1:2–2:23; 3:1–9; 5:9–6:9. The first section of 1:2—2:23 is helpful to illustrate this identification; it contains all five of these characteristics. In 1.3, there is the "What profit" question followed by a poem in 1:4–11 and an "I-Narrative" in 1:12—2:20. The "What profit" question of 2:22 is preceded and followed by 2:21 and 2:23. In a similar manner 3:1–19 also shows these characteristics framed within in the pivotal rhetorical "what profit" question. In 3:9, the "what profit" question appears after the poem has already appeared in 3:1–8. An "I-Narrative" follows the question in 3:10–18. The concluding "What profit" question is preceded by a statement concerning vanity found in the same v. 19. Ibid., 237.

11. Johnson, "The Rhetorical Question as a Literary Device in Ecclesiastes," 249. Qoheleth offsets this bleak reality that humanity faces. It appears that God allows humanity joy in order to take their minds off of the dismal and short existence that they inevitably face.

Rhetorical questions also seek to induce audience participation. "The more a question requires audience involvement, the more likely it is to appear at strategic points in a pericope."[12] For example, 2:24 invites the reader to take part in the argument that the author is building. "There is nothing better for mortals than to eat and drink, and find enjoyment in their toil. This also, I saw, is from the hand of God." A rhetorical question follows this assertion in v. 25. "For apart from him who can eat or who can have enjoyment?" Raymond Johnson believes that the shift to an interrogative statement shows Qoheleth's attempt to make contact with the audience. Questions such as 1:3, "What do people gain from all the toil at which they toil under the sun?" also fulfill this role. An additional element to the force of this question is the fact that it moves the reader not only to formulate an answer internally but also to wonder about the intent of the question itself. Either through repetition or ambiguity, rhetorical questions used in this manner draw the audience into the argument and worldview of the author.[13]

Qoheleth also pulls the reader into the vortex of the author's argument through literary gaps destabilizing the reader's norms. Once in the gap, the reader is susceptible to accepting the author's norms. As already noted, asking a question spurs the audience to participate, but it also makes the reader vulnerable. The gaps in the text entrap the reader. These gaps create uncertainty and suspense resulting in the destabilization of the reader's norms. For example in 1:3, the text asks, "What do people gain from all the toil at which they toil under the sun?"[14] The text does not immediately answer

---

12. Johnson, "The Rhetorical Question as a Literary Device in Ecclesiastes," 251.

13. Ibid., 251.

14. A few brief comments about this very central verse to the argument of Ecclesiastes are in order. Key words in this verse would be gain, toil, under the sun, and the word used for people. The word *yitron* from the root *ytr*, in the NRSV translated as "gain," appears ten times in Ecclesiastes and is absent from the rest of the Hebrew Bible. It may also be possible that for Qoheleth this word also had the commercial connotation of profit. This understanding would seem to fit with other portions of the text, particularly 4:7–8, that emphasize the emptiness of toil and its yield, or lack thereof. The word used for toil (used twenty-two times in the book) means hard work. This word is congruent with Qoheleth's emphasis on the strenuous consistent strain that humanity exerts but yielding no fruitfulness, simply vanity or emptiness. The phrase "under the sun" is also another common phrase of Qoheleth appearing twenty-nine times in the text. Qoheleth uses this phrase to speak of the broad span of life experience: the good and adversity from the hand of God, the enjoyment, and difficulties that humanity faces. Thus, this rhetorical question encapsulates part of Qoheleth's message: endeavoring to address a mindset in his audience, he intimates via rhetorical questions the understanding that all the toil, hard work, strain which humanity experiences in this life does not really bring

this question but leaves the reader to ponder the answer as the argument develops. While in this vulnerable area of suspense the author can begin to rebuild the norms that he has destabilized.[15]

Having covertly destabilized the reader's norms, Qoheleth also seeks to reconstruct those norms to his preference. Ecclesiastes 1:2—2:26 is a good example of how he accomplishes this task. As stated above, 1:3 draws the reader into uncertainty and ambiguity. The previously held and unchallenged norm of toil resulting in gain is placed in other contexts. The first new context is that of 1:4–11 where the recurring nature of the cosmos receives the focus. Yet the reader does not yet receive an answer. The next context is that of 1:12—2:21 and its "I narratives" giving sundry experiences and giving consideration to the norm of toil producing gain. In this section the question in 2:15 brings a preliminary reorientation, "Then I said to myself, 'What happens to the fool will happen to me also; why then have I been so very wise?' And I said to myself that this is also vanity." Verse 22 repeats the question once again with, "What do mortals get from all the toil and strain with which they toil under the sun?" In 2:24-26, Qoheleth gives an alternative to the previously held but now destabilized norm. The response to the question on 1:3 is found in 2:24-26. Eat, drink, and find enjoyment in toil because all of this is from the hand of God. While not a reversal of the norm that toil brings gain, this section refocuses the passage on seizing the opportunity for joy.[16]

The rhetorical question has a vital role in Qoheleth's argument. It, however, fits within a larger rhetorical strategy that Qoheleth employs. Douglas Miller discerns that Qoheleth seeks to influence his readers to take a different viewpoint from the one they have. The author "sees the members of this group have become trapped into viewing every part of their lives, even their religious practice, as a means of manipulating their own success and security."[17] He desires that his audience view life, work, pleasure, wisdom and the religious service in a way that will cause them to be steadfast in both the good and bad days. Ecclesiastes 7:14 says, "In the day of prosperity be joyful, and in the day of adversity consider: God has

---

any gain or ultimate satisfaction. Whybray, *Ecclesiastes*, 36–38.
    15. Johnson, "The Rhetorical Question as a Literary Device in Ecclesiastes," 252–53.
    16. Ibid., 255–57.
    17. Miller, "What the Preacher Forgot: The Rhetoric of Ecclesiastes," 224.

made the one as well as the other, so that mortals may not find out anything that will come after them."[18]

ETHOS

The second prong of Qoheleth's rhetorical strategy is ethos. The author, Miller argues, leans more upon ethos, "the persuasive power of the author's own credibility manifested in the writing itself... cultivating trust between author and reader,"[19] than pathos (emotions) or logos (a logical flow of argument). He establishes this ethos by competence, status, and benevolence. Qoheleth's competence appears in the life experience that he shares with the audience and also with his use of literary devices such as the rhetorical question (discussed above). Assuming Solomon's persona helps him to establish status since Solomon was known for his wisdom, work, and pleasure. The reader sees the author's benevolent character in the fact that he is willing to share the observations and conclusions from his years of life experience with the reader. Qoheleth utilizes pathos in service to ethos as he makes mention of the emotions experienced in the different situations of life, his own frustrations with the journey of life, and his repeated use of הבל. As to logos (the logical flow of argument), the argument appears to be logical but in reality there are a number of conclusions that possibly have their authority in the ethos that the author has developed with the audience.[20]

Eric Christianson

Eric Christianson adds to this understanding of the author's use of ethos. The author uses his self-revelation, particularly in the first two chapters, not only to bolster credibility and persuasiveness but also to cause the reader to wrestle with similar self-probing questions.[21]

The reader, Christianson argues, truly comes to know Qoheleth. There appears to be an interaction between the author and the reader in which the reader experiences Qoheleth's character via the self-divulgence

---

18. Ibid., 224.
19. Ibid.
20. Ibid., 224–28.
21. Christianson, *A Time to Tell: Narrative Strategies in Ecclesiastes*, 173–74.

The Rhetorical Strategy of Ecclesiastes

that transpires in the text; transference of identity takes place. Christianson writes, "I refer to transference of identity, the reader's to the narrator's, whereby a self is recognized whose experience is identifiable and able to be appropriated."[22] An examination of chapters 1:12—2:26 provides an example of this transference.

In chapters 1:12—2:26 Qoheleth exposes much information about the author as this section begins with a poem contemplating the world's circular nature. These reflections result in the reader being drawn into the present experience of the narration. The story telling of this passage is the crucial aspect of this passage as Qoheleth exhibits a reflection on his past through his self-divulging narration. Furthermore, the use of the first person accentuates the story as the author speaks to the reader in solitude, uninhibited by an intermediary.[23]

Qoheleth had royal status, made vineyards, parks, and gardens and amassed great wealth; he had arrived to an enviable place of status, intellectually and socially. His intellectual status contributed to his self-assessment of greatness. He says in 1:16, "I said . . . Behold, I have become great and increased in wisdom more than all who were before me over Jerusalem . . . ." Placing this statement to the test is what begins chapter 2.[24] Yet, he finds himself despairing life in 2:17–20. Each benchmark that he used to define himself, his work and reputation, will likely go to a fool after his death. As he surveys these realities, Qoheleth considers his own self with all of its trappings to be an empty, perplexing vexation.[25]

Qoheleth transparently reflects on his past through his story telling. This divulgence is far from superficial because the reader views the intimation of Qoheleth's self via the deep level of vulnerability in the text.

Elizabeth Stone makes the following poignant remark about the aforementioned: "Like a candle flame in mist, we cannot see him or touch him or name him, and yet he is there. And as surely as food gives fragrance and drums resound, [K]oheleth gives us his own particular light, whether he is one or many men, whether the page has felt the point of one or many pens."[26] This self-disclosure is intentional and ripe with rhetorical purpose. Christianson writes,

22. Ibid., 173–74.
23. Ibid., 206.
24. Ibid.
25. Ibid., 207.
26. Stone, "Old Man Koheleth," 98–102.

And so is established a focal point for readers: Does he smile wryly at his past? Does he frown at his folly? Does he weep? ... His narrated experience is a way of observing the development of the self over the expanse of time. As autobiography it becomes a way for readers to examine the arenas in which the formation of the self might take place. We look hard at Qoheleth's self (he gives us no choice) and our gaze is returned, with the (frightening?) prospect that the quality of our own selves will be reflected (to be הבל).[27]

By this self-divulgence, particularly in the first two chapters, the author intentionally leads the reader to a point of introspective examination.[28] In so doing, the reader becomes sufficiently prepared for the re-examination of accepted norms and beliefs that occur in the book. The audience comes to a point of affirming or rejecting the previously held norms and beliefs. Thus, the reader and the reader's beliefs are now sufficiently prepared to experience destabilization.

DESTABILIZATION

The third prong in the rhetorical strategy is destabilization. The author seeks to shake his audience's beliefs and values. To this end, Qoheleth proceeds very carefully because he does not want to alienate them. He must demonstrate that he thinks similarly with them on certain frustrations of life yet also express that he does not share their values and conclusions about the proper approach to life. He brings this destabilization, in part, by his use of the rhetorical question (see above) and his use of the persona of Solomon (see above) who stands as a symbol of that which is considered הבל—work, wisdom, and pleasure.[29] He also creates this sense of destabilization via rhetoric of contradiction and rhetoric of ambiguity.

Douglas Ingram

Douglas Ingram, in his book *Ambiguity in Ecclesiastes*, suggests that Qoheleth purposefully includes ambiguity in the text in order to engulf the reader in the development of meaning.[30] Ingram defines ambiguity as key

---

27. Christianson, *A Time to Tell: Narrative Strategies in Ecclesiastes*, 211–12.
28. Ibid., 212.
29. Miller, "What the Preacher Forgot: The Rhetoric of Ecclesiastes," 228–30.
30. Ingram distinguishes meaning from significance. Significance would be that

words, recurring phrases, or section of the book that cause the reader to supply the meaning of the text because the key word or recurring phrase is indeterminate. This indeterminacy is caused when a word or phrase could have more than one meaning or when the word or phrase does not communicate "any coherent meaning."[31] He writes, "I believe that Ecclesiastes is ambiguous by design precisely to engage the reader in the process of creating or discerning meaning . . . ."[32]

One of the examples of ambiguity in Ecclesiastes would be the word הבל. Kathleen Farmer ponders how one book could possibly have such different interpretations and consequently points to הבל and its inherently ambiguous nature. "Ecclesiastes has been understood in radically different ways by different readers in part because the thematic metaphor 'all is הבל' is fundamentally ambiguous."[33] Likewise, Douglas Miller concurs, "[T]he approach taken to הבל dramatically shapes the way the entire book is understood."[34] To demonstrate how the word adds ambiguity to Ecclesiastes (and in so doing also intensifies de-stabilization), I will give attention to two crucial recurring phrases followed by a survey of thoughts by scholars concerning this word and its role in Ecclesiastes.

The appearance of the phrase הכל הבל occurs six times in Ecclesiastes. Ingram notes that none of these requires a particular translation, to the exclusion of other possibilities; its occurrences are ambiguous. This phrase appears in the *inclusio* in 1:2 and 12:8. Ingram understands the phrase with its use of הכל to be referring to all the activity that takes place.[35]

Ingram also notes the occurrence (three verses where this phrase appears with 1:14b, 2:11c, 2:17b) of these words with the phrase ורעות רוח הכל הבל. He posits that an examination of the additional phrase may give

---

which comes forth as a later reader giving consideration to the meaning in terms of her or his present contemporary situation. Meaning, for Ingram, is "that which a reader may discern of what could have been meant by the author." Ingram, *Ambiguity in Ecclesiastes*, 40.

31. Ibid., 2.
32. Ibid., 42.
33. Farmer, *Who Knows What Is Good?* 146.
34. Miller, "Qohelet's Symbolic Use of הבל," 437–54.
35. Fox asserts that this reading is referring to what takes place in human experience, not all activity in existence. Fox, *A Time to Tear Down*, 40. Christianson, on the other hand, gives a much broader reading to include not only the human activity but everything—without exception. Christianson, *A Time to Tell*, 89.

A Polemical Preacher of Joy

insight into the meaning of the recurring phrase הכל הבל.[36] In all the occurrences where this phrase appears the author is ruminating on the deeds done under the sun. The question is how are these deeds to be understood? Are they ephemeral because they lack duration, futile because there is no lasting worth, or is it another meaning? Another appearance of the expression הכל הבל is in 3:19.[37] A majority of scholars understand this phrase to speak of the transience of life. After examining these six appearances, it is clear that none of them demands a particular translation.[38] The understanding of these phrases rests on how the reader approaches the book itself.

Another phrase גם־זה הבל appears fifteen times in the text. Whereas the previous phrase referred to everything as הבל, this phrase speaks about particular specific situations.[39] The ambiguity is present; the meaning of the phrase is unclear. In what follows I will briefly examine each of these occurrences to demonstrate what Ingram argues is the intentional injection of ambiguity into the text by the author.

The phrase in 2:1 גם־הוא־הבל could speak of two different possibilities. The author could be referring to the noun טוֹב, which also contains some ambiguity, or speak of examining pleasure.[40] The phrase in 2:15 הבל־גם־הוא may refer to the greatness of Qoheleth's wisdom or the realization that he experiences the same end as the fool or anticipation of the thought in v. 16 that the wise receive no more remembrance than the fool.[41] The text, in 2:19, possibly speaks of the work that Qoheleth accomplished, the profit he earned from it, or that someone else may reap the results of all his labor.[42] The use of the phrase in 2:21 is similar. Here הבל could be speaking of the portion חלק or perhaps to the fact that an individual who did not work for it will gain the portion or possibly to the fact that the individual who expended his labor with wisdom, knowledge, and skill only has his portion pass to someone else.[43] The use of הבל in 2:23 most likely refers

---

36. Ingram, *Ambiguity in Ecclesiastes*, 111.
37. Ibid., 115.
38. Ibid., 115.
39. Ibid., 115–17.
40. Ibid., 117.
41. Ibid., 117.
42. Ibid., 117.
43. Ibid., 117.

to the situation of life being full of pain and their work a chasing after the wind.[44]

In 3:19, the word is more appropriately understood to convey "meaningless" or "futile" or "incomprehensible." The presence of this phrase in 2:26 may simply place a blanket of doubt on the previous positive statements uttered in this section of the book. Likewise, the possibilities of meaning for הבל are many. Does it speak of the idea that sinners accumulate in order to give to the good or to the larger idea that it is God who grants wisdom, knowledge, and pleasure to the good and assigns to the sinner the function of gathering to give to the good?[45]

The exact phrase that ends chapter two occupies 4:4. Does the phrase, here, possibly refer to humanity's jealousy, to the profit that is gained and the skill necessary to reach this goal, or to the fact that the profit and work is the ultimate result of jealousy? The use of the phrase in 4:8 is also in question. Does הבל refer to טובה? Is it the fact that Qoheleth does not partake of טובה? Is it the fact that no one is ever satisfied with all of one's wealth? Similar questions could be asked of the use of the phrase in 4:16. The presence of this phrase in 5:10 could refer to the תבואה, resulting in the lover of money not being satisfied with it, or to the situation where the lover of money and gain ultimately does not obtain income. Which is it? The answer is uncertain.[46]

The phrase in 6:2 is slightly different in that it does not include the particle גם. In this context it functions similarly to the phrase in 2:26. Does the word הבל speak of the fact that a stranger will partake in a man's wealth, to the fact that the man will not be able to enjoy his own wealth, or to the entire situation? In 6:9, this phrase serves as the middle of the book. Again, it is unclear what the phrase means in this verse. Does it refer to the sight of the eyes, to the wandering of the desire, or to the entirety of the better-than saying in the first portion of the verse?[47]

In 7:6, הבל refers directly to the laughter of fools or the better-than saying contained in 7:5. In 8:10, the word הבל again may refer to the previous clause, which refers to the one who has been forgotten, or it may speak of the verse in its entirety. In 8:14 Qoheleth speaks of a situation where the

---

44. Ibid., 117.
45. Ibid., 117.
46. Ibid., 118–19.
47. Ibid., 119–20.

A Polemical Preacher of Joy

righteous experience what the wicked should receive and vice versa.[48] The preceding brief treatment of these two phrases has illustrated the ambiguity of the word הבל.

Further demonstrating the ambiguity of this word, scholars differ on their understanding of this key word. Graham Ogden looks at the specific use of the word in Ecclesiastes and concludes, "The term *hebel* in Qoheleth has a distinctive function and meaning; it conveys the notion that life is enigmatic, and mysterious; that there are many unanswered and unanswerable questions."[49] Crenshaw contends that the word "shows two nuances: temporal (ephemerality) and existential (futility or absurdity)."[50] Whybray agrees with the rendering in the NRSV, everything is vanity. Whybray, therefore, writes,

> Elsewhere Qoheleth never employs this extremely emphatic form of speech, nor does he speak in such a general way of everything as "vanity": he applies the word only to specific, clearly defined situations. Consequently it cannot be affirmed with certainty that v. 2 expresses Qoheleth's own thought: the verse is undoubtedly an interpretation of his thought, but may well be a misunderstanding or at least an over-simplification of it.[51]

More recent commentaries continue to wrestle with the translation of this word. Tremper Longman in his commentary reads the word to convey "meaningless" and states that "the book of Ecclesiastes leaves no doubt about Qoheleth's ultimate conclusion—everything is completely meaningless."[52] Seow writes that Qoheleth "does not mean that everything is meaningless or insignificant, but that everything is beyond apprehension and comprehension."[53] "The activities in the world and their unpredictable consequences," Seow continues, "are said to be *hebel*. . . . They are unpredictable, arbitrary, and incomprehensible."[54] Ian Provan affirms that Qohe-

---

48. Ingram, *Ambiguity in Ecclesiastes*, 120-21. Fox sees this verse as ambiguous. "It is unclear whether *hebel* is predicated of the merry noise of fools (in which case the observation is rather trite) or of the rebuke of the wise, judged absurd because their wisdom is vulnerable to lust for gain (v. 7)." Fox, *A Time to Tear Down*, 38.

49. Ogden, *Qoheleth*, 23.

50. Crenshaw, *Ecclesiastes*, 57.

51. Whybray, *Ecclesiastes*, 35.

52. Longman, *The Book of Ecclesiastes*, 61.

53. Seow, *Ecclesiastes*, 59.

54. Ibid., 102.

leth has more than ephemerality in mind when he uses this word; "It is also the elusive nature of reality, that is, the way in which it resists our attempts to capture it and contain it, to grasp hold of it and control it."[55]

Again, the word in a number of places in the text has a multiplicity of meaning possibilities. As stated above, Ingram writes, "I believe that Ecclesiastes is ambiguous by design precisely to engage the reader in the process of creating or discerning meaning. . . ."[56] I would add that the author uses this intentional ambiguity to further create a literary atmosphere of destabilization. This ambiguity, with its multiple possible meanings and indeterminacy, facilitates the author bringing into question the audience's deeply held values.

Bernard Lee

Another way in which this destabilization comes about is via rhetoric of contradiction; the author contradicts conventionally held beliefs.[57] An example of this rhetoric of contradiction appears in 1:12–18:

> 12 I, the Teacher, when king over Israel in Jerusalem, 13 applied my mind to seek and to search out by wisdom all that is done under heaven; it is an unhappy business that God has given to human beings to be busy with. 14 I saw all the deeds that are done under the sun; and see, all is vanity and a chasing after wind. 15 What is crooked cannot be made straight, and what is lacking cannot be counted. 16 I said to myself, "I have acquired great wisdom, surpassing all who were over Jerusalem before me; and my mind has had great experience of wisdom and knowledge." 17 And I applied my mind to know wisdom and to know madness and folly. I perceived that this also is but a chasing after wind. 18 For in much wisdom is much vexation, and those who increase knowledge increase sorrow.

55. Provan, *Ecclesiastes, Song of Songs*, 52.

56. Ingram, *Ambiguity in Ecclesiastes*, 42. Farmer argues that the word is a metaphor, and that metaphors are "intentionally provocative figures of speech which can be understood in quite different ways. . . . Like all other metaphors, it invites its hearers to look for qualities that two essentially unlike things have in common. Both the speaker and the hearer of a metaphor know that the two entities . . . are alike in some ways and unlike in other ways." Farmer would prefer that translations preserve this metaphor quality by allowing the reader to choose. Farmer, *Who Knows What Is Good?* 143.

57. This is a term used by Bernard Lee in his thesis. Lee, "Toward a Rhetoric of Contradiction in the Book of Ecclesiastes." I acknowledge my indebtedness to this work.

In this text, Bernard Lee argues, the reader discovers an individual betwixt two realities: a reality where deeds of wisdom do not (necessarily) have significance and an insatiable quest to find meaning in the aforementioned deeds. This is the quandary that grips the mind of Qoheleth and, consequently, the mind of the reader; he persists in his recommendation that all should pursue wisdom but finds no demonstrable benefit to those who heed such exhortation. He states his quandary in 2:16 when he states that there is no lasting remembrance of the wise man as with the fool; wisdom is thus placed in the same class as folly.[58]

Qoheleth has great difficulty with this unresolved tension. The source of his grief is the injustice that he identifies in this dilemma: there is no reward to the one who walks in wisdom. In 2:21 there is the sobering realization that a wise person could labor all of his life and ultimately leave all the fruits of his labor to a fool.[59]

Qoheleth's many observations, according to Lee, about wisdom's lack of reward continue the tension and contradiction between his epistemological expectations and his experiential knowledge of life. He continues to search for a resolution to this tension and continues to find the notion that there is no demonstrable reward of wisdom over folly to be extremely troubling. Lee writes, "Locked in the clutches of contradiction, he searches the world to find a solution to break the impasse. Until he should succeed, [K]ohelet remains suspended in the paradox of his advice to be wise in the face of impending death."[60] I would argue that this rhetoric of contradiction and this paradox de-stabilizes the reader's paradigm about wisdom and its value because it has traditionally been viewed as a valuable virtue and one that would lead to benefit and success in this life.

ANTI-APOCALYPTIC GENRE

The fourth prong of rhetorical strategy that I address is the use of the anti-apocalyptic genre. The previous prongs are present throughout the book or, in the case of the ethos prong, impact the rest of the book. This fourth prong, however, is embedded in three specific passages of the text. Without the identification of this rhetorical strategy, much of the message (and rhetorical strategy) of Qoheleth is not understood. One must consider that

---

58. Lee, "Toward a Rhetoric of Contradiction in the Book of Ecclesiastes," 99.
59. Ibid., 112.
60. Ibid., 111.

genre is flexible, anchored to authorial will, and centered on the *foci* of setting and function. The setting and function of Qoheleth (see above discussion) alerts the reader to the presence of the anti-apocalyptic genre. This prong also overlaps with the de-stabilization prong in that it seeks to refute the commonly held apocalyptic thought of the day. The previous chapter examined three passages: 7:1–10; 3:10–22; and 9:1–10 and expounded how they demonstrate the use of an anti-apocalyptic genre. This section does not seek to re-exegete these passages but rather to highlight the anti-apocalyptic nature of these passages as part of the overall rhetorical strategy.

Qoheleth's purpose, Perdue argues, in 7:1–10 is to contest a theology of despair, held by the apocalyptic seers, and stress that adhering to such a theology is ill-advised since humanity's knowledge is limited. It is likely, Perdue argues, that these theologians of despair had an apocalyptic view that was despondent over the situation of the present. Although Qoheleth does not dispute that the situation is difficult, he does jettison the theology of gloom and despair. This rejection serves to destabilize a belief of which the reader would be aware.[61]

Quite the contrary to the apocalyptic seers who purport to know what the Deity has determined and to be able to move toil to success, the poem in 3:10–22 furthers the conclusion that human events do not fall into a cosmic order of time and are unknowable to people.[62] Qoheleth argues against their emphasis on "the justice of God, earthly retribution, moral dualism (the wicked and the righteous), and the understanding of the correlation of time and event for a successful outcome."[63] Humanity can know that God has worked, but they cannot ascertain in what way God has worked. With this refutation of apocalyptic seer thought, Qoheleth has extinguished any hope that God reveals God's will via special revelation.

Challenging the apocalyptic thought of the day, the author, in 9:1–10, encourages his audience not to seek the deliverance of the afterlife; there is one fate to both the wicked and the fool. Apocalyptic thought presents the hope that the imminent future would bring both divine intervention on behalf of the righteous and an eschatological judgment upon evil. In 9:1–3, Qoheleth rebuffs this false notion by asserting that the same end belongs to individuals who follow wisdom and individuals who follow folly. Opposing the anticipation of a divine in-breaking of eschatological retribution,

---

61. Perdue, "Wisdom and Apocalyptic: The Case of Qoheleth," 245–46.
62. Ibid., 252–53.
63. Ibid., 247.

Qoheleth paints the picture of an ephemeral life leading to the universal fate of oblivion. With each of these anti-apocalyptic passages, the author dismantles key components of the contemporary apocalyptic thought. This dismantling along with the de-stabilization prong especially prepares the reader to receive a reconstruction of the proper view and approach toward this life.

RE-STABILIZATION

The fifth prong in the rhetorical strategy is re-stabilization. Having deconstructed the faulty views of his audience, Qoheleth moves to reconstruct a theology of joy. The anti-apocalyptic passages (examined above) contain this theology of joy; these passages include an overlapping of anti-apocalyptic genre and re-stabilization prongs.

For Qoheleth, in 7:1–10, the one who is truly wise recognizes that the individual was born to experience the suffering that leads to death. In light of this fact, the wise response is to taste of joy if and when one can do so.[64] Qoheleth's opponents, Perdue asserts, are those who consider the present situation as more dismal than the past and that the situation is so bleak that it precludes rejoicing. The wise course of action, therefore, is to go to the house of mourning, a truly pessimistic point of view. Qoheleth's response acknowledges the dismal state of affairs but contends that the proper response is to seek to enjoy this present life, now.[65]

In light of the perennial and futile search of 3:10–15, what is humanity to do? Rather than alter the present situation through unique revelation via a seer, humanity should enjoy the journey that God has given. "There is nothing better for them than to be happy and enjoy themselves as long as they live." This is a statement of resignation in light of the impervious realities of life. The author stresses the importance of his exhortation by listing simple staples of life as opportunities for joy: eat, drink, and take pleasure in work. Here the author is emphasizing that humans cannot even understand the present with all of its intricate mysteries nor can they know the future, so Qoheleth points to the portion that humans have in this life: enjoy life if and when possible.[66]

---

64. Ibid., 246.
65. Ibid.
66. Rasiah Sugirtharajah, from a post-colonial interpretation, also sees a similar understanding in the Qoheleth's perspective on life and the present oppression. For

Having deconstructed the false expectations given by the apocalyptic seers, Qoheleth, in 9:1–10, endeavors to rebuild a proper hope. He endeavors to direct the reader to the present and the value of this present life. The response to this transitory and enigmatic existence is what Qoheleth emphasizes in 9:7–10—joy. In these verses Qoheleth gives his most forceful exhortation or command to enjoy this life. He wants his audience to orientate their lives in light of the untimely certainty of death.[67] He argues that humanity's portion חלק is to enjoy their present situation and the activities therein, when they can.[68]

Robert K. Johnston[69] gives further understanding of Qoheleth's emphasis on joy beyond the anti-apocalyptic passages. He writes of the proper manner to understand Ecclesiastes as well as gives structural and thematic concerns. He concludes that Qoheleth's purpose in writing the text is to discourage humans from their pursuit of conquering life. Contrary to the understanding that commentators such as Crenshaw have concerning Ecclesiastes, Johnston sees Qoheleth as summoning the wisdom tradition's return to its foundation, "the enjoyment of life itself." (As such, Qoheleth has a truly pastoral concern in his writing.) He accomplishes this goal by emphasizing the many limitations and unanswerable questions in this disconcerting life. Instead of this futile aspiration of conquering life and its hidden order, Qoheleth wants his readers to trust in the joy that God provides via creation and life.

The very structure of the book, with the exception of the title (1:1), epigram (1:2; 12:8), and epilogue (12:9–14), also testifies to the central

---

Sugirtharajah, Ecclesiastes is a writing that seeks to protect and maintain the rule of the establishment. He has a similar dating of the text and sees it as composed under Ptolemaic rule. Qoheleth is understood as one of those Jewish elite who had benefited from the colonial Hellenistic power and amassed wealth, herds, and slaves. (2:4–8) From this background and from this indebtedness to the colonial powers, Qoheleth encouraged the people to accept the present conditions and to be loyal to the king (10:20). He tells his colonized audience to simply be happy as much as they can and that the present difficulties would not change. (3:12; 4:1–3; 5:12) Although Sugirtharajah utilizes a different method of interpretation from that used in this paper, he does arrive at similar conclusion. The message of Ecclesiastes is far from apocalyptic: there is no hope of change; make the most of the present difficult situations that you can. Sugirthirajah, *Postcolonial Criticism and Biblical Interpretation*, 80–81. Although Sugirtharajah does not use this term, in one regard he too concludes that Ecclesiastes is anti-apocalyptic.

67. Ogden, *Qoheleth*, 167.
68. Perdue, "Wisdom and Apocalyptic: The Case of Qoheleth," 253.
69. Johnston, "'Confessions of a Workaholic': A Reappraisal of Qoheleth," 15–28.

A Polemical Preacher of Joy

message of Ecclesiastes.[70] Qoheleth encourages the reader to let enjoyment, rather than toil and labor, be the focus of life.[71] Within this structure Qoheleth develops some themes: humanity's work is profitless, death is an equalizing element in human existence regardless of social status, humanity's ability to know is limited, and the proper response to this reality is to embrace the gift of joy. A primary theme is the limitation of humanity's work. Humanity's destiny, whether rich or poor, wise or fool, is essentially death (2:1; 3:19; 5:12–16). This life, which leads to the equalizing element of death, is governed by a moral order that one cannot decipher (7:15; 8:14). Even the stalwart hope of wisdom does not necessarily bring certainty to life (4:13–16; 9:13–16). With these contradictions and tensions in mind the idea of humanity conquering life is a foolish dream. This futile venture is foolish because it infringes on the inscrutable sovereignty of God (3:11; 6:10, 11). Additionally, there is the fact that humans cannot know what their direction should be or what their future will be (6:12, 7:29; 9:11–15).[72]

In light of these undeniable limitations, Qoheleth stresses his counsel to enjoy the life God has granted. In short, the lesson is that humanity should not attempt to master life but rather try to "see" (ponder) and rejoice in all the good that God has brought.[73] Having highlighted the problems and frustrations that the reader faces in life, Qoheleth now sets forth an alternative. He directs the reader to accept the realities that are beyond his/her control and to decide to change his/her point of view. He discredits the idea of toil as a way to gain security (4:7–8), so that in its place can be a toil that has enjoyment (4:9–12). Instead of pleasures that disappoints, he presents pleasures via the simple things of life (2:24). Qoheleth presents a theology of divine gift; he speaks of the importance of receiving the gift of enjoyment from God.[74]

As stated above, Whybray considers Qoheleth to be a preacher of joy and identifies the seven texts (2:24; 3:12, 22; 5:17; 8:15; 9:7–9; 11:9,10; 12:1) that encourage the reader to follow after pleasure and enjoyment; these joy

---

70 At the beginning of the book (1:3–11), the reader encounters a poem emphasizing the fact that toil and work is profitless—utilizing rhetorical questions (discussed above). The book ends in 11:9—12:7 with a poem urging the reader to enjoy life.

71. Johnston, "'Confessions of a Workaholic': A Reappraisal of Qoheleth," 18.

72. Ibid., 21.

73. Ibid., 21.

74. Miller, "What the Preacher Forgot: The Rhetoric of Ecclesiastes," 230–32.

statements show greater intensity with the progression of the book.[75] These punctuating statements about joy serve as a Leitmotiv, and the respective contexts for these joy statements lead to the conclusion that the ability to enjoy life is a gift from God. One needs to accept the unalterable lot that one has in life, its relative brevity, and the fact that humanity cannot tell the future. In light of and in spite of these unchangeable facts, Qoheleth encourages the reader to pursue enjoyment, which is a gift from God.[76]

SUMMARY

In the process of furthering a message of joy, Qoheleth uses an intertwined rhetorical approach. It is a five- pronged rhetorical strategy that includes rhetorical questions, ethos, de-stabilization, anti-apocalyptic genre, and re-stabilization.

This chapter has discussed two overarching functions of the rhetorical question in Ecclesiastes: the disputational and psychological functions. These rhetorical questions can serve to solidify consensus with the reader and persuade. One primary way that Ecclesiastes uses rhetorical questions to build consensus is with the double question. Rhetorical questions in Ecclesiastes also serve as pivotal persuasive devices as they introduce, amplify, or conclude an argument. Another especially important role of the rhetorical question in Ecclesiastes is the psychological impact on the reader. These

---

75. The increasing emphatic nature of these joy statements appear in the text. In 2:24, there is the simple statement, "There is nothing better for mortals than to eat and drink, and find enjoyment in their toil." The following two statements of joy include an assertive phrase in the beginning. "I know that there is nothing better for them than to be happy and enjoy themselves as long as they live." (3:12) Yet another assertive phrase appears in 3:22. "So I saw that there is nothing better than that all should enjoy their work . . ." The fourth statement increases the intensity ever so slightly as 5:18 declares, "This is what I have seen to be good; it is fitting to eat and drink and find enjoyment in all the toil with which one toils under the sun the few days of the life God gives us . . . ." In 8:15, Qoheleth puts more of a personal endorsement behind his statement of joy. "So I commend enjoyment, for there is nothing better for people under the sun than to eat, drink, and enjoy themselves, for this will go with them in their toil through the days of life that God gives them under the sun." In the next cluster of joy statements, Qoheleth commands. "Go, eat your bread with enjoyment, and drink your wine with a merry heart . . . ." (9:7). "Let your garments always be white; do not let oil be lacking on your head" (9:8). "Enjoy life with the wife whom you love, all the days of your vain life that are given under the sun, because this is your portion in life and in your toil at which you toil under the sun" (9:9). Whybray, "Qoheleth, Preacher of Joy," 87–88.

76. Ibid., 87–98.

A Polemical Preacher of Joy

questions impact the mood of the reader, and they also affect the audience in terms of contact and victimization as well as reconstructing the norms. Rhetorical questions also seek to induce audience participation. Once the reader is pulled into the vortex of the author's argument through literary gaps, the rhetorical questions serve to destabilize the reader's norms.

Qoheleth leans more upon ethos, than pathos (emotions) or logos (a logical flow of argument). He establishes this ethos by competence, status, and benevolence. Eric Christiansen adds that the author's self-revelation, particularly in the first two chapters, not only bolsters credibility and persuasiveness but also causes the reader to wrestle with similar self-probative questions.

Qoheleth induces destabilization, in part, by his use of the rhetorical question and his use of the persona of Solomon. He also creates this sense of destabilization via a rhetoric of contradiction and a rhetoric of ambiguity. Douglas Ingram, in his book *Ambiguity in Ecclesiastes*, suggests that the author purposefully includes ambiguity in the text in order to engulf the reader in the development of meaning. Another way in which this destabilization comes about is via rhetoric of contradiction, as explained by Bernard Lee in his thesis "Toward a Rhetoric of Contradiction in the Book of Ecclesiastes"; the author contradicts conventionally held beliefs about the effectiveness of wisdom.

Qoheleth also utilizes an anti-apocalyptic genre in the process of furthering his message of joy. This genre appears in 7:1–10, 3:10–22, and 9:1–10. Qoheleth's purpose in 7:1–10 is to refute a theology of despair, held by the apocalyptic seers, because humanity's knowledge is limited. Quite the contrary to the apocalyptic seers who purport to know what the Deity has determined and to be able to move toil to success, the poem in 3:10–22 furthers the conclusion that human events do not fall into a cosmic order of time and are unknowable to people. Challenging the apocalyptic thought of the day, the author, in 9:1–10, encourages his audience not to seek the deliverance of the afterlife.

Having deconstructed the false expectations given by the apocalyptic seers, Qoheleth moves to re-stabilize his audience's theology; he constructs a theology of joy. The author, in 9:1–10, endeavors to rebuild a proper hope. He endeavors to direct the reader to the present and the value of this present life. The response to this transitory and enigmatic existence is what Qoheleth emphasizes in 9:7–10—joy. Instead of this futile aspiration of conquering life and its hidden order, Qoheleth wants his readers to trust in the joy that God provides via creation and life. Additionally, Qoheleth, within the overall book structure, develops some themes: humanity's work is profitless, death is an equalizing element in human existence regardless of social status, humanity's ability to know is limited, and the proper response to this reality is to embrace the gift of joy.

At the outset, this book posed three queries to begin the discussion: How is the reader to interpret Ecclesiastes? What is the message of the author? What is the genre of this book? A central response to these questions has been that Qoheleth employs an anti-apocalyptic genre in Ecclesiastes, as a part of his overall message of joy. In chapter one, a focused survey of scholarship illustrated that the scholarly deliberation of Ecclesiastes's message (function) is varied and that the debate on its genre(s) is also diverse. The environment is ripe for another suggestion. Interacting with genre theorists in and out of the field of biblical studies, chapter two presented a definition for genre: Genre is flexible, anchored to authorial will, and centered on the *foci* of setting and function. Chapter three examined a selection of Second Temple texts to demonstrate this point: the "line of demarcation" between wisdom and apocalyptic (or at least our perceived line of demarcation between these two types of literature) is very permeable. From this observation, attention turned in chapter four to key passages in Ecclesiastes that exhibit this anti-apocalyptic genre. Chapter five, above, has demonstrated Qoheleth's intertwined five-pronged rhetorical strategy, which includes the anti-apocalyptic genre. This presence of the anti-apocalyptic genre does not answer all of the questions about Ecclesiastes, but the presentation of it is intended to further the scholarly discussion of this profoundly intriguing book.

Bibliography

Allison, Dale C. Jr. "The Background of Romans 11:11-15 in Apocalyptic and Rabbinic Literature." *Studia Biblical et Theologica* 10 (1980) 229-34.
Aune, David. *Prophecy in Early Christianity and the Ancient Mediterranean World*. Grand Rapids: Eerdmans, 1983.
Amir, Yehoshua. "The Figure of Death in the 'Book of Wisdom.'" *Journal of Jewish Studies* 30 (1979) 157-78.
Anderson, William, H. U. "The Curse of Work in Qoheleth: An Expose of Genesis 3:17-19 in Ecclesiastes." *Evangelical Quarterly* 70 (1998) 99-13.
———. "Philosophical Considerations in a Genre Analysis of Qoheleth." *Vetus Testamentum* 48 (1998) 289-300.
Archer, Gleason L., Jr. "Linguistic Evidence for the Date of Ecclesiastes." *Journal Evangelical Theological Society* 32 (1969) 167-81.
Argall, Randall. *1 Enoch and Sirach: A Comparative Literary and Conceptual Analysis of the Themes of Revelation, Creation and Judgment*. Atlanta: Scholars, 1995.
Armstrong, James F. "Ecclesiastes in Old Testament Theology." *Princeton Seminary Bulletin* 94 (1983) 16-25.
Barton, George A. *A Critical and Exegetical Commentary on the Book of Ecclesiastes*. International Critical Commentary. Edinburgh: T. & T. Clark, 1912.
Bartholomew, Craig G. "Qoheleth in the Canon?! Current Trends in the Interpretation of Ecclesiastes." *Themelios* 24 (1999) 4-20.
———. *Reading Ecclesiastes: Old Testament Exegesis and Hermeneutical Theory*. Rome: Biblical Institute Press, 1998.
Bauer, Walter. *A Greek-English Lexicon of the New Testament and Other Early Christian Literature*. Translated and adapted by W. F. Arndt and F. W. Gingrich, and augmented by F. W. Gingrich and F. Danker. 2nd ed. Chicago: University of Chicago Press, 1979.
Bawarshi, Ani. "The Genre Function." *College English* 62.3 (2000) 335-60.
Bergant, Dianne. *What Are They Saying About Wisdom Literature?* New York: Paulist, 1984.
Biblia Hebraica Stuttgartensia Stuttgart: Deutsche Bibelgesellshaft, 1977.
Boccaccini, Gabriele. *Middle Judaism: Jewish Thought, 300 B.C.E. to 200 C.E.* Minneapolis: Fortress, 1991.
Bridges, Charles. *An Exposition of the Book of Ecclesiastes*. London: Banner of Truth Trust, 1960.
Brown, Francis, et al. *The New Brown, Driver, and Briggs Hebrew and English Lexicon of the Old Testament*. Lafayette, IN: Associated Publishers and Authors, 1981.

Bibliography

Brueggemann, Walter. *The Message of the Psalms.* Minneapolis: Augsburg, 1984.

———. "The Social Significance of Solomon as a Patron of Wisdom." In *The Sage in Israel and the Ancient Near East*, edited by John Gammie and Leo G. Perdue, 117–32. Winoma Lake, IN: Eisenbrauns, 1990.

Burkes, Shannon. "Wisdom and Apocalypticism in the Wisdom of Solomon." *Harvard Theological Review* 95 (2002) 21–44.

Chandler, Daniel. "An Introduction to Genre Theory." 1997. Online: http://www.aber.ac.uk/media/Documents/intgenre/chandler_genre_theory.pdf [accessed June 2008]

Charlesworth, James H., ed. *The Old Testament Pseudepigrapha.* New York: Doubleday, 1983.

Christianson, Eric S. *A Time to Tell: Narrative Strategies in Ecclesiastes.* Journal for the Study of the Old Testament: Supplement Series 280. Sheffield, UK: Sheffield Academic Press, 1998.

Childs, Brevard. *Introduction to the Old Testament as Scripture.* Philadelphia: Fortress, 1979.

Clemens, David M. "The Law of Sin and Death: Ecclesiastes and Genesis 1–3." *Themelios* 19 (1994) 5–8.

Cohen, Ralph. "History and Genre" *New Literary History* 17 (1986) 203–17.

Collins, Adella Yarbo. "Introduction." *Semeia* 36 (1986) 1–11.

Collins, John. *The Apocalyptic Imagination: An Introduction to the Jewish Matrix of Christianity.* New York: Crossroad, 1987.

———. "Apocalyptic Literature." In *Early Judaism and Its Modern Interpreters*, edited by Robert A. Kraft and George W. E. Vickelsburg, 345–70. Society of Biblical Literature Monograph Series 1. Philadelphia: Fortress, 1986.

———. "The Biblical Precedent for Natural Theology." *Journal of the American Academy of Religion* 45 (1977) Supplement B, 46.

———. "Cosmos and Salvation: Jewish Wisdom and Apocalyptic in the Hellenistic Age." *History of Religion* 17 (1977) 121–42.

———. "Daniel and His Social World." *Interpretation* 39 (1985) 131–43.

———."The Genre Apocalypse in Hellenistic Judaism," In *Apocalypticism in the Mediterranean World and the Near East*, edited by D. Hellholm, 531–48. Tübingen: Mohr/Siebeck, 1983.

———. "The Jewish Apocalypses." *Semeia* 14 (1978) 21–60.

———. *Jewish Wisdom in the Hellenitic Age.* Louisville, KY: Westminster John Knox, 1997.

———. "Towards The Morphology of a Genre" *Semeia* 14 (1978) 1–20.

———. "Wisdom, Apocalypticism, and Genric Compatibility." In *Ssearch of Wisdom: Essays in Memory of John G. Gammie*, edited by Leo G. Perdueet al., 165–85. Louisville: Westminster John Knox, 1993.

Corley, Jeremy. "Wisdom Versus Apocalyptic and Science in Sirach 1,1–10." In *Wisdom and Apocalypticism in the Dead Sea Scrolls and in the Biblical Tradition*, edited by F. Garcia Martinez, 269–85. Leuven: Leuven University Press, 2003.

Coughenour, Robert. "Enoch and Wisdom: A Study of the Wisdom Elements in the Book of Enoch." PhD diss., Case Western Reserve University, 1972.

———. "The Woe Oracles in Ethiopic Enoch." *Journal for the Study of Judaism* 9 (1978) 192–97.

Crenshaw, James. "Method in Determining Wisdom's Influence upon 'Historical' Literature." *Journal of Biblical Literature* 88 (1969) 129–42.

———. *Ecclesiastes: A Commentary*. Philadelphia: Westminster, 1987.

———. "Prolegomenon." In *Studies in Ancient Israelite Wisdom*, edited by Harry M. Orlinsky, 1-36. New York: KTAV, 1976.

———. "Qoheleth in Current Research." *Hebrew Annual Review* 7 (1983) 41-56.

———. "Wisdom in the OT." *The Interpreter's Dictionary of the Bible*, edited by G. A. Buttrick, 4 vols, supplementary volume, 954-55. Nashville: Abingdon, 1962.

Davies, Philip R. "Reading Daniel Sociologically." In *The Book of Daniel in the Light of New Findings*, edited by A. S. van der Woude, 345-61. Leuven: Leuven University Press, 1993.

———. "The Social World of Apocalyptic Writings." In *The World of Ancient Israel: Social, Anthropological, and Political Perspectives*, edited by Ronald E. Clements, 251-71. Cambridge: Cambridge University Press, 1989.

Davis, Barry C. "Death, An Impetus for Life: Ecclesiastes 12:1-8." *Bibliotheca Sacra* 148 (1991) 298-18.

Dahood, Mitchell. "The Phoenician Background of Qoheleth." *Biblica* 7 (1966) 264-82.

Dell, Katherine. *The Book of Job as Skeptical Literature*. Berlin: de Gruyter, 1991.

Devitt, Amy. "Genre: New Conceptions of an Old Concept." *College Composition and Communication* 44 (1993) 573-86.

Dibelius, Martin. *A Commentary on the Epistle of James*. Translated by Michael Williams. Philadelphia: Fortress, 1976.

Eaton, Michael. *Ecclesiastes, An Introduction and Commentary*. Downers Grove, IL: InterVarsity, 1983.

Elgvin, Torleif. "Wisdom with and without Apocalyptic." In *Sapiential, Liturgical and Poetical Texts from Qumran. Proceedings of the Third Meeting of the International Organization for Qumran Studies Oslo 1998*, edited by D.K. Falk and F. García Martínez, 15-38. Leiden: Brill, 2000.

Farmer, Kathleen. *Who Knows What is Good? A Commentary on the Books of Proverbs and Ecclesiastes*. Grand Rapids: Eerdmans, 1991.

Fishelov, David. *Metaphors of Genre: The Role of Analogies in Genre Theory*. University Park, PA: The Pennsylvania State University, 1993.

Fontaine, Carole. "The Sage in Family and Tribe." In *The Sage in Israel and the Ancient Near East*, edited by John Gammie and Leo G. Perdue, 155-64. Winona Lake, IN: Eisenbrauns, 1990.

Fowler, Alastair. *Kinds of Literature: An Introduction to the Theory of Genres and Modes*. Cambridge: Harvard University Press, 1982.

Fox, Michael V. "Aging and Death in Qoheleth 12." *Journal for the Study of the Old Testament* 42 (1988) 55-77.

———. "Frame-Narrative and Composition in the Book of Qohelet." *Hebrew Union College Annual* 48 (1968) 83-106.

———. "The Meaning of Hebel for Qohelet." *Journal Biblical Literature* 105 (1986) 409-27.

———. *Qohelet and His Contradictions*. Decatur, GA: Almond, 1989.

———. "Qoheleth's Epistemology." *Hebrew Union College Annual* 58 (1987) 137-55.

———. *A Time to Tear Down and a Time to Build Up: A Rereading of Ecclesiastes*. Grand Rapids: Eerdmans, 1999.

Fredricks, Daniel C. *Qoheleth's Language: Re-evaluating Its Nature and Date*. Lewiston, NY: Mellen, 1988.

Bibliography

Gammie, John. "From Prudentialism to Apocalypticism: The Houses of the Sages amid the Varying Forms of Wisdom." In *The Sage in Israel and the Ancient Near East*, edited by John Gammie and Leo G. Perdue, 479-98. Winona Lake, IN: Eisenbrauns, 1990.

Garret, Duane. *Proverbs, Ecclesiastes, Song of Songs*. Nashville: Broadman, 1993.

Gerhart, M. "Genre as Praxis: An Inquiry." *PreText* 4 (1983) 273-94.

———. *Genre Choices, Gender Questions*. Norman, OK: University of Oklahoma Press, 1992.

———. "Generic Studies: Their Renewed Importance in Religious and Literary Criticism." *Journal of the American Academy of Religion* 45 (1977) 309-27.

Gilbert, Maurice. "Wisdom Literature." In *Jewish Writings of the Second Temple Period*, edited by Michael E. Stone, 283-324. Philadelphia: Fortress, 1984.

Ginsberg, Christian D. *Song of Songs and Coheleth*. New York: Schocken, 1968.

Ginsberg, H. Louis. *Studies in Koheleth*. New York: Jewish Theological Seminary of America, 1950.

Goff, Matthew J. "Wisdom, Apocalypticism, and the Pedagogical Ethos of 4QInstruction." In *Conflicted Boundaries in Wisdom and Apocalypticism*, edited by Benjamin G. Wright III and Lawrence M. Wills, 57-68. Leiden: Brill, 2005.

Goldberg, Louis. *Ecclesiastes*. Grand Rapids: Zondervan, 1983.

Gordis, Robert. *Koheleth—The Man and His World: A Study of Ecclesiastes*. 3rd ed. New York: Schocken, 1968.

Grabbe, Lester. *Wisdom of Solomon*. Sheffield, UK: Sheffield Academic Press, 1997.

Gunkel, Hermann. "Fundamental Problems of Hebrew Literary History." In *What Remains of the Old Testament and Other Essays*, translated by A. Dallas, 52-68. New York: MacMillian, 1928.

———. *What Remains of the Old Testament and Other Essays*. Translated by A. Dallas. New York: Macmillan, 1928.

Hanson, Paul. "Apocalypticism." In *The Interpreter's Dictionary of the Bible*. Supplemental Volume, 29-30. Nashville: Abingdon, 1962.

———. *The Dawn of Apocalyptic: The Historical and Sociological Roots of Jewish Apocalyptic Eschatology*. Philadelphia: Fortress, 1979.

———. "Jewish Apocalyptic Against Its Near Eastern Environment." *Revue Biblique* 78 (1971) 33-58.

———. *Old Testament Apocalyptic*. Nashville: Abingdon, 1987.

Harrington, Daniel J. "4QInstruction and 4 Ezra." In *Wisdom and Apocalypticism in the Dead Sea Scrolls and in the Biblical Tradition*, edited by F. García Martínez, 343-56. Leuven: Leuven University Press, 2003.

———. *Invitation to the Apocrypha*. Grand Rapids: Eerdmans, 1999.

———. *Wisdom Texts from Qumran*. London: Routledge, 1996.

Hartin, Patrick J. "Who is Wise and Understanding among You?" (James 3:13). An Analysis of Wisdom, Eschatology, and Apocalypticism in the Letter of James." In *Conflicted Boundaries in Wisdom and Apocalypticism*, edited by Benjamin G. Wright III and Lawrence M. Wills, 149-68. Leiden: Brill, 2005.

Hellholm, David "The Problem of Apocalyptic Genre." *Semeia* 36 (1986) 13-64.

Hirsch, Eric D. *Validity in Interpretation*. New Haven: Yale University Press, 1967.

Holm-Nielsen, Svend. "The Book of Ecclesiastes and the Interpretation of It in Jewish and Christian Theology." *Annual of the Swedish Theological Institute* 10 (1975-76) 38-96.

Horsley, Richard. "The Politics of Cultural Production in Second Temple Judea: Historical Context and Political-Religious relations of the Scribes Who Produced *1 Enoch*, Sirach, and Daniel." In *Conflicted Boundaries in Wisdom and Apocalypticism*, edited by Benjamin G. Wright III and Lawrence M. Wills, 123-45. Leiden: Brill, 2005.

Ingram, Douglas. *Ambiguity in Ecclesiastes*. London: T. & T. Clark, 2006.

Jackson-McCabe, Matt. "A Letter to the Twelve Tribes in the Diaspora: Wisdom and 'Apocalyptic' Eschatology in the Letter of James." In *The Society of Biblical Literature 1996 Seminar Papers*, 504-17. Society of Biblical Literature Seminar Paper 35. Atlanta: Scholars, 1996.

Johnson, Elizabeth. *The Function of Apocalyptic and Wisdom Traditions in Romans 9-11: Rethinking the Questions*. Atlanta: Scholars, 1989.

Johnson, Raymond E. "The Rhetorical Question as a Literary Device in Ecclesiastes (Qoheleth, Reader-Response, Literary Criticism)." Ph.D., Southern Baptist Seminary, 1986.

Johnson, Timothy. *Now My Eyes See You: Unveiling an Apocalyptic Job*. Sheffield, UK: Sheffield Phoenix Press, 2009.

Johnston, Robert K. "Confessions of a Workaholic: A Reappraisal of Qoheleth." *Catholic Biblical Quarterly* 38 (1976) 14-28.

Kaiser, Walter Jr. *Ecclesiastes: Total Life*. Chicago: Moody, 1979.

Keil, Carl F., and Franz Delitzsch. *Ecclesiastes*. Translated by M. G. Easton. Grand Rapids: Eerdmans, 1980.

Kerferd, George. "The Sage in Hellenistic Philosophical Literature (399 B.C.E.-199 C.E.)." In *The Sage in Israel and the Ancient Near East*, edited by John Gammie and Leo G. Perdue, 343-54 Winona Lake, IN: Eisenbrauns, 1990.

Kidner, Derek. *A Time to Mourn and a Time to Dance*. Downers Grove, IL: InterVarsity, 1976.

———. *The Wisdom of Proverbs, Job and Ecclesiastes*. Downers Grove, IL: InterVarsity, 1985.

Kittel, Gerhard, and Gerhard Friedrich, eds. *Theological Dictionary of the New Testament*. Translated by Geoffrey W. Bromiley. 10 vols. Grand Rapids: Eerdmans, 1964-76.

Knibb, Michael. "Apocalyptic and Wisdom in 4 Ezra." *Journal for the Study of Judaism* 13 (1982) 56-74.

Koch, Klaus. *The Rediscovery of Apocalyptic*. Translated by M. Kohl. London: Allenson, 1972.

Köhler, Ludwig, and Walter Baumgartner. *The Hebrew and Aramaic Lexicon of the Old Testament*. Leiden: Brill, 1994.

Kreueger, Thomas. *Qoheleth*. Minneapolis: Fortress, 2004.

Laws, Sophie. *A Commentary on the Epistle of James*. San Francisco: Harper & Row, 1980.

Lee, Bernard. "Toward a Rhetoric of Contradiction in the Book of Ecclesiastes." MA thesis, The University of Calgary, 1997.

Lemaire, Andre. "The Sage in School and Temple." In *The Sage in Israel and the Ancient Near East*, edited by John Gammie and Leo Perdue, 165-81. Winona Lake, IN: Eisenbrauns, 1990.

Leupold, Herbert. *Exposition of Ecclesiastes*. Grand Rapids: Baker, 1966.

Loader, James A. *Ecclesiastes*. Translated J. Vried. Grand Rapids: Eerdmans, 1998.

———. *Polar Structures in the Book of Qoheleth*. Berlin: de Gruyter, 1979.

Lohfink, Nobert. *Kohelet*. Wurzburg: Echter, 1980.

Longman, Tremper III. *The Book of Ecclesiastes*. Grand Rapids: Eerdmans, 1998.

Bibliography

Maltby, A. "The Book of Ecclesiastes and the After-Life." *Evangelical Quarterly* 35 (1963) 39–44.

Martínez, F. García. "Wisdom and Qumran: Worldly or Heavenly?" In *Wisdom and Apocalypticism in the Dead Sea Scrolls and in the Biblical Tradition*, edited by F. García Martínez, 1–16. Leuven: Leuven University Press, 2003.

McNeille, Alan. *An Introduction to Ecclesiastes with Notes and Appendices.* Cambridge: Cambridge University Press, 1904.

Milik, J. T. "Problemes de la Litterature Henochique a la Lumiere des Fragments Arameens De Qumran" *Harvard Theological Review* 64 (1971) 333–78.

Miller, Carolyn. "Genre as Social Action." In *Genre and the New Rhetoric*, edited by A. Freeman and P. Medway, 23–42. Bristol, PA: Taylor & Francis, 1994.

Miller, Douglas B. "Qoheleth's Symbolic Use of הבל." *Journal Biblical Literature* 117 (1998) 437–54.

———. *Symbol and Rhetoric in Ecclesiastes.* Leiden: Brill, 2002.

———. "What the Preacher Forgot: The Rhetoric of Ecclesiastes." *Catholic Biblical Quarterly* 62 (2000) 215–35.

Murphy, Frederick J. "Sapiential Elements in the Syriac Apocalypse of Baruch." *The Jewish Quarterly Review* 4 (1986) 311–27.

Murphy, Roland. *The Book of Job: A Short Reading.* New York: Paulist, 1999.

———. *Ecclesiastes.* Dallas: Word, 1992.

———. *Ecclesiastes, Song of Songs.* Hermeneia. Philadelphia, Fortress, 1988.

———. "Qoheleth Interpreted: The Bearing of the Past on the Present." *Vetus Testamentum* 32 (1982) 331–37.

———. "Recent Research on Proverbs and Qoheleth." *Currents in Research: Biblical Studies* 1 (1993) 119–40.

———. *The Tree of Life.* 2nd ed. Grand Rapids: Eerdmans, 1996.

———. *Wisdom Literature: Job, Proverbs, Ruth, Canticles, Ecclesiastes, and Esther.* Grand Rapids: Eerdmans, 1981.

———. "Wisdom Theses." In *The Papin Festschrift Essays in Honour of Joseph Papin*, edited by Joseph Armenti, 187–200. Villanova: Villanova University Press, 1976.

Nasuti, Harry. *Defining the Sacred Songs: Genre, Tradition and the Post-Critical Interpretation of the Psalms.* Journal for the Studies of the Old Testament 218. Sheffield, UK: Sheffield Academic Press, 1999.

Nickelsburg, George. "Apocalyptic Message of 1 Enoch 92–105." *Catholic Biblical Quarterly* 39 (1977) 309–28.

———. "Enoch as Scientist, Sage, and Prophet: Content, Function, and Authorship in 1 Enoch." *The Society of Biblical Literature 1999 Seminar Papers*, 203–30. Society of Biblical Literature Seminar Papers 38. Atlanta: Society of Biblical Literature, 1999.

———. "Enochic Wisdom: An Alternative to the Mosaic Torah?" In *Hesed Ve-Emet: Studies in Honor of Ernest S. Frerichs*, edited Jodi Magness and Seymour Gitin, 123–30. Atlanta: Scholars, 1998.

———. *Jewish Literature between the Bible and the Mishnah.* Philadelphia: Fortress, 1981.

———. *Resurrection, Immortality and Eternal Life in Intertestamental Judaism.* Cambridge: Cambridge University Press, 1972.

———. "Social Aspects of Palestinian Jewish Apocalypticism." In *Social Aspects of Palestinian Jewish Apocalypticism in the Mediterranean World and the Near East: Proceedings of the International Colloquim on Apocalyptcisim, Uppsala, 1979*, 2nd ed., edited by David Hellholm, 641–54. Tübingen: Mohr Siebeck, 1983.

———. "Wisdom and Apocalypticism in Early Judaism: Some Points for Discussion." In *Conflicted Boundaries in Wisdom and Apocalypticism*, edited by Benjamin G. Wright III and Lawrence M. Wills, 17–37. Leiden: Brill, 2005.
Ogden, Graham. *Qoheleth*. Sheffield, UK: JSOT, 1987.
Perdue, Leo G. "Wisdom and Apocalyptic: The Case of Qoheleth." In *Wisdom and Apocalypticism in the Dead Sea Scrolls and in the Biblical Tradition*, edited by F. García Martínez, 231–58. Paris: Leuven University Press, 2003.
———. *Wisdom and Creation*. 1994. Reprint. Eugene, OR: Wipf and Stock, 2009.
———. *Wisdom in Revolt*. Sheffield, UK: Sheffield Academic Press, 1991.
Perry, Theodore. *Dialogues with Kohelet*. University Park, PA: The Pennsylvania State University Press, 1993.
Pope, Marvin. *Job*. Garden City, NY: Doubleday, 1965.
Provan, Ian. *Ecclesiastes, Song of Songs*. Grand Rapids: Zondervan, 2001.
Ranston, Harry. *Ecclesiastes and the Early Greek Wisdom Literature*. London: Epworth, 1925.
Rodd, Cyril S. *The Book of Job*. Philadelphia: Trinity, 1990.
Rosmarin, Adena. *The Power of Genre*. Minneapolis: University of Minnesota Press, 1985.
Rowland, Christopher. *The Open Heaven: A Study of Apocalyptic in Judaism and Early Christianity*. 1982. Reprint. Eugene, OR: Wipf and Stock, 2002.
Rudman, Dominic. "A Contextual Reading of Ecclesiastes 4:13–16." *Journal of Biblical Liteature* 116 (1997) 57–73.
Russell, D. S. *Apocalyptic: Ancient and Modern*. Philadelphia: Fortress, 1978.
———. *Divine Disclosure*. London: SCM, 1992.
Sacchi, Paolo. *Jewish Apocalyptic and Its History*. Translated by William J. Short. Journal for the Study of the Pseudepigrapha 20; Bresica, Italy: Paideia, 1990.
Sacks, Sheldon. *Fiction and the Shape of Belief*. Berkley: University of California Press, 1964.
Salters, Robert B. "A Note on the Dating of Ecclesiastes." *Catholic Biblical Quarterly* 61 (1999) 47–52.
Sanders, E.P. "The Genre of Palestinian Jewish Apocalypses." In *Apocalypticism in the Mediterranean World and the Near East*, edited by David Hellhom, 447–60. Tübingen: Mohr, 1989.
Schoors, Antoon, ed. *Qoheleth in the Context of Wisdom*. Leuven: Leuven University Press, 1998.
Schuessler, Fiorenza, Elisabeth. "The Phenomenon of Early Christian Apocalyptic: Some Reflections on Method." In *Apocalypticism in the Mediterranean World and the Near East: Proceedings of the International Colloquim on Apocalypticism, Uppsala, 1979*, edited by David Hellhom, 2nd ed., 295–316. Tübingen: Mohr Siebeck, 1989.
Scott, Robert Balgarnie Young. *Proverbs/ Ecclesiastes*. Garden City, NY: Doubleday, 1965.
———. *The Way of Wisdom in the Old Testament*. New York: Macmillan, 1971.
Seow, Choon Leong. *Ecclesiastes*. Garden City, NY: Doubleday, 1997.
———. "Linguistic Evidence and the Dating of Qohelet." *Journal of Biblical Literature* 115 (1996) 646–50.
———. "Qoheleth's Autobiography." In *Fortunate the Eyes that See: Essays in Honor of David Noel Freedman*, edited by A. B. Veck et al., 275–87. Grand Rapids: Eerdmans, 1995.
———. "Qohelet's Eschatalogical Poem." *Journal of Biblical Literature* 118 (1999) 209–34.
Shead, Andrew G. "Reading Ecclesiastes 'Epilogically.'" *Tyndale Bulletin* 48 (1997) 67–91.

Bibliography

Shekan, Patrick, and Alexander Di Lella. *The Wisdom of Ben Sira*. New York: Doubleday, 1987.

Sheppard, Gerald T. "The Epilogue to Qoheleth as Theological Commentary." *Catholic Biblical Quarterly* 39 (1977) 182–89.

Shields, Martin A. "Ecclesiastes and the End of Wisdom." *Tyndale Bulletin* 50 (1999) 117–39.

Smith, Jonathan Z. "Wisdom and Apocalyptic." In *Map Is Not Territory*, 67–87. Chicago: University of Chicago Press, 1978.

Sneed, Mark. "The Social Location of the Book of Qoheleth." *Hebrew Studies* 39 (1998) 41–51.

Spangenberg, Izak J. J. "A Century of Wrestling with Qohelet." In *Qohelet in the Context of Wisdom*, edited by A. Schoors, 61–91. Leuven: Leuven University Press, 1998.

———. "Irony in the Book of Qoheleth." *Journal for the Study of the Old Testament* 72 (1996) 57–69.

Stone, Elizabeth. "Old Man Koheleth." *Journal of Bible and Religion* 10 (1942) 98–102.

Stone, Michael. "Enoch, Aramaic Levi." *Journal for the Study of Judaism in the Persian, Hellenistic, and Roman Periods* 19 (1988) 159–70.

———. *Fourth Ezra*. Minneapolis: Fortress, 1990.

———. *Jewish Writings of the Second Temple Period: Apocrypha, Pseudepigrapha, Qumran Sectarian Writings, Philo, Josephus*. CRINT 2.2. Assen: Van Gorcum, 1984.

———. "Lists of Revealed Things in Apocalyptic Literature." In *Magnalia Dei, the Mighty Acts of God: Essays on the Bible and Archaeology in Memory of G. Ernest Wright*, edited by Frank Moore Cross et al., 414–51. Garden City, NY: Doubleday, 1976.

Sugithirajah, Rasiah S. *Postcolonial Criticism and Biblical Interpretation*. Oxford: Oxford Press, 2002.

Swales, John. *Genre Analysis: English in Academic and Research Settings*. New York: Cambridge University Press, 1990.

Tanzer, Sarah. "Response to George Nickelsburg, 'Wisdom and Apocalypticism in Early Judaism.'" In *Conflicted Boundaries in Wisdom and Apocalypticism*, edited by Benjamin G. Wright III and Lawrence M. Wills, 39–49. Leiden: Brill, 2005.

Tiller, Patrick A. "The Rich and the Poor in James: An Apocalyptic Ethic." In *Conflicted Boundaries in Wisdom and Apocalypticism*, edited by Benjamin G. Wright III and Lawrence M. Wills, 169–80. Leiden: Brill, 2005.

Todorov, Tzvetan. "The Origin of Genres." *New Literary History* 8 (1976) 159–70.

Von Rad, Gerhard. *Old Testament Theology*. Translated by D. M. G. Stalker. 2 vols. Peabody, MA: Prince, 1962.

———. *The Problem of the Hexateuch and Other Essays*. Translated by E. W. Trueman Dicken. London: SCM, 1966.

———. *Wisdom in Israel*. Translated by James D. Martin. Nashville: Abingdon, 1972.

Webb, Robert. "'Apocalyptic': Observation on a Slippery Term." *Journal of Near Eastern Studies* 49 (1990) 115–26.

Westermann, Claus. *The Living Psalms*. Translated by J. Porter. Grand Rapids: Eerdmans, 1996.

———. *The Structure of the Book of Job: A Form-Critical Analysis*. Translated by Charles A. Muenchow. Philadelphia: Fortress, 1981.

Whitley, Charles F. *Koheleth: His Language and Thought*. Berlin: de Gruyter, 1979.

Whybray, Roger N. *Ecclesiastes*. Grand Rapids: Eerdmans, 1989.

———. *The Intellectual Tradition in the Old Testament*. Berlin: de Gruyter, 1974.

———. "Qoheleth, Preacher of Joy." *Journal for the Study of the Old Testament* 23 (1982) 87–98.
Wright, Addison. "The Riddle of the Sphinx: The Structure of the Book of Qoheleth." *Catholic Biblical Quarterly* 30 (1968) 313–34.
Wright, Benjamin G., III. "Putting the Puzzle Together: Some Suggestions Concerning the Social Location of the Wisdom of Ben Sira." In *Conflicted Boundaries in Wisdom and Apocalypticism*, edited by Benjamin G. Wright III and Lawrence M. Wills, 89–112. Leiden: Brill, 2005.

www.ingramcontent.com/pod-product-compliance
Lightning Source LLC
Chambersburg PA
CBHW050028240426
43662CB00046B/1699